Composing for the Screen in Germany and the USSR

WITHDRAWN
UTSA Libraries

I0789786

CULTURAL POLITICS AND PROPAGANDA

COMPOSING FOR THE SCREEN IN GERMANY AND THE USSR

EDITED BY **ROBYNN J. STILWELL** AND **PHIL POWRIE**

Indiana University Press
Bloomington & Indianapolis

This book is a publication of

Indiana University Press
601 North Morton Street
Bloomington, IN 47404-3797 USA

http://iupress.indiana.edu

Telephone orders 800-842-6796
Fax orders   812-855-7931
Orders by e-mail iuporder@indiana.edu

© 2008 by Indiana University Press
All rights reserved

No part of this book may be reproduced or utilized in any form or by any means, electronic or mechanical, including photocopying and recording, or by any information storage and retrieval system, without permission in writing from the publisher. The Association of American University Presses' Resolution on Permissions constitutes the only exception to this prohibition.

The paper used in this publication meets the minimum requirements of American National Standard for Information Sciences—Permanence of Paper for Printed Library Materials, ANSI Z39.48-1984.

Manufactured in the United States of America

Library of Congress Cataloging-in-Publication Data

Composing for the screen in Germany and the USSR : cultural politics and propaganda / edited by Robynn Stilwell and Phil Powrie.
   p. cm.
Includes bibliographical references and index.
ISBN 978-0-253-34976-7 (cloth)
ISBN 978-0-253-21954-1 (pbk.)
1. Motion picture music—Germany—History and criticism. 2. Motion picture music—Soviet Union—History and criticism. 3. Music and state. I. Stilwell, Robynn Jeananne. II. Powrie, Phil.
ML2075.C66 2007
781.5′420943—dc22

Library
University of Texas
at San Antonio

CONTENTS

Introduction

As a medium, cinema is now over a century old; the musical genre of "film music" is at least that old, arguably older than the medium itself, extending back through magic lantern shows and Victorian melodrama into the entire history of theatrical presentation. Music provides shock absorbers for the suspension of disbelief and an underlining, highlighting, *underscoring* of visual and verbal signals from the abstract and structural to the narrative and emotional. The vocabulary and syntax of musical gesture has changed less than those of the visual medium to which it has been allied, and much of its specificity (and even its generality) has been taken as given.

Despite the long history of film music, serious academic study is still fairly new, really only coming into its own as a discipline in the past two decades. That is not to say that there has not been a substantial amount written on the relationship between music and the screen, but for much of the past century, it has been mostly prescriptive, occasionally descriptive, and only recently analytical. Because of the relative volume of the writing, there is a tendency to think we know what the history and technique of film music is, or at least that the ground has been fairly well mapped.

The problem with this conception is that it breaks down so quickly. For one thing, there is not so much a "body" of literature as a wealth of materials scattered among trade papers, fan magazines, philosophical treatises, and only occasionally music journals.[1] Much of the writing, particularly during the decade of the 1920s, is of a practical nature, as music directors from studios and theaters, from the centers and the front lines alike, discussed the technique of accompanying silent movies. At the same time, film theorists were struggling to understand their new medium and its specificity, including the reasons (some implicit, some explicit) why another medium—music—seemed so intricately intertwined with the flickering images on the silver screen. Once sound film and the modern technique of film composition, wedding sound and image on a single strip of film, became well-established by the beginning of World War II, both the broader aesthetic musings of the philosopher and the nuts-and-bolts technical writing of the composer and musician dwindled and a middleground critical literature arose. However, the split between those who are interested in film as a medium (who often ignore the sonic element, including music) and the musically inclined (who often ignore the screen) remains a consistent divide even today.

Undoubtedly the period in which the relationship between image, narrative, and music was under the greatest scrutiny in the literature was that surrounding the coming of sound. Everything that had been established in the fledgling film medium was thrown into question. The flexibility and multiplicity of performative film music—each audience was presented with a potentially different and new experience—was reduced to a single multi-faceted, repeatable work, an experience somewhere between a theatrical piece and a painting. This had obvious disadvantages in its limitation to a single statement, but also great advantages in the relative flexibility of the act of composition. The interaction of the various interrelated media shifted from the point of performance and reception to that of conception and creation. For those who would argue that film was an art, not merely a commercial commodity, this was a significant shift of control, in line with many impulses within modernist artistic circles.

Of course, this period of flux in film production and aesthetics took place during one of the greatest periods of political upheaval of the twentieth century. Film as a modern art emerged after World War I and the Soviet Revolution of 1917, and the transition to sound occurred roughly a decade later as the political forces that led to World War II began to converge. It is perhaps not surprising that the two countries that produced the highest concentration of serious writing on the subject of film music were Germany and the USSR.

By the advent of sound film, both Germany and the USSR had distinct national cinemas that were thriving: Germany had a level of production and refinement of style rivaled only by Hollywood; the Soviet Union, although more restricted by the technology and its own deprivation of the time, had some of the most vigorous and adventurous thinkers engaged in debate about cinema and the arts more broadly. Both the German and Russian cultures were long predisposed to explicit theorizing about aesthetics and the role of the arts in society; and political developments in these two nations brought art's role in society directly into question at a time when cinema was emerging as a major art and changing so fundamentally in its constitution as a multimedia art.

The volume of writing by such key figures as Sergei Eisenstein, Theodor

Adorno, and Hanns Eisler, and the overtly political context of the music and films produced in those countries at this time, has led us, perhaps, to an over-confidence that we really *know* about the film music of the period. How did the theorizing stack up to the practice of film scoring?

This question can be posed at a number of levels, from the positioning of the theorist in the political/industrial structure to the details of the finished film-music product. Eisenstein embraced communism but was often in conflict with Stalin's regime over everything from the usual attacks of "formalism" to essentially commercial issues such as budgeting and resources; his writings are prescriptive and written alongside the development of sound-film technique and aesthetics, and as such are tinged with optimism and idealism. Eisler's communist ideals brought him more sharply in conflict with the Nazi Party (and later the U.S. House Un-American Activities Committee); he was writing after escaping Germany and on the cusp of the Cold War, and his distaste for the industrial practices of Hollywood tinges—and sometimes paints in broad brushes—his comments in *Composing for the Films* with frustration and resistance. A lack of proper attention to that context can cause one to overlook salient details in Eisler's own film scores: for example, reading his proscription of the technique, one would assume that Hanns Eisler would *never* utilize mickey-mousing—the close correlation of musical line and rhythm to onscreen movement—in his film scores; one would be wrong, as there are certainly examples in several of his scores. While it may be occasionally amusing to observe the gap between what a theorist says and what that theorist as a composer does ("don't do as I do, do as I say"), the gap also may enlighten us about the pervasiveness of certain music-image relationships as well as national and nationalistic concepts of how meaning should be made.

In cultures that were so accustomed to thinking about the relationship between art, cultural, and national identity as were Germany and the new Soviet Union, it is not surprising that the dominant political parties wished to shore up their newly won power by "naturalizing" their agendas, or placing their ideologies in a larger context of the nations' cultural histories. There has been considerable work in this area, but little of it addresses the role of music.[2] Music became a key ingredient in the propaganda machines developed by the National Socialists and Stalin, an art both to regulate and exploit. Indeed, it is impossible to speak of film music in these countries during the early sound era *without* considering the political implications of compositional choice and the relationship between music and image. Even in films which do not overtly deal with political subjects—the German *Bergfilm* genre is an excellent example—the combination of music and images can do more to construct a larger sense of a people's identity than the narrative itself. Propaganda was not, then, an imposition from above in these regimes so much as a harnessing of the modes of thinking already pervasive in the artistic life of the culture, and the manner of that harnessing diverged. Both nations drew on ideals of a mythic past in order to promote a sense of inevitability and continuity of the current ruling powers with the roots of the culture. In Germany, the Nazi cult of the *Volk* managed to unite the ostensibly divergent arenas of folk culture and high art through the Wagnerian concept of the *Gesamtkunstwerk*. Wagner's own fascination with Germanic mythology articulated in the massive Ring cycle of operas and his grandiose visions uniting theatrical spectacle and music were inspirations for the Nazi machine, although the influence of Wagner's musical style has perhaps been exaggerated, as several essays in the collection attest. The concurrent, and at times contradictory, nineteenth-century German aesthetic impulse toward "pure" or "absolute" music—that which transcended material meaning and achieved the ineffable or sublime—seemed to transcend musical boundaries in the Nazi aesthetic, such as the abstractly glorious images of divers unhampered by gravity in Leni Riefenstahl's *Olympia* (1938). Well-established tropes of power—particularly military power—and mystery may have been prized by the propagandists, but a wide variety of musical means were allowed and even embraced by the Nazi Party, so long as the musicians were not Jewish.

The Communist Party under Stalin had a greater cultural challenge, to unite a more fragmented group of peoples under a single regime. The Soviet Union did not have Germany's strong history of technological and artistic development, so the drive of modernity was faced with a steeper climb. While Germany was looking to the past to create unity, the Soviet Union was looking to the future. This relative lack of musical foundation may in part be responsible for an artistic policy both more restrictive stylistically, and more vague and arbitrary. In Socialist Realism, modernity was embraced, but modernism was not. Music was a useful tool for teaching, but its ability to slip its own boundaries and make new and unexpected meanings was a constant challenge, both for those policing the arts and for composers who could not always control how their work was seen. The continuing debate over Shostakovich's music—whether, for instance, the Fifth Symphony is a capitulation to Socialist Realism or an ironic thumbing of the nose—demonstrates that historical distance does not always clarify matters. However, when united with imagery, as in film, we are able to refine the focus somewhat more easily with the additional lens.

It is worth reviewing work done in these areas before outlining what this volume proposes. Both German and Russian cinemas have had considerable attention devoted to them since the mid-1990s.[3] In the case of German cinema, over twenty volumes were published from the mid-1990s to 2004.[4] None of these address the intersection between music and cinema, however, even if some deal with musical genres, such as opera and operetta.[5] Until 2004, the treatment of music and film was confined to a small number of journal articles, book chapters, or conference pieces that tended to adopt a music historical rather than analytical musicological perspective; they gave, for example, historical accounts of composers or genres, rather than an analysis of how the music functioned in the films concerned.[6] Lutz Koepnick's 2002 volume on the crossover between Hollywood and German cinema in the period 1930–50 showed a willingness to engage rather more with music, if only briefly; there is, for example, a section on Peter Kreuder's score for *Glückskinder* (Lucky Kids, Paul Martin, 1936) within the context of Nazi musical politics (Koepnick memorably but problematically points out how "Nazi film music beat audiences into delightful submission"),[7] and a section on one of the composers treated by Robert Peck in chapter 1, Giuseppe Becce, with a short analysis of Becce's score for *Der Kaiser von Kalifornien* (The Emperor of California, Luis Trenker, 1936).[8]

Amongst the small number of pieces on music in the German cinema in this period, special mention should be made of Caryl Flinn's work in the 1990s, collected and expanded in a volume published in 2004.[9] Her 1992 work, *Strains of Utopia*, was, with Claudia Gorbman's *Unheard Melodies*, one of the key works to elaborate the function of music in film, dealing in particular with music's nostalgic function. That book focused on Hollywood cinema; the 2004 volume analyzes music's function in the New German Cinema with a focus on the way music, far from being an unheard melody (to reprise Gorbman's view of its function), encourages active participation in historical remembrance and the celebration of alterity. She suggests that "musical citations are made in such exaggerated ways that they generate the impression of inculcated, clichéd codes rather than articulations of character emotions, diegetic context, or ambient mood."[10] Musical elements, by being foregrounded, fragmented, and placed in new contexts, raise questions that Flinn links to issues of identity and history. History, in this view, is no longer a teleological grand narrative, anchored in seamless plenitude, but a collection of disarticulated fragments, ruins gesturing to a lost and profoundly problematic past. This is exemplified by the use of ca-nonical art music, such as Beethoven's Ninth Symphony, which signals "an acoustic icon of official German culture"[11] in a variety of films. It can equally be the sparse, disjunctive, and often silence-laden collages of Peer Raben's scores for Fassbinder's films. These include his own often kitschy compositions, as well as fragments of pre-existing music, where music signals melodramati-cally what the characters cannot or will not say.

Whereas Flinn ranges widely across musical styles in her cultural studies analysis of the New German Cinema, Roger Hillman's volume focuses more specifically on the use of art music in many of the same films, and makes many of the same points about its status as a cultural icon anchored in a problematic past.[12] Given the substantial work done on the German cinema of the 1970s and 1980s by Flinn and Hillman, our own volume concentrates mainly on pre-war cinema.

Work on Russian cinema has been less concentrated in the last few years, after a post-glasnost surge in the early to mid-1990s; but it is still substantial, with two major general volumes on Russian cinema,[13] and a number of more specialized volumes, many of them appearing in I.B.Tauris's Russian cinema series, KINO.[14] Importantly, however, none of these volumes address the intersection between music and film (with the exception of the volume on Shostakovich), even if there is some work on the Stalinist musical (as there is on the Nazi musical).[15] Like much of the work on film music in German cinema, Tatiana Egorova's volume is a historical survey, and there has been even less work on music and Russian film in article form than for German cinema.[16]

This volume therefore has one root purpose: to examine more closely film music from this vibrant, productive, politically charged yet largely still unresearched period where the relationship between film and music is concerned. The contributors have approached their subjects from a variety of perspectives, from single works by long-recognized artists to the output of an entire generation of composers in the German film industry; from unraveling theoretical writings to the active composition of film scores as an analytical process. They have done archival work, close readings of films, style comparison, and political histories. This variety of methodology is a strength when exploring an underexplored field—*particularly* if the presumption persists that we know more than we actually do. In order to gain a fuller understanding of this complex period, we need to come at it from a number of different angles.

Film historian Robert Peck tackles the broadest of scopes in "Film Music in the Third Reich," drawing together recent work in the field to give a composite picture centered on film music. As he points out, writing on film music is notably sparse compared to the amount of attention lavished on other aspects of the cinema during that period. Whereas in American or British culture, for instance, the stylistic similarity of film music to art music meant that film music was regarded as slightly more deserving of scholarly attention than popular music, the situation in German music studies is more that of falling between two stools. Because of the obvious cultural implications of jazz during the Weimar Republic and the Third Reich, or the potentially subversive overtones of cabaret and musical theater, they have tended to be much more popular foci of scholarly research. Peck outlines some of the policy issues and looks closely at the agencies of regulation and censorship in the German film industry from 1933 to 1945, with new research on the *Reichsmusikprüfstelle* (Reich Music Examination Office), a section of the Propaganda Ministry. He then traces the careers of five composers—Giuseppe Becce, Werner Egk, Winfried Zillig, Franz Grothe, and Peter Kreuder—who were prominent at the time, either specifically for film music (Becce) or for their activities outside the film industry. They are of particular interest because of the continuity of their work and careers despite regime changes; they did not suddenly change their style or approach in 1933 to accommodate the new regime, and then return to normal after 1945.

Musicologist Reimar Volker challenges received wisdom by focusing on a single case study, examining Herbert Windt's "Wagnerian" score for Leni Riefenstahl's iconic Nazi film *Triumph des Willens* (Triumph of the Will, 1935). The film's obvious propagandistic content but stunning aesthetic beauty has made it an uncomfortable if fascinating object of study for film scholars; however, as is often the case, the music is not addressed in any depth, if at all. The spectacular nature of the visuals—they are there to be looked at and marveled over as images, not merely moments within a story—means that music can be even more crucial to the audience's emotional relationship with the imagery than in a more conventionally narrative film. Claudia Gorbman's concept of "mutual implication"[17] is amplified in the case of the spectacular: the images are infused by the audience's emotional engagement by the music, and the music gains rhetorical power from association with particular imagery. In a more mainstream Anglo-American cinematic example, one might think of David Lean's images of the desert set against Maurice Jarre's quasi-Orientalist/French-Wagnerian *Lawrence of Arabia* theme. There is nothing "authentic" or specifically iconic—in Peircean terms—about that relationship; it is entirely arbitrary (symbolic), but has welded itself together in the public consciousness of most moviegoers. One can argue that Richard Wagner's anti-Semitic and—in the eyes of some—proto-fascist philosophies are closer to the Nazi ideology than Jarre's faux Saint-Saëns is to Lean's Lawrence epic (although a few more terms in the equation might prove that Jarre's stylistic lineage is just as implicated in Lean's colonialist fantasies, via Saint-Saëns's biblical exoticism in *Samson et Delila*); however, the process of associating music with image is still a combination of building on old tropes and creating new ones.

The centrality of Richard Wagner's music to long-held conceptions of Nazi aesthetics—some of which hinge merely on Hitler's personal affection for the composer—leads to the frequent assumption that Windt's style in a central product of Nazi propaganda/art must be Wagnerian. Volker's analysis creates a much more subtle picture of both Windt's score and of Nazi musical ideology. Volker finds that a closer look at Herbert Windt's background and his assignments prior to the rally recorded in *Triumph des Willens* suggests that the composer did not merely adhere to the Wagner-Bruckner sound world. Instead, Windt was a leader in the first phase of Nazi cultural politics "marked by the quest, and need, for authentic and innovative art forms capable of reflecting the 'new' spirit and aesthetic the Nazi movement felt compelled to propagate"— making him quite literally an avant-garde composer, not a musical reactionary merely recapitulating Wagner's style of the previous century.

German studies scholar Marc Weiner also deals with a composer on the leading edge of an artistic movement, though in a much different fashion. Just as Windt's participation in popular *U(nterhaltungs)-Musik* has meant that a close examination of the cultural and political context has at times overshadowed the nuance of musical style and history, Alban Berg's position as one of the leading *E(rnste)-Musik* composers in Germany during the 1920s and 1930s has frequently meant that cultural and political context has been relegated to the margins (and footnotes) of Berg studies. Since he composed in the serial or twelve-tone method developed by his teacher, the Jewish Arnold Schoenberg, who left Germany in 1933 and settled in Los Angeles in 1934, Berg's music has often been studied as a quasi-scientific, mathematical product best understood as a matrix of predetermined choices mingled with personal fingerprints that are the markers of "genius." However, Berg's style hewed closely to the expressionistic, highly emotive style of Schoenberg's pre-serial composition, and his attraction to the lyrical, dramatic, and theatrical forms of song, concerto, and opera have made his music sit particularly uncomfortably in the realm of "absolute" or "pure" music to which German musical culture, and the "science" of musicology that emerged from it in the nineteenth century, aspired—except for the awkward issue of Wagner and his drive to create the *Gesamtkunstwerk* that many theorists of both film and music feel would have been realized in film.

Berg's opera *Lulu* is notable for its inclusion of a film interlude. Ironically, this inclusion is for a *silent* film. By 1935, this was forward-looking for opera but backward-looking for film. Weiner notes the remarkable second "silence" of the film interlude: that the critical response to the insertion of film within an opera (as opposed to filmed operas) is practically unheard. Weiner analyzes critical silence as revealing of widespread assumptions regarding the two art forms that characterized the arts as "diametrically opposed in their aesthetic quality and social function." He argues that the transgressive, socially volatile content of the film interlude plays on the critique of the new medium, film, as licentious and potentially anarchical, disgusting, even "American," associated with an audience that was excluded from high culture, such as opera. The film interlude becomes not merely a novelty, but a recursive symbol of class and aesthetic division.

This politically charged aesthetic polarization of *E-Musik* and *U-Musik* lies alongside the polarization between the urgent, urban modernism of composer Edmund Meisel's work in Leftist theater and cinema (including a controversial score to Eisenstein's *Bronenosets Potyomkin* [Battleship Potemkin, 1925]) and the romanticized nature of the conservative-nationalist ideology represented by the popular *Bergfilm* genre. Christopher Morris's finely nuanced reading of Meisel's score for *Der heilige Berg* (The Holy Mountain, 1926) explores these tensions not only in Meisel's film composition, but in an accompanying article he wrote to promote the film. As Morris explores, the musical signifiers of nature, inherited from nineteenth-century German Romanticism, are often cyclical, both continuously in motion and repetitive, spinning a sense of timelessness; but these musical characteristics, with just a subtle shift of emphasis and rhythm, can transmute motion from flow to flywheel, nature to technology. Beyond style, on a structural level, Meisel's score, with its abrupt shifts that highlight rather than smooth over the technological intervention of editing, can seem primitive and awkward, or as precursors to the modernist "reforms" of film music technique that were proposed some twenty years later by Adorno and Eisler. In Morris's analysis, *Der heilige Berg* begins to resemble a lenticular postcard, continually shifting between two different images: the film is "haunted by these tensions between tradition and progress, high art and popular culture."

Composer Ed Hughes has a unique perspective on both the writings and film score compositions of Hanns Eisler: in 2001, Hughes was commissioned by the Bath International Music Festival to compose a new score for the 1929 Joris Ivens short film *Regen* (Rain), Eisler's scoring of which became the basis for a practical exploration in an appendix of *Composing for the Films*. Eisler's work was to some extent a reaction to and against Sergei Eisenstein's analysis of the music/image relationship in *Aleksandr Nevskiy* (Alexander Nevskiy, 1938, about which see more in Julie Hubbert's and Rebecca Schwartz-Bishir's essays). Considering Eisenstein's and Eisler's writings, and Eisler's and his own film scores, Hughes investigates the multifarious workings of rhythm within the frame, in film editing, in Eisler's score, and in Hughes's own score, *Light Cuts through Dark Skies*.

The modern application and transformation of principles from earlier in the century is yet more foregrounded in musicologist Björn Heile's examination of Mauricio Kagel's work as a composer who is also a filmmaker. Building on the principles of serialism,[18] Kagel created a series of films in which he treated all aspects of film—image and sound (sound and music) alike—as parameters in a process of multiple serialism. Kagel's work questions particularly the hierarchical relationship that privileges sight over sound, organized sound (music) over noise, and even the chain of cause and effect over random chance. His films do not reject the creation of symbolic relationships by juxtaposing image and sound/sound and image, but problematize those relationships; the oft-noted eerie similarity in result that emerged from mid-century musical experiments in total serialism and chance composition converge in Kagel's work, even as they often delight in the incongruities in a manner that harkens back to the Dadaists of the 1920s and even the Marx Brothers. Kagel conceptualized film as an integrally related multimedia art form, which he likened to "the only possible continuation of opera."

While German culture was steeped in operatic metaphors and aspirations, integration, and organicism, Soviet culture was more volatile and charged with the energetic force of a newly forged nation changing fast from a medieval feudal system to a modern communist state. The futuristic drive of the machine and a culture in which dance was more central than opera created a different sensibility. Russian culture has always been influenced by other European cultures—Italian, French, German—but the new Soviet state, revolutionary tendencies in philosophical thinking, and new technologies meant different metaphors and approaches: fewer aesthetic musings, more manifestos.

Sergei Eisenstein's emphasis on "rhythm, rhythm, rhythm, above all else rhythm" is the focus of Julie Hubbert's close examination of his writing on image/music relationships. Eisenstein's arguments are less concerned with meaning, or organic narrative cohesion of the sort generated by leitmotivic, or thematic, scoring popular in Hollywood, or even the local coincidence of movement and music often derided as "mickey-mousing"—and perhaps suggested in Eisenstein's infamous pictorial analysis of *Aleksandr Nevskiy*, and more with large-scale, abstract structural movement. While that kind of structural rhythm is associated with more abstract filmmaking—like Ivens's *Regen* or Dziga Vertov's *Chelovek s kino-apparatom* (Man with a Movie Camera, also 1929)—Eisenstein argued that those tenets could and should be observed in narrative film as well. Hubbert not only teases out some of the implications of those arguments for film scoring, but traces similarities in Eisenstein's writing to the works of George Antheil, Erik Satie, and Kurt London, suggesting that Eisenstein's work is somewhat less idiosyncratic than is generally perceived.

Eisenstein's iconic collaboration with Sergei Prokofiev on *Aleksandr Nevskiy* is the subject of Rebecca Schwartz-Bishir's essay. Similarly to Volker's closer look at the concept of "Nazi musical style," Schwartz-Bishir's examination of "Prokofiev's successful compromise with Socialist Realism" takes a look at the contradictory nature of Prokofiev's compositional technique and his resolution of his more modernist tendencies with Socialist Realism, under the ironic guise of representing Teutonic barbarism. Some of Prokofiev's more radical recording techniques appear to have been influenced by the composer's visit to the Disney studios in Hollywood, and even his decision against the authentic in favor of a decidedly inauthentic representation has clear echoes of Hollywood film scoring's approach to the exoticism of the other and of the past.

Just as Heile's work on Kagel's more recent work demonstrates that the organizing principles of total serialism and the creation of symbolic connections still permeated the artistic climate of Germany half a century later, so does Mitchell Morris's look at Russian emigré Slava Tsukerman's film *Liquid Sky*, set in New Wave Soho, demonstrate that the aesthetics of the earlier Soviet period were still influencing artistic choices as late as 1982. This is seen from the echoes of constructivism in the design to the use of the "Laurel Waltz" of eccentric American composer Anthony Philip Heinrich (himself a German immigrant of the nineteenth century) in an ironic/nostalgic manner reminiscent of Dmitri Shostakovich dropping Vincent Youmans's foxtrot "Tea for Two" into his ballet *The Golden Age*. As with Eisenstein, some sequences in the film subordinate traditional narrative to "rhythmic" structures that articulate meaning through juxtaposition or layering. The dissolution of the normal music/image hierarchies and the "fortuitous" collision of the Russian *ostranenie* with the (post-)punk "do-it-yourself" attitude (and Brechtian *Verfremdung*) help create an incipient "post-modernism" that is rooted in older Russian/Soviet aesthetics in a work consciously framed as a *Gesamtkunstwerk* by its controlling creator. German and Soviet ideals emerge from an American underground.

The essays in this book are united by their desire to investigate areas of the film musical terrain that are often overlooked—either because they are out of the way and unexplored, or more often because we have assumed that we know what they are like. They are also interested in making connections between theory and practice, and between theory and culture. The history of film music is a vast, still largely uncharted territory. This volume is intended to begin shading in the topography while serving as a call for others to take up their cartographic pencils and join us.

Notes

1. See Marks, "Film Music," and Stilwell, "Film Music," for a closer examination of the literature of film music.

2. See for example Welch, *Propaganda and the German Cinema*; Petley, "Film Policy"; and a key volume covering both cinemas, Taylor, *Film Propaganda*.

3. In the following brief survey, we refer principally to English-language books.

4. These include the following: Allan and Sandford, *DEFA*; Alter, *Projecting History*; Bergfelder, *International Adventures*; Bergfelder et al., *The German Cinema Book*; Davidson, *Deterritorializing the New German Cinema*; Elsaesser, *A Second Life*; Elsaesser, *BFI Companion to German Cinema*; Elsaesser, *Weimar Cinema and After*; Feinstein, *The Triumph of the Ordinary*; Ginsberg and Thompson, *Perspectives on German Cinema*; Hake, *German National Cinema*; Koepnick, *The Dark Mirror*; Kuzniar, *The Queer German Cinema*; O'Sickey and von Zadow, *Triangulated Visions*; Oksiloff, *Picturing the Primitive*; Shandley, *Rubble Films*; Silberman, *German Cinema*; Welch, *Propaganda and the German Cinema*.

5. See for example Elsaesser, "Transparent Duplicities: Pabst's *The Threepenny Opera*," and Elsaesser, "It's the End of the Song: Walter Reisch, Operetta, and the Double Negative."

6. This is the case for jazz in the swing-film in Hoffmann, "Liebe, Jazz und Übermut," and the conference collection of the 11th Internationaler Filmhistorischer Kongress, held in Hamburg in 1998 (see Hagener and Hans, *Als die Filme singen lernten*). This volume has a number of pieces on German cinema from a historical perspective: on early music film (Sannwald, "Der Ton macht die Musik"; Quaresima, "Tankstelle und Hinterhof"), on specific composers (Werner Richard Heymann, Friedrich Hollaender, Ralph Benatzky, and Mischa Spoliansky) in the case of Bolte, "Vom Kabarett zum Film," or singers (Claus, "Von Gilbert zu Goebbels"). There is less of a historical perspective in Vossen's analysis the year before of Richard Tauber's voice in *Die große Attraktion* (The Big Attraction, Max Reichmann, 1931), where she argues that the function of Tauber's voice is to legitimize what was regarded as a foreign medium (Vossen, "*Die große Attraktion*").

7. Koepnick, *The Dark Mirror*, 46.

8. Ibid., 42–46, 121–25, respectively.

9. The volume contains the following pieces by Flinn: "Music and the Melodramatic Past"; "Camp, Music, and the Production of History"; "The Legacy of Modernism"; "Strategies of Remembrance"; "Embracing Kitsch"; as well as a new essay on opera in the films of Kluge (chapter 4). She has pursued work in this area with "The Music That Lola Ran To."

10. Flinn, *The New German Cinema*, 3.

11. Ibid., 13.

12. Hillman, *Unsettling Scores*. This includes some earlier work (see "Beethoven, Mahler, and the New German Cinema" and "Cultural Memory on Film Soundtracks"), but most of it is new material.

13. Gillespie, Russian Cinema; Taylor, *The BFI Companion to Eastern European and Russian Cinema*.

14. Beumers, *Russia on Reels;* Gillespie, *Early Soviet Cinema;* Haynes, *New Soviet Man;* Lawton, *Before the Fall;* Roberts, *Forward Soviet!;* Sargeant, *Vsevolod Pudovkin;* Widdis, *Visions of a New Land;* Woll, *Real Images;* Youngblood, *The Magic Mirror;* and the second edition of Taylor's 1979 classic (Taylor, *Film Propaganda*). The Kino series also has short volumes on Russian filmmakers: see Beardow, *Little Vera;* Beumers, *Burnt by the Sun;* Graffy, *Bed and Sofa;* Kepley, *The End of St Petersburg;* Neuberger, *Ivan the Terrible;* Roberts, *The Man with the Movie Camera;* Synessios, *Mirror;* Taylor, *The Battleship Potemkin;* Woll, *The Cranes Are Flying;* Youngblood, *Repentance*. See also an interesting volume on Shostakovich's film scores: Riley, *Dmitri Shostakovich*.

15. See Anderson, "Why Stalinist Musicals?"; Taylor, "But Eastward, Look, the Land is Brighter"; Gillespie, "The Sounds of Music."

16. Egorova, *Soviet Film Music*. Articles or book chapters: Merritt, "Recharging *Alexander Nevskiy*," reviews Prokofiev's score, with reference to the influence of the Disney studio, and comments on the disjunction between music and image; Baier, "Der visuelle Ton," discusses Meisel's scores for films by Sergei Eisenstein, Walther Ruttmann, and Ilya Trauberg; Schlegel, "Das stalinistische Hollywood," shows how Aleksandrov's musical film comedies are similar in form to Hollywood musicals (echoing Eagle, "Socialist Realism and American Genre Films"); Thiel, "Versiegelte Klänge," reviews Tarkovsky's use of art music, and his occasional forays into more modern music, such as that composed by Vyacheslav Ovtchinnikov and Eduard Artemyev.

17. Gorbman, *Unheard Melodies*, 15.

18. While serialism may be seen as the aesthetic antithesis of the *Gesamtkunstwerk* because of its precise control of all parameters (modern(ist)/scientific vs. Romantic/emotional), serialism—particularly multiple or "total" serialism—itself may be seen as an internalization of the totalizing impulse that expands outward in the *Gesamtkunstwerk*. As serialized parameters expand beyond the aural into the visual, the resemblance becomes even more striking.

References

Allan, Seán, and John Sandford, eds. *DEFA: East German Cinema, 1946–1992*. New York: Berghahn Books, 1999.

Alter, Nora M. *Projecting History: German Nonfiction Cinema, 1967–2000*. Ann Arbor: University of Michigan Press, 2002.

Anderson, Trudy. "Why Stalinist Musicals?" *Discourse* 17/3 (1995): 38–48.

Baier, Christian. "Der visuelle Ton: Der Filmkomponist Edmund Meisel." *Neue Zeitschrift für Musik* 156/4 (1995): 16–21.

Beardow, Frank. *Little Vera*. London: I. B. Tauris, 2003.

Bergfelder, Tim. *International Adventures: German Popular Cinema and European Co-productions in the 1960s*. New York: Berghahn Books, 2004.

Bergfelder, Tim, Erica Carter, and Deniz Gokturk, eds. *The German Cinema Book*. London: British Film Institute, 2002.

Beumers, Birgit. *Russia on Reels: The Russian Idea in Post-Soviet Cinema*. London: I. B. Tauris, 1999.

———. *Burnt by the Sun*. London: I. B. Tauris, 2000.

Bolte, Marie-Luise. "Vom Kabarett zum Film: Thesen zum Filmsong und vier Komponisten-Porträts." In *Als die Filme singen lernten: Innovation und Tradition im Musikfilm 1928–1938*, ed. Malte Hagener and Jan Hans. München: CineGraph text + kritik, 1999, 39–47.

Brown, Royal S. *Overtones and Undertones: Reading Film Music*. Berkeley: University of California Press, 1994.

Buhler, James, Caryl Flinn, and David Neumeyer, eds. *Music and Cinema*. Hanover, N.H.: Wesleyan University Press, 2000.

Chion, Michel. *Audio-Vision: Sound on Screen.* Trans. Claudia Gorbman. New York: Columbia University Press, 1994.

———. *The Voice in Cinema.* Trans. Claudia Gorbman. New York: Columbia University Press, 1999.

Claus, Horst. "Von Gilbert zu Goebbels: Hans Steinhoff zwischen Operette und Tonfilm mit Musik." In *Als die Filme singen lernten: Innovation und Tradition im Musikfilm 1928–1938,* ed. Malte Hagener and Jan Hans. München: CineGraph text + kritik, 1999, 105–20.

Davidson, John E. *Deterritorializing the New German Cinema.* Minneapolis: University of Minnesota Press, 1999.

Eagle, Herbert. "Socialist Realism and American Genre Films: The Mining of Codes in *Jazzman.*" In *The Red Screen: Politics, Society, Art in Soviet Cinema,* ed. Anna Lawton. New York: Routledge, 1992, 249–63.

Egorova, Tatiana K. *Soviet Film Music: An Historical Survey.* Trans. Tatiana A. Ganf and Natalia A. Egunova. Contemporary music studies, 13. Australia: Harwood Academic Publishers; Amsterdam: OPA, Overseas Publishers Association , 1997.

Eisler, Hanns, and Theodor W. Adorno. *Composing for the Films.* 1947. Reprint, London: Athlone Press, 1994.

Elsaesser, Thomas. *BFI Companion to German Cinema.* London: British Film Institute, 1999.

———. "It's the End of the Song: Walter Reisch, Operetta and the Double Negative." In Thomas Elsaesser, *Weimar Cinema and After: Germany's Historical Imaginary.* London: Routledge, 2000, 330–58.

———. "Transparent Duplicities: Pabst's *The Threepenny Opera.*" In Thomas Elsaesser, *Weimar Cinema and After: Germany's Historical Imaginary.* London: Routledge, 2000, 311–29. Previously published in *The Films of G. W. Pabst: An Extra-Territorial Cinema.* New Brunswick, N.J.: Rutgers University Press, 1990, 103–15.

———. *Weimar Cinema and After: Germany's Historical Imaginary.* London: Routledge, 2000.

Elsaesser, Thomas, with Michael Wedel. *A Second Life: German Cinema's First Decades.* Amsterdam: Amsterdam University Press, 1996.

Feinstein, Joshua. *The Triumph of the Ordinary: Depictions of Daily Life in the East German Cinema, 1949–1989.* Chapel Hill: University of North Carolina Press, 2002.

Flinn, Caryl. "Camp, Music, and the Production of History: *Anita* and Rosa von Praunheim." In *Queering the Canon: Defying the Sights in German Literatures and Culture,* ed. Christoph Lorey and John L. Plews. Columbia: Camden House, 1998, 350–82.

———. "Embracing Kitsch: Werner Schroeter, Music and *The Bomber Pilot.*" In *Film Music: Critical Approaches,* ed. Kevin. J. Donnelly. Edinburgh: Edinburgh University Press, 2001, 129–51.

———. "The Legacy of Modernism: Peter Raben, Film Music and Political After Shock." In *Cinesonic: The World of Sound in Film,* ed. Philip Brophy. North Ryde: Australian Film Television and Radio School, 1999, 171–88.

———. "The Music That Lola Ran To." In *Sound Matters: Essays on the Acoustics of Modern German Culture,* ed. Nora M. Alter and Lutz Koepnick. New York: Berghahn Books, 2004, 197–213.

———. "Music and the Melodramatic Past of New German Cinema." In *Melodrama: Stage/Picture/Screen,* ed. Jacky Bratton, Jim Cook, and Christine Gledhill. London: British Film Institute, 1994, 106–18.

———. *The New German Cinema: Music, History, and the Matter of Style.* Berkeley: University of California Press, 2004.

———. *Strains of Utopia: Gender, Nostalgia, and Hollywood Film Music.* Princeton: Princeton University Press, 1992.

———. "Strategies of Remembrance: Music and History in the New German Cinema." In *Music and Cinema,* ed. James Buhler, Caryl Flinn, and David Neumeyer. Hanover, N.H.: Wesleyan University Press, 2000, 118–41.

Gillespie, David. *Early Soviet Cinema: Innovation, Ideology and Propaganda.* London: Wallflower, 2000.

——. *Russian Cinema.* Harlow, Essex: Longman, 2003.

Gillespie, David C. "The Sounds of Music: Soundtrack and Song in Soviet Film." *Slavic Review* 62/3 (2003): 473–90.

Ginsberg, Terri, and Kirsten Moana Thompson, eds. *Perspectives on German Cinema.* New York: G. K. Hall; London: Prentice Hall International, 1996.

Gorbman, Claudia. *Unheard Melodies: Narrative Film Music.* Bloomington: Indiana University Press, 1987.

Graffy, Julian. *Bed and Sofa.* London: I. B. Tauris, 2001.

Hagener, Malte, and Jan Hans, eds. *Als die Filme singen lernten: Innovation und Tradition im Musikfilm 1928–1938.* München: CineGraph text + kritik, 1999.

Hake, Sabine. *German National Cinema.* London: Routledge, 2001.

Haynes, John. *New Soviet Man: Gender and Masculinity in Stalinist Soviet Cinema.* Manchester: Manchester University Press, 2003.

Hillman, Roger. "Beethoven, Mahler, and the New German Cinema." *Musicology Australia* 20 (1997): 84–93.

——. "Cultural Memory on Film Soundtracks." *Journal of European Studies* 33/3–4 (2003): 323–32.

——. *Unsettling Scores: German Film, Music, and Ideology.* Bloomington: Indiana University Press, 2006.

Hoffmann, Bernd. "Liebe, Jazz und Übermut: Der swingende Heimatfilm der 1950er Jahre." In *Heimatlose Klange? Regionale Musiklandschaften—heute,* ed. Thomas Phleps. Beiträge zur Popularmusikforschung; 29/30. Karben: Coda, 2002, 259–86.

Kalinak, Kathryn Marie. *Settling the Score: Music and the Classical Hollywood Film.* Madison: University of Wisconsin Press, 1992.

Kepley, Vance. *The End of St Petersburg.* London: I. B. Tauris, 2003.

Koepnick, Lutz. *The Dark Mirror: German Cinema Between Hitler and Hollywood.* Berkeley: University of California Press, 2002.

Kuzniar, Alice A. *The Queer German Cinema.* Stanford, Calif.: Stanford University Press, 2000.

Lawton, Anna. *Before the Fall: Soviet Cinema in the Gorbachev Years.* Philadelphia: Xlibris, 2002.

Marks, Martin. "Film Music: The Material, Literature, and Present State of Research." *Notes* 36 (1979): 282–325.

Merritt, Russell. "Recharging *Alexander Nevsky;* Tracking the Eisenstein-Prokofiev War Horse." *Film Quarterly* 48/2 (1994): 34–48.

Neuberger, Joan. *Ivan the Terrible.* London: I. B. Tauris, 2000.

O'Sickey, Ingeborg Majer, and Ingeborg von Zadow, eds. *Triangulated Visions: Women in Recent German Cinema.* Albany: State University of New York Press, 1998.

Oksiloff, Asseka. *Picturing the Primitive: Visual Culture, Ethnography, and Early German Cinema.* London: Palgrave, 2002.

Quaresima, Leonardo. "Tankstelle und Hinterhof: 'Genre'-Entwicklung als Modernisierungsprogramm." In *Als die Filme singen lernten: Innovation und Tradition im Musikfilm 1928–1938,* ed. Malte Hagener and Jan Hans. München: CineGraph text + kritik, 1999, 61–71.

Petley, Julian. "Film Policy in the Third Reich." In *The German Cinema Book,* ed. Tim Bergfelder, Erica Carter, and Deniz Gokturk. London: British Film Institute, 2002, 173–81.

Riley, John. *Dmitri Shostakovich.* London: I. B. Tauris, 2004.

Roberts, Graham. *The Man with the Movie Camera.* London: I. B. Tauris, 2000.

——. *Forward Soviet! History and Non-Fiction Film in the USSR.* London: I. B. Tauris, 1999.

Sargeant, Amy. *Vsevolod Pudovkin: Classic Films of the Soviet Avant-Garde.* London: I. B. Tauris, 2000.

Sannwald, Daniela. "Der Ton macht die Musik: Zur Definition und Struktur des frühen Ton-films." In *Als die Filme singen lernten: Innovation und Tradition im Musikfilm 1928–1938,* ed. Malte Hagener and Jan Hans. München: CineGraph text + kritik, 1999, 29–38.

Schlegel, Hans-Joachim. "Das stalinistischen Hollywood: Zu Grigorij Aleksandrovs Musikfilmkomödien." In *Als die Filme singen lernten: Innovation und Tradition im Musikfilm 1928–1938,* ed. Malte Hagener and Jan Hans. München: CineGraph text + kritik, 1999, 138–49.

Shandley, Robert R. *Rubble Films: German Cinema in the Shadow of the Third Reich.* Philadelphia: Temple University Press, 2001.

Silberman, Marc. *German Cinema: Texts in Context.* Detroit: Wayne State University Press, 1995.

Stilwell, Robynn J. "Film Music Scholarship since 1980: A Critical Review." *Journal of Film Music* 1/1 (2002): 19–61.

Synessios, Natasha. *Mirror.* London: I. B. Tauris, 2001.

Taylor, Richard. *The Battleship Potemkin.* London: I. B. Tauris, 2000.

———, ed. *The BFI Companion to Eastern European and Russian Cinema.* London: British Film Institute, 2000.

———. "But Eastward, Look, the Land Is Brighter: Towards a Topography of Utopia in the Stalinist Musical." In *100 Years of European Cinema: Entertainment or Ideology?,* ed. Diana Holmes and Alison Smith. Manchester: Manchester University Press, 2000, 11–26.

———. *Film Propaganda: Soviet Russia and Nazi Germany.* 2nd ed. London: I. B. Tauris, 1998.

Thiel, Wolfgang. "Versiegelte Klange: Gedanken zur musikalischen Konzeption in den Filmen von Andrej Tarkowski." In *Film und Musik,* ed. Regina Schlagnitweit and Gottfried Schlemmer. Wien: Synema, 2001, 125–35.

Vossen, Ursula. "Die große Attraktion: Opern- und Operettensanger im deutschsprachigen Tonfilm." In *MusikSpektakelFilm: Musiktheater und Tanzkultur in deutschen Film, 1922–1937,* ed. Katja Uhlenbrock. München: CineGraph text + kritik, 1998, 105–22.

Welch, David. *Propaganda and the German Cinema, 1933–1945.* 1983; reprint, London: I. B. Tauris, 2001.

Widdis, Emma. *Visions of a New Land: Soviet Film from the Revolution to the Second World War.* New Haven, Conn.: Yale University Press, 2003.

Woll, Josephine. *Real Images: Soviet Cinema and the Thaw.* London: I. B. Tauris, 2000.

———. *The Cranes Are Flying.* London: I. B. Tauris, 2003.

Youngblood, Denise J. *The Magic Mirror: Moviemaking in Russia, 1908–1918.* Wisconsin Studies in Film. Madison: University of Wisconsin Press, 1999.

———. *Repentance.* London: I. B. Tauris, 2001.

PART

GERMANY

ONE

Film Music in the Third Reich

ROBERT E. PECK

Writing in 1995, Pamela Potter remarked on the paucity of writing on music in the Third Reich, especially as compared with that on the other arts of the period.[1] Such a comparison is especially striking in relation to work on Third Reich cinema, often referred to as "Nazi film." Much of the musical scholarship is concerned with the more celebrated and controversial personalities of the period—such as Furtwängler, von Karajan, Schoenberg, Pfitzner, Hindemith, Richard Strauss, and others—and their relations with the political authorities. In Germany it has long been the practice to make a clear distinction between "serious" music, i.e., orchestral, choral, and operatic music, as represented by such composers—designated *E-Musik* (for *ernst*)—and popular and commercial music—*U-Musik* (for *Unterhaltung*, entertainment). Music historians dealing with this period have looked predominantly at the serious side, but considerable work has also been done on popular music. Within this body of literature the subject of film music is rarely mentioned. Similarly, in the scholarly literature concerned with film, rarely is there any reference to the music. Interest is normally focused on narrative concerns or the propaganda aspect, or on particular stars and directors. Film composers, if mentioned at all, are named merely in passing when listing the production crew of individual films. Although some attention has been paid to the film *musical* as a genre,[2] very little has been paid to music as a significant feature of the films of all genres.

Given the interest that both these areas of cultural life in the Third Reich have received separately, it seems curious that the area where they coincide has been largely overlooked by music historians and film researchers alike. This by no means reflects the importance ascribed to film music at the time. Film composers were—unlike, for example, cinematographers and production designers—recognized by the industry as of major importance to the production. This is indicated by the "league tables" published at the end of every calendar year, recognizing the output of screenwriters, directors, and composers, but no other contributors.[3] Over 200 composers contributed to the films of this period, many of them already well known from their other activities, either as conductors and musical directors, or as composers of operas, operettas, and popular songs.

Second, virtually every feature film contained not only background or illustration music, but also diegetic music integrated into the narrative by way of dances, songs, choral pieces, or concerts. This extended beyond light entertainment and musical films to include melodramas, war, history, and adventure films. It would be extremely difficult to name a single film where this was not the case, which may well be unique within the filmic conventions of European cinema.

Third, cinema was—together with radio and the recording industry, with which it maintained close links—a principal source of hit songs and dance melodies. Popular film music was regularly broadcast on special radio programs[4] and marketed on gramophone records. Indeed, the list of hit songs of the thirties and forties that were introduced to the public through films is virtually endless.

Finally, articles on musical technique and policy, as well as features on and by individual composers, were from an early date published in the film trade press, providing another clear indication of the importance attached to film music by the industry in Germany.

In what follows, we shall review the institutional context of German cinema of the period, while focusing on a number of key composers, both "serious" and popular. As we shall see, in all cases, their careers, while being affected to some extent by political constraints, were not disrupted during the Nazi period. A case in point is Giuseppe Becce.

E-Musik 1: Becce

It is particularly fitting to start with this composer, as he is credited as the first to write a film-specific score in Germany. That was in 1913; the Italian-born

Becce was an accomplished musician who had premiered his first operetta in Bremen in 1910 at the age of twenty-three, and two years later his first opera in Breslau.[5] Moving to Berlin to continue his studies, he was engaged by the pioneering filmmaker Oskar Messter, who was producing a film about Richard Wagner. On the strength of Becce's physical resemblance to the eponymous composer, he was cast in the title role.[6] As the Wagner estate was demanding exorbitant royalties, Wagner's own music could not be used, whereupon Becce was commissioned to write a special score for the film. He went on to compose for the screen for the next five decades.[7] His filmography numbers 184 titles, making him one of the most prolific film composers of all time. Becce is perhaps best known internationally for his invention of the Kinothek (*Kino* = cinema + *Bibliothek* = library), a ten-volume collection of original scores published between 1919 and 1929 to provide cinema musicians with piano and orchestral arrangements to illustrate typical, recurring situations and moods in silent films.[8]

During the period of the Third Reich alone, Becce wrote the music for over fifty films, of which some thirty-three were German or German co-productions. The others were made in Italy, Austria, Czechoslovakia, France, and the USA. His work ranged across all genres, but he seemed to have a particular affinity for mountain films, both features and documentaries, collaborating with Arnold Fanck on *Die weiße Hölle von Piz Palü* (The White Hell of Pitz Palu, 1929) and *Kampf um den Berg—Eine Hochtour vor 20 Jahren* (Battle for the Mountain, 1940), and with Leni Riefenstahl on *Das blaue Licht* (The Blue Light, 1932). His most enduring working relationship was with Luis Trenker, collaborating on several mountain films—such as *Der Sohn der weißen Berge* (Son of the White Mountain, 1930), *Berge in Flammen* (Mountains on Fire, 1931)—and also on others merely set in the mountains—such as *Der Feuerteufel* (The Fire Devil, 1940)—or with an alpine reference, such as *Der Kaiser von Kalifornien* (The Emperor of California, 1936). Between 1933 (*Der Rebell*, The Rebel) and 1945 (*Monte Miracolo*), Becce and Trenker made eight films together.

In 1933 Becce collaborated with the little-known director Franz Wenzler on another mountain film, *Gipfelstürmer* (Assault on the Summit), about the conquest of the north face of the Matterhorn.[9] Possibly linked with this project, the same year and with the same director, he wrote the music for *Hans Westmar*, a film biography of the Nazi icon Horst Wessel. This was one of the few blatantly Nazi films of the period, and has hence received considerable attention from film historians. On this project, Becce shared credit for the music with Ernst "Putzi" Hanfstaengl, a longtime companion of Hitler and member of his inner circle, who at the time held the post of foreign press chief of the Nazi party.

Two years later Becce worked again with Wenzler, on the German-Italian co-production *Hundert Tage* (Hundred Days, 1935), from the historical play *Campo di Maggio* by Benito Mussolini and Giovacchino Forzano, first staged in 1931. This was a much more elaborate affair than the previous two films, with clear political resonances for the contemporary audience and an all-star cast including Werner Krauss as Napoleon and Gustav Gründgens as Fouché.[10]

After the war Becce composed for another twenty-two films. His last project, the alpine documentary *Zauber der Dolomiten* (The Magic of the Dolomites, Hans J. Gnamm, 1959), signaled a fitting conclusion to a career in which he had achieved a unique specialization in this genre.[11] In 1961 Becce was awarded the German equivalent of the OBE (*Bundesverdienstkreuz*), and in 1971, at the age of eighty-four, received the lifetime service award of the German film industry. He died in West Berlin in 1973.[12] Apart from its longevity, Becce's career is not atypical for the period. Many composers began writing film music during the silent era and carried on into the postwar period, with little indication that the events of the Third Reich ever impinged significantly upon their professional activities. Before turning to other composers, we shall consider the institutional framework.

The German Cinema and Nazism

The silent cinema was international. A film, simply by translating its intertitles, could in theory be marketed anywhere. Putting the dialogue on the sound track immediately imposed severe restrictions. Hollywood productions, which had previously dominated the world market, suddenly became less attractive to audiences who had to read subtitles while listening to a foreign language. As soon as the technology permitted, it was far preferable to listen to dialogue spoken in one's own language. The non-anglophone countries reaped the benefits, in particular the German-speaking regions, comprising most of central Europe plus the peripheral areas within the German (and former Austro-Hungarian) sphere of influence. These represented the largest potential market of the time outside the United States itself and helped the German film industry to acquire a dominant position on the continent. Throughout the 1930s, Germany produced an average of 140 films a year, putting it well ahead of its European competitors and second only to Hollywood.[13] At the outbreak of World War II, film output was reduced considerably, but production levels for the entire duration of the Third Reich still averaged out at approximately 100 films per year. All these films needed a musical score, and thanks to the established practice of composing for the silent cinema, sufficient experienced contributors were available for the task. When the Nazis came to power, they thus inherited a flourishing film industry, in which music played a major part.

What happened next, in the conventional view, is that the nature of filmmaking in Germany changed dramatically, with all production from that date onward harnessed to the Nazi cause. Yet between 1933 and 1945 probably not more than 4 percent of total output could have been recognized as products of the Third Reich in terms of any overt Nazi content, such as uniforms, emblems, "Hitler" salutes, slogans, songs, or—without the iconography—by clearly conveying a specifically Nazi message. Such films have frequently been given pride of place in standard works on the "Nazi" cinema, creating the impression that they characterized the era rather than being exceptional cases. Moreover, these same films were, on the whole, unsuccessful and frequently disowned by the Propaganda Ministry. Hence, although an explicit and recognizable Nazi cinema did exist, it was neither typical nor numerically significant.

A similar situation existed in the field of music, as Pamela Potter has observed: "For many years . . . music in Nazi Germany was commonly perceived as a strictly controlled regimen of march music, Wagner operas, and Beethoven symphonies, devoid of any atonal music, jazz, or any other remnants of 'Weimar culture.'"[14] Such a conventional view is expressed, for example, by Erwin Kroll: "They regaled us with Blood and Soil music, with marching songs, victory cantatas and hymns to Hitler."[15]

This conception of Nazi cultural policy as an extreme, totalitarian phenomenon is somewhat misleading. It is certainly true that there was no shortage of songs glorifying the Nazis and "hymns to the Führer," together with a large number of new marches.[16] But the explicitly Nazi music—like its celluloid counterparts—developed in addition to, and not by displacing, the existing mainstream. Normal production activities in both media carried on much as before.

The notion that by the end of 1933 the Nazis had consolidated control over the arts, and that they immediately proceeded to infuse these with their particular ideology, is not entirely consistent with the facts. This is due partly to a common misconception about the nature of "the Nazis," namely that they constituted a homogeneous and coherent movement. It is well known that initially the party, and later the state apparatus that it controlled, was riven with internal conflicts, both personal and ideological. The contradictions were endemic and ran deep. Hence any reference to "Nazism" or "the Nazis" has to be approached with some caution, as it implies a degree of consensus which was rarely achieved. In the cultural sphere especially, this was clearly illustrated by the unconcealed antagonism between Alfred Rosenberg, the leading Hitlerian ideologue, and Joseph Goebbels.

In 1921 Rosenberg had become editor of the official party newspaper, the *Völkischer Beobachter*, and in 1929 he founded the militant Combat League for German Culture (*Kampfbund für deutsche Kultur*). Rosenberg and his followers took an aggressively reactionary position, articulated in a variety of publications under their control. Quotations later used to illustrate the extreme and perverse policies regarding the arts have been taken mainly from these sources. Where music was concerned, their attacks were directed at all modern or modernist tendencies. Specifically, this meant the "musical bolshevism" associated with Kurt Weill, the modernist school pioneered by Stravinsky, the twelve-tone system of Arnold Schoenberg and other composers such as Alban Berg and Anton Webern.[17] Also targeted was jazz and swing music, seen as the American "product of negroid sub-humanity and Jewish commercialism (*Geschäftsgeist*)."[18]

Goebbels took a very different line from Rosenberg: conciliatory rather than confrontational, pragmatic rather than doctrinaire, creative rather than regressive. This automatically put them on a long-term collision course. When, after the seizure of political power, the struggle for political advantage had run its course, Goebbels held all the cards.[19] First, as head of the newly formed Ministry of Propaganda, he held a government post, which Rosenberg did not, mistakenly believing that his position in the party was more important. Second, Goebbels was president of the Reich Chamber of Culture, which he had created in 1933, and was thus effectively in control of all the artistic and media professions. Rosenberg was awarded the grandiose title of "The Führer's Plenipotentiary for the Entire Intellectual and Ideological Education and Training of the Nazi Party," while the organization that was created to go with the title (whose full designation was abbreviated DBFÜ) was more commonly known as "the Rosenberg Office."[20] Although this left him at some disadvantage with regard to the arts, it did not deter him and his followers from continuing their attacks unabated on their perceived enemies. During the subsequent years those in the Rosenberg camp continued to churn out invective against their various targets in the columns of their publications.

In 1934, in an address to the Chamber of Culture, Goebbels declared that it would be a mistake to assume that its purpose was "to promote any particular direction in the arts, either modern or reactionary, liberal or anti-liberal."[21] In the same speech he announced that Jews, because of their "outlook (*Ansicht*) and experience . . . were on the whole unsuitable to manage Germany's cultural heritage." That the Jews should be expelled from the cultural professions was one of the few things that both factions could agree on. The agency through which this was to be realized was the Reich Chamber of Culture (RKK), an umbrella organization comprising seven individual chambers, including a Film Chamber (RFK) and a Music Chamber (RMK).[22] Membership in one of the appropriate chambers was mandatory in order to practice any of these professions, Jews being explicitly barred. The immediate consequence of this measure was a massive hemorrhage of talent from all the affected fields.[23]

The number of film composers expelled from the profession during 1933 can be estimated on the following basis: Of the 116 composers working on films released in 1933 and 1934, sixty (52 percent) did not compose for any films after that date. The great majority of these had probably been denied access to the RMK, and hence were effectively expelled, because of their race or on other grounds. There may have been others, however, who had voluntarily left the country or the profession, as well as some composers who had not sought or received any commissions after 1934. Even if the true figure is fewer than sixty, there can be no doubt that the expulsion of so many Jewish composers drastically depleted the available pool of talent and experience, although it does not appear to have affected in any way the kind of music being produced, refuting the contention that Jews constituted a foreign body in German cultural life.

While the Chamber of Music was responsible for controlling access to the profession and day-to-day administrative affairs, the formulation and implementation of music policy was in the hands of the of the Propaganda Ministry, specifically *Abteilung M* (the Music Section). Goebbels once described this relationship as that between the "engine room" and the "bridge."[24] Within the Music Section the key agency was the *Reichsmusikprüfstelle* (Reich Music Examination Office). Its remit was as follows:

> To test new musical publications from opera to popular dance music, including recordings; *to supervise film music;* to eliminate the music of enemy states and music which is un-German; to promote contemporary German composition; to supervise musical programming in the Reich, i.e., to write reports evaluating musical works for other offices.[25]

Meyer has claimed that by "March 1936 all musical film scores and song texts had to be submitted to the censor ten days before shooting could begin,"[26] but no authority is cited for this. If true, the censor in question would not have been the *Prüfstelle,* since no material was vetted prior to publication. According to the deputy director of the Music Section, Fritz von Borries, there was no pre-censorship of musical works; music writers and publishers were only obliged to submit material for examination if specifically asked to do so.[27] The *Prüfstelle* was certainly responsible for the blacklisting of music, but, as von Borries stated in 1944, fewer than a hundred works were blacklisted.[28] There were no instances of *E-Musik* on the black list. Popular music, or *U-Musik,* was clearly the problem area where all of the transgressive pieces were to be found. What was considered objectionable was "the performance of so-called hot style (*Hot-Stil*) and the undignified mimicking of alien models that offend the healthy instincts of the German people, such as actual or imitation Negro music, as well as tasteless lyrics."[29]

What these criteria tell us, in conjunction with the brevity of the blacklists, is that "undesirable" music was rather rare in Nazi Germany. Only if the jazz was too "hot" (which was seldom) or if the classics were "distorted" (which was never) would the agency intervene. But by 1936, with the Jewish and other "unacceptable" composers gone, those who remained knew where the lines had been drawn and were unlikely to cross them. It was only the jazz musicians who sometimes tried to see how far they could go. Hence the rationale that von Borries put forward to justify the existence of the *Prüfstelle* was that without an agency to police the lines, they could be crossed at will; with an agency this rarely happened. The agency was there, according to von Borries, in order to watch over and monitor the creative process. From this standpoint, supervision was by no means intended to thwart innovation, but rather to channel it into new directions, promoting new music to represent a resurgent new Germany. Accordingly, one of the most important functions of the Prüfstelle was to oversee the programmes of concert performances, to ensure that contemporary work was being given sufficient exposure:

> It is the purpose of concerts to introduce the public—a public that for the most part is extremely mistrustful and dismissive—to contemporary music. This demands much effort and patience. . . . But to admit defeat in the face of public rejection would be to condemn the world of music (*Musikkultur*) to stagnation. Only through new works, which embody in their form and structure as yet unknown artistic approaches, can the living stream of music be kept flowing.[30]

This mission statement is a clear expression of the policy behind Goebbels's desire to discover and sponsor musical talent. In 1941, in an attempt to win back artists who had deserted Germany, Goebbels even approached Hermann Scherchen, a socialist who virtually personified the notion of musical bolshevism and who had emigrated to Switzerland in 1933. He was offered the post of orchestral director of the Leipzig Gewandhaus, but declined.[31]

E-Musik 2: Werner Egk

Only a small group of film composers, with a limited number of films to their credit, could be regarded as having "modernist tendencies," associated either with the style of Stravinsky or with the atonal music of Arnold Schoenberg.[32] Within this category, the case of Werner Egk is particularly illuminating, as he is the only major orchestral composer of the period to have written music for film, even though it was only one film. This rather unusual surname was adopted in his early twenties by the man born Werner Joseph Meyer, as an acronym referring to his wife: "Elisabeth geborene (*née*) Karl," possibly because he considered the all-too-common "Meyer" to be unsuitable for an artist destined for greatness.[33] Egk did, in fact, become one of the most prominent German composers of the 1930s and 1940s, although today he seems to have been largely forgotten, unlike his teacher and friend Carl Orff. Together with Orff, Egk was an enthusiastic follower of Stravinsky, and this influence was conspicuous in his work throughout his career.

His first opera, *Die Zaubergeige* (The Magic Violin), was first performed in 1935. It was enthusiastically received by Fritz Stege, the highly influential music critic representing the Goebbels position and a major adversary of Alfred Rosenberg and his followers. Stege publicly praised the danceable sequences, and "henceforth treated the composer as a paradigm for music and musicians in

Nazi Germany."[34] The following year Egk, together with Carl Orff and Richard Strauss, was commissioned to write the music for the 1936 Berlin Olympics in order, as Grunberger says, "to provide aural chiaroscuro for the mammoth athletic junket."[35] For this he was awarded a Gold Medal in the Olympic "orchestral music" competition.[36] Both Egk's *Olympische Festmusik* (Olympic Festival Music) and Strauss's *Olympic Hymn* are heard in passing in Leni Riefenstahl's 1938 film *Olympiade*.[37] Riefenstahl herself mentioned Egk's fanfares in her appeal to the West German Censorship Board (*Filmbewertungsstelle*) in January 1958, against their refusal to certify the film for disribution.[38] What she called the "background music" was provided by Herbert Windt, who had earlier worked with her on *Triumph des Willens* (Triumph of the Will).[39] Any uncertainty regarding the acceptability of Egk's modernist style was finally dispelled in 1938, when Hitler and Goebbels attended a performance of his second opera, *Peer Gynt*. According to Grunberger, "at the final curtain the audience did not know whether to boo or cheer,"[40] until the Führer warmly invited him to his box and announced: "Egk, I am pleased to make the acquaintance of a worthy successor to Richard Wagner!"[41] Egk received a commission worth RM 10,000 and *Peer Gynt* was placed on the repertoire of opera houses all over the Reich.[42]

Egk's brief involvement with film music came in 1940, when he was commissioned to write the score for a Ufa production, *Jungens* (Boys, Robert A. Stemmle). The plot resembled a *Boy's Own* or *Famous Five* adventure story, in which a group of boys expose the activities of a smuggling ring operating on the Baltic coast. The parts were played by pupils of the Adolf Hitler School in Sonthofen, wearing their Hitler Youth uniforms.[43] Thus it was another of the relatively few films that contained overtly Nazi images, but according to Hull, it was "light on propaganda and [gave] an appealing and unusual view of everyday life in 1941."[44] It is somewhat surprising that a composer of Egk's standing should have accepted a commission for a film that was clearly a third-rate production: no stars, no production values, no mass appeal. After the war Egk gave the following account of his foray into film:

> The film *Jungens* was just a routine job for the eminent film director R. A. Stemmle, as was the music that I wrote at his request. The film was about a group of boys pursuing a gang of smugglers on their own initiative and ultimately capturing them. The kind of music required was a conventional illustration score, e.g. for a sand storm, a scene in a pub, and so forth. Among other things I also had to write the music and words of a Hitler Youth song in the style of an actual Hitler Youth song, as we were not permitted to use an existing Hitler Youth song in this unpolitical adventure film.[45]

When *Jungens* was viewed by Goebbels in February 1941, his comment was: "Not a masterpiece. But what the hell. . . ."[46] The film appears to have been considerably less than "not a masterpiece." It was a flop at the box office and has now vanished into oblivion, mentioned only occasionally in the literature as an example of the (very insignificant) youth film genre.[47] Two years later the Reich Youth Leader, Artur Axmann, proposed another Hitler Youth film to Goebbels, who rejected the suggestion out of hand, observing in his diary: "So far we have four failed youth films; I think that's sufficient."[48]

A few months later Goebbels appointed Egk to replace Paul Graener as head of the Composers' Section, a post he held until the end of the war. In 1948, he wrote the music for one more film, *Der Herr vom anderen Stern* (The Gentleman from the Other Star, Heinz Hilpert, 1948), with Heinz Rühmann.[49] He continued composing and performing into the 1960s, and died in 1983.[50]

E-Musik 3: Winfried Zillig

Whereas there was always a degree of residual ambiguity about the acceptability of Stravinsky, the same could not be said about the atonal dissonance of the Schoenberg school. Because Schoenberg was Jewish, his work ideally lent itself to a racial interpretation in Rosenberg's journals, where one could find statements such as "atonality contradicts the rhythm of the blood and soul of the German people,"[51] and that "in so far as atonists . . . are Jewish, they obey a law of their race [and] must attempt to destroy generically alien harmony."[52] But as Potter has shown, despite the ravings "against the 'destroyers' of 'Germanic' tonality, atonal and twelve-tone works continued to be heard and created throughout the Third Reich."[53]

Winfried Zillig had been a pupil of Schoenberg in Vienna in 1925, and accompanied him to Berlin in 1927.[54] But as a non-Jew, he was never targeted by the Nazis. Thus, after 1933, he continued to pursue a highly successful career, first holding the position of orchestral director of the Düsseldorf opera and from 1937 the same position in Essen; then, from 1940, he was effectively in charge of all musical activities in Reichsgau Wartheland, centered on Poznan. Between 1934 and 1945, Zillig also found the time to write the score for seven feature films, across a wide range of genres.[55] The first of these, *Der Schimmelreiter* (Rider on a White Horse, Hans Deppe and Curt Oertel, 1934), was probably the best known. Although classified as a "political" film, it was re-released in Germany after the war as a modern classic.

Zillig was also successful with his operas *Rosse and Das Opfer*, both exemplifying the dodecaphonic system. "Their musical austerity should have aroused strong condemnation,"[56] but as John has pointed out, the reality of music in the Nazi state was much more complex than the profusion of literature directed against *entartete* music would lead us to believe.[57] Atonality was not to be censured, but rather acknowledged as a new, revolutionary style to be co-opted by the new state and its revolutionary political movement.[58] Accordingly, Zillig was commissioned to write incidental music for the Reich Theatre Festival in Heidelberg, then the most prestigious event in the German theater calendar,[59] and had a cycle of songs and other chamber and orchestral works performed in the twelve-tone scale.[60]

Attacks on those following in the Schoenberg tradition nevertheless continued, as could be expected, from reactionary quarters. The most trenchant and sustained criticism came not from the Rosenberg Office and its sympathizers, but from the ranks of the film composers. Alois Melichar, one of Germany's most eminent and prolific composers for film (forty-one scores between 1933 and 1945), is perhaps better known today for his polemical writings than for his music. Melichar addressed the following advice, inter alia, to the aspiring film composer:

> Good film music must have the character of truly popular music. Don't write as if you won't be understood for another fifty years. Write for your own time. Write clearly, simply, transparently, and honestly! If you try this you will realize how far, far more difficult it is to write this way than to construct music by means of the "twelve tone technique," the "trope system," etc., that may look wonderful on paper—and which will be praised to the skies by "progressive" critics—but which, if performed, sounds absolutely dreadful![61]

After the war Zillig composed further concertos, string quartets, song cycles, sonatas, an opera, and the music for numerous radio plays. He also continued to write music for films, contributing scores for at least fourteen projects between 1948 and 1962. He received the German equivalent of an Oscar (*Deutscher Filmpreis*) for the film *Jonas* (Ottomar Domnick), co-scripted by Hans Magnus Enzensberger, in 1957.[62] The sound track for his last film, *Panamericana: Traumstraße der Welt* (Panamericana: Dream Highway of the World, 1968), was released on the Red Seal label in 1996.[63]

In 1947 he accepted the post of principal conductor of Hessian Broadcasting (Frankfurt), and from 1959 until his death in 1963 he was head of the Music Department of North German Broadcasting (Hamburg). From these influential positions, he continued to promote the music of the Schoenberg tradition, which had never really suffered any setbacks since that composer's emigration in 1933.[64]

U-Musik: Grothe and Kreuder

The situation of jazz music in the Third Reich was almost as confused and contradictory as that of "serious" modern music. Officially discouraged and reviled as racially polluted, it remained enormously popular with a wide public and could not be suppressed without arousing serious resentment. The authorities therefore first turned a blind eye, allowing it to thrive as an underground culture, and then later co-opted it for morale and propaganda purposes.[65] As we have seen, it was the practitioners of jazz music who were most likely to push at the boundaries of the acceptable and who occasionally fell afoul of the

Prüfstelle. Perhaps in order to clarify exactly where these boundaries lay, Hans Hinkel, then general secretary of the Chamber of Culture, issued the following directive, published in the film trade press:

> The public has a right to enjoy cheerful, relaxing music. Any other kind of musical presentation that puts special effects, silly antics or clowning around in the spotlight is not acceptable. Neither is any kind of effeminate performance by backing groups using falsetto voices, whispering or other such devices that convey an unmanly impression.[66]

As in the case of *E-Musik*, Hinkel reiterated the importance of innovation, but within the established limits: "With regard to the style of musical performance, there is no reason to restrict the healthy development of [new] sounds and rhythms. What is important is not whether the saxophone (still incorrectly regarded as a Negro instrument) or mutes in horns are used, but rather how they are used in the context of the work as a whole."[67]

Although these guidelines applied to *U-Musik* generally, it is significant that they were published in the film trade press, since, as Thiel has noted, "the lion's share of film music commissions went to specialists in the circle of the U-musicians."[68] Indeed, within this circle of musical directors and bandleaders there was a so-called "songwriting elite" (*Schlager-Prominenz*), all of whom were contributors of film music. Among the names repeatedly found in this context are Franz Doelle, Georg Haentzschel, Peter Kreuder, Theo Mackeben, Franz Grothe, Peter Ingelhoff, Friedrich Schröder, Leo Leux, and Michael Jary. They all figure in the various histories of jazz and popular music in the Third Reich, often with no mention of their contributions to the cinema. Between them, however, they account for hundreds of feature film scores, while some also wrote the music for documentaries and culture films. Within this group, the two most significant figures were undoubtedly Franz Grothe and Peter Kreuder.

Grothe was born into a highly musical Berlin family and benefited from an excellent musical education. After the early death of his father, he began work as a jazz pianist while still a teenager. He was soon able to join the celebrated Dejas Béla orchestra, and when the Nazis came to power he was well established in the jazz world as a performer, composer, and arranger.[69] By then he had already written the music for some twelve films, including *Die große Attraktion* (The Big Attraction, Max Reichmann, 1931), starring Richard Tauber. His credits even included a number of foreign and international productions, for example *L'Amour chante* (Love Songs, Robert Florey, 1930) and *La ragazza dal livido azzurro* (The Girl with the Bruise, E. W. Emo, 1933).

With his career as film composer flourishing, Grothe accepted an offer from Universal in the autumn of 1936, but found Hollywood uncongenial and returned to Europe eighteen months later. While working together on the comedy *Napoleon ist an allem schuld* (It's All Napoleon's Fault, Curt Goetz), he fell in love with and married the newly arrived Norwegian singer and film actress Kirsten Heiberg, who went on to become a star of the German cinema.[70] Between 1938 and 1945 Grothe wrote the music for eight of her fourteen films, including a number of hit songs.

Throughout this period, Grothe continued to compose and perform in the jazz idiom, walking the tightrope of what was and what was not officially acceptable. In this arena he collaborated frequently with his lifelong friend and fellow Berliner Georg Haentzschel, whose career paralleled Grothe's. Beginning as a jazz pianist in the mid-twenties, he worked freelance with a number of bands and for Berlin Radio. In 1928, he was chosen to replace the regular pianist of an American band touring Germany, headed by Lud Gluskin.[71] In 1937, Haentzschel also began writing film music, and by the end of the war had contributed to twelve films, including the celebrated Münchhausen (Josef von Báky, 1943).

In 1941, with the war entering its third year, Goebbels decided to relax the rules on popular music, particularly with regard to broadcasting, because "the people, and in particular the soldiers at the front, require some distraction from the hardships and exertions of daily life."[72] In the consequent restructuring of the German Broadcasting Corporation (*Reichsrundfunkgesellschaft*) two of the ten new sections were given the highest priority: Group A, Light Dance and Entertainment Music, headed by Georg Haentzschel, and Group B, Sophisticated (*gehobener*) Entertainment Music (including film music and contemporary operettas) headed by Franz Grothe.[73]

The next stage of the process was to create an elite corps of popular musicians to broadcast regularly, primarily for the benefit of the armed forces, who were beginning to satisfy their need for popular music from neutral and enemy stations, using their military receivers. It was also meant for the pleasure of civilian fans of light popular music,[74] for as Goebbels now conceded, "Rhythm is fundamental to music. We are not living in the Victorian age (*Biedermeierzeit*), but in a century that takes its tune from the thousandfold humming of machines and the roar of motors."[75] The German Dance and Entertainment Orchestra (*Deutsche Tanz- und Unterhaltungsorchester*, or DTU) was to have the status in popular music equivalent to that of the Berlin Philharmonic in the classical sector, and Franz Grothe was to be its Furtwängler.[76] Bringing together the best dance and jazz musicians in the country, its principals were deemed to be providing an essential contribution to the war effort and public morale, and were hence exempted from military service. Some, in fact, were already in uniform and had to be requisitioned from the Wehrmacht. The new orchestra, with Franz Grothe as musical director and Georg Haentzschel as principal conductor, began broadcasting on the national programme (*Großdeutscher Rundfunk*) in June 1942.[77]

The end of the war found Grothe in Bavaria, where he spent the next several years playing in American clubs.[78] Resuming his career, Grothe went on to write another 87 film scores, as well as composing for stage, radio, and television. Altogether he contributed to over 167 films, of which 59 were made during the years of the Third Reich.[79]

Peter Kreuder, three years older than Grothe, was born in the Rhineland (Aachen) and appears to have been a genuine musical prodigy, having given a recital of Mozart at the Guildhall (*Gürzenich*) in Cologne at the age of six.[80] By his early twenties, however, he had discovered the charms of popular music and had become a celebrated jazz pianist in Berlin, working in bars and clubs. In the late 1920s, Kreuder was providing piano accompaniment to the songs of Marlene Dietrich, and in 1929 wrote for her the chanson "Mein blondes Baby."[81] The following year he was working with her again, this time on *The Blue Angel* as musical assistant to Friedrich Hollaender. He wrote his first original film score in 1931, for *Kadetten* (Cadets), a film directed by Georg Jacoby and set in Lichterfelde, the German counterpart of the British Sandhurst or the American West Point.

His first major success came in 1933 with *Mazurka* (Willi Forst), and two years later in Paris he was awarded what was then the equivalent of the European Oscar (*Weltfilmpreis*) for *Das Mädchen Johanna* (Gustav Ucicky), a film about Joan of Arc. Also in 1935 he collaborated with Leni Riefenstahl on a Nuremberg rally film, a kind of postscript to *Triumph des Willens*, called *Day of Freedom: Our Wehrmacht*. In her memoirs Riefenstahl describes his score as "spirited" (*schmissig*).[82] He also provided numbers for the infantry music corps, while at the same time subverting his civilian arrangements with syncopation and swing elements, a practice which in 1940 landed him on the *Prüfstelle* blacklist.[83] In all he wrote the music for 188 films, 33 of which were made under the Third Reich. But it is for his popular songs—some 1,500 of them—for which he will be best remembered.[84]

The careers of the five composers reviewed above—Becce, Egk, Zillig, Grothe, and Kreuder—all began before 1933 and continued well past 1945. Apart from their involvement with film music, they have only one thing in common: none of them were Jewish. As long as they were acceptable racially, they were allowed to pursue their respective careers with relatively little constraint. Leading representatives of the schools and genres officially out of favor—or even proscribed—seem hardly affected by the strictures of Nazi policy.

This by no means suggests that the nature of the Third Reich was harmless, or even benign, to those other than the Jews. But it does call into question the conventional view that for most people and most professions in Germany life was turned upside down in 1933 and then returned to normal after 1945. What is most striking are the *continuities* before, during, and after this period. There can be little doubt that the leaders of the Third Reich would have dearly loved to have brought about revolutionary changes, and in some areas they achieved this. On the whole, however, they were prevented from doing so—largely through their own internal schisms, and their lack of vision and consistency. The notion that the Third Reich was a monolithic entity, rigidly coordinated and super-efficient, is itself a creation of Nazi propaganda—and one that has been largely accepted by posterity.

What has been so extensively documented in the case of orchestral and popular music also doubtless holds true for film music. In spite of all its innumerable pronouncements, the Nazi regime made no serious attempt to formulate coherent policy in this area, nor any real effort to enforce ideologically determined standards of musical taste. Its greatest impact took the form of massive purges directed against the Jews and others perceived as enemies. For everyone else, as Potter has observed, "the transition of musical life from the Weimar Republic to the Third Reich displayed more continuities than caesuras"[85]—and, one might add, from the Third Reich to the Federal Republic as well.

Notes

1. Potter, "Nazi Seizure," 39.
2. See for example Uhlenbrok, *MusikSpektakelFilm,* and Belach, *Wir tanzen um die Welt.*
3. See for example *Film-Kurier* (31 December 1942), 5.
4. These were noted regularly in the trade press, e.g., *Film-Kurier* (5 February 1943), 2.
5. Simeon, "Giuseppe Becce," 35.
6. London, *Film Music,* 240.
7. Siebert, *Filmmusik,* 45ff.
8. See London, *Film Music,* 50–61.
9. Drewniak, *Der deutsche Film,* 567.
10. See Leiser, *Nazi Cinema,* 54–55.
11. Simeon, "Giuseppe Becce," E4.
12. Drewniak, *Der deutsche Film,* 921.
13. Nineteen thirty-one had the highest output during the interwar period with 200 productions, 1938 the lowest with 114; see Bauer, *Deutscher Spielfilmalmanach,* iii.
14. Potter, *Most German,* 25.
15. Kroll, "Verbotene Musik," 310.
16. See for example von Bormann, "Das nationalsozialistische Gemeinschaftslied"; Frommann, *Die Lieder der NS-Zeit;* Meyer, *A Generation Led Astray;* Niedhart and Broderick, *Lieder in Politik.*
17. For a detailed account of this concept and its implications see John, *Musik-Bolschewismus.*
18. Kroll, "Verbotene Musik," 515.
19. This dispute has been studied extensively. See for example Bollmus, *Das Amt Rosenberg,* and Brenner, "Die Kunst im politischen Machtkampf."
20. On the structure and activities of the Rosenberg Office, see de Vries, *Sonderstab Musik,* 23ff.
21. Dahm, "Anfänge und Ideologie der Reichskulturkammer," 78–79.
22. The others were literature, theater, broadcasting, press, and visual arts.
23. More applicants were denied access to the RKK in music than in any of the other affected fields, the figures being as follows: music 2,310, film 750, theater 535, writing 1,303, press 420, art 1,657. Record held at the Berlin Document Center, quoted by Levi, *Music in the Third Reich,* 4.
24. Sington and Weidenfeld, *The Goebbels Experiment,* 236.
25. Ellis, "The Propaganda Ministry," 233; emphasis added.

26. Meyer, *Politics*, 207.

27. Borries, "Die Reichsmusikprüfstelle," 52.

28. Ibid., 52.

29. Ibid., 53.

30. Ibid., 60.

31. John, *Musik-Bolschewismus*, 379.

32. During the Weimar years Stravinsky had been extremely popular in Germany and he was frequently on tour there. At the same time, he was under relentless attack by Rosenberg's Combat League as one of the foremost representatives of everything they detested about contemporary music. When the Nazis came to power Stravinsky suddenly found his work disappearing from the programs and his lucrative personal engagements being cancelled. In June 1933 he expressed his amazement that he had received no German invitations for the coming season, especially since (as he put it) "my negative stand on Communism and Judaism—to put it mildly—is generally well known" (Evans, "Die Rezeption," 99). He was indeed well known as a prominent supporter of Italian fascism, "with reactionary, anti-democratic, and to some extent anti-semitic convictions" (Fetthauer, *Musikverlage*, 27374). However, after submitting his proof of ancestry (*Ariernachweis*) to refute rumors that he was Jewish, he was, over the next few years, able to re-establish his previous position. Understandably then, he was incensed when his *Histoire du soldat* was included in the 1938 *"entartete Musik"* (Degenerate Music) Exhibition, the musical counterpart to the notorious 1937 exhibition of "entartete Kunst" (Degenerate Art) in Munich. Organized by Hans Severus Ziegler, deputy Gauleiter of Thuringia and head of the Gau cultural office, it was a measure of the general confusion and lack of consensus that Stravinsky had been lumped together with composers such as Webern, Schoenberg, Krenek, and the like.

33. Kater, *Composers*, 4.

34. Ibid., 7.

35. Grunberger, *A Social History*, 525.

36. See Riethmüller, *"Komposition,"* 25868, and Kater, *Composers*, 13–14.

37. Graham, *Leni Riefenstahl*, 177.

38. Ibid., 288.

39. See Volker, "Von oben sehr erwünscht."

40. Grunberger, *A Social History*, 518.

41. Kater, *Composers*, 10.

42. Prieberg, *Musik im NS-Staat*, 320ff.

43. Drewniak, *Der deutsche Film*, 590.

44. Hull, *Film in the Third Reich*, 191.

45. Vogelsang, *Filmmusik im Dritten Reich*, 15.

46. *Tagebücher*, entry for 2 March 1941, 1/9, 167.

47. Cadars and Courtade, *Le Cinéma nazi*, 144ff.

48. *Tagebücher*, entry for 29 June 1943, 2/8, 562.

49. Thiel, *Filmmusik in Geschichte*, 211.

50. *Riemann Musiklexikon*, 311.

51. Meyer, "The Nazi Musicologist," 654.

52. Ibid., 654.

53. Potter, *Most German*, 20.

54. Levi, *Music in the Third Reich*, 104.

55. *Glenzdorfs internationales Film-Lexikon*, 1943.

56. Levi, *Music in the Third Reich*, 105.

57. John, *Musik-Bolschewismus*, 380.

58. Ibid., 379.

59. Levi, *Music in the Third Reich*, 105.

60. Stuckenschmidt, "Musik unter Hitler," 45, quoted by Wulf, *Musik im Dritten Reich*, 332.

61. *Film-Nachrichten*, 17 March 1945

62. Vogelsang, *Filmmusik im Dritten Reich*, 296.

63. Catalogue no. 09026626592.

64. Heister, in Sarkowicz, *Hitlers Künstler*, 335.

65. This is an extraordinary story that has been told in considerable detail by Kater, *Different Drummers*, the first volume of his trilogy on music in the Third Reich.

66. Hinkel, *Film-Kurier*, 3.

67. Ibid.

68. Thiel, *Filmmusik in Geschichte*, 155.

69. Pacher, "Franz Grothe," xv.

70. Ibid., xvi.

71. Kater, *Different Drummers*, 7.

72. "Der Rundfunk im Krieg," in *Zeit ohne Beispiel*, quoted by Bergmeier and Lotz, *Hitler's Airwaves*, 142.

73. Drechsler, *Die Funktion der Musik*, 4243.

74. Kater, *Different Drummers*, 127.

75. *Film und Funk* (19 March 1942), quoted by Bergmeier and Lotz, *Hitler's Airwaves*, 144.

76. Bundesarchiv [BA] R55/200, quoted in ibid, 144

77. Bundesarchiv [BA] R55/1224, quoted in ibid, 147.

78. Pacher, "Franz Grothe," xvii.

79. Only one composer had a larger number of films to his credit during this period, Werner Bochmann with sixty-nine.

80. Kühn, "Peter Kreuder," 692.

81. Pacher, *Sehn Sie*, 288.

82. Riefenstahl, *Memoiren*, 245.

83. Kühn in Heister and Klein, Musik und Musikpolitik, 223.

84. After the war Kreuder, through his acquaintance with Eva Peron, emigrated to Argentina, and after her death in 1951 he moved to Brazil. While in South America he carried on his composing and performing unabated, holding the post of musical director of radio stations in São Paulo, Rio de Janeiro, and Buenos Aires, as well as writing the scores for numerous Latin American films. He finally returned to Germany in 1955 to continue his career there.

85. Potter, *Most German*, 2.

References

Bauer, Alfred. *Deutscher Spielfilmalmanach 1929–1950*. München: Filmladen Christoph Winterberg, 1950.

Belach, Helga, ed. *Wir tanzen um die Welt. Deutsche Revuefilme 1933–1945*. München: Carl Hanser, 1979.

Bergmeier, Horst J. P., and Rainer E. Lotz. *Hitler's Airwaves: The Inside Story of Nazi Radio Broadcasting and Propaganda Swing*. New Haven, Conn.: Yale University Press, 1997.

Bollmus, Reinhard. *Das Amt Rosenberg und seine Gegner: Zum Machtkampf im nationalsozialistischen Herrschaftssystem*. Stuttgart: Deutsche Verlags-Anstalt, 1970.

Bormann, Alexander von. "Das nationalsozialistische Gemeinschaftslied." In *Die Deutsche Literatur im Dritten Reich. Themen, Traditionen, Wirkungen,* ed. H. Denkler and K. Prümm. Stuttgart: Reklam, 1976, 256–80.

Borries, Fritz von. "Die Reichsmusikprüfstelle und ihr Wirken für die Musikkultur." In *Jahrbuch der deutschen Musik 1944*, ed. H. von Hase and A. Dreetz. Leipzig: Gremeinsamer Verlag von Breitkopf und Härtel; Berlin: Hesses Verlag, 1944, 49–55.

Brenner, Hildegard. "Die Kunst im politischen Machtkampf der Jahre 1933–34." *Vierteljahreshefte für Zeitgeschichte* 10/1 (1962): 17–42. Reprinted in translation as "Art in the Political Power Struggle of 1933 and 1934." In *Republic to Reich*, ed. H. Holborn. New York:

Vintage Books, 1972, 395–432.

Cadars, Pierre, and Francis Courtade. *Le Cinéma nazi*. Paris: E. Losfeld, 1972.

Dahm, Volker. "Anfänge und Ideologie der Reichskulturkammer." *Vierteljahreshefte für Zeitgeschichte* 34 (1986): 53–84.

de Vries, Willem. *Sonderstab Musik: Music Confiscation by the Einsatzstab Reichsleiter Rosenberg under the Nazi Occupation of Western Europe*. Amsterdam: Amsterdam University Press, 1996.

Drechsler, Nanny. *Die Funktion der Musik im deutschen Rundfunk, 1933–1945*. Pfaffenweiler: Centaurus-Verlagsgesellschaft, 1988.

Drewniak, Boguslaw. *Der deutsche Film 1938–1945: Ein Gesamtüberblick*. Düsseldorf: Droste Verlag, 1987.

Ellis, Donald W. "The Propaganda Ministry and Centralized Regulation of Music in the Third Reich: The 'Biological Aesthetic' as Policy." *Journal of European Studies* 5 (1975): 223–38.

Evans, Joan. "Die Rezeption der Musik Igor Strawinskys in Hitlerdeutschland." *Archiv für Musikwissenschaft* 55/2 (1998): 91–109.

Fetthauer, Sophie. *Musikverlage im "Dritten Reich" und im Exil*. Hamburg: Von Bockel Verlag, 2004.

Frommann, Eberhard. *Die Lieder der NS-Zeit*. Köln: Papy Rossa Verlag, 1999.

Glenzdorfs internationales Film-Lexikon. Biographisches Handbuch für das gesamte Filmwesen. Bad Münder: Prominent-Filmverlag, 1960/61.

Goebbels, Joseph. *Die Tagebücher von Joseph Goebbels*. München: K.G. Saur, 1998.

Graham, Cooper C. *Leni Riefenstahl and Olympia*. Metuchen, N.J.: Scarecrow, 1986.

Grunberger, Richard. *A Social History of the Third Reich*. Harmondsworth: Penguin, 1974.

Heister, Hanns-Werner, and Hans-Günter Klein, eds. *Musik und Musikpolitik im faschistischen Deutschland*. Frankfurt am Main: Fischer Taschenbuch Verlag, 1984.

Hinkel, Hans. "Richtlinie für die Ausführung von Unterhaltungsmusik." *Film-Kurier*, 16 November 1942, p. 3.

Hull, David Stewart. *Film in the Third Reich*. Berkeley: University of California Press, 1969.

John, Eckhard. *Musik-Bolschewismus: Die Politisierung der Musik in Deutschland 1918–1938*. Stuttgart, Weimar: Verlag J. B. Metzler, 1994.

Kater, Michael H. *Composers of the Nazi Era: Eight Portraits*. New York: Oxford University Press, 2000.

———. *Different Drummers: Jazz in the Culture of Nazi Germany*. New York: Oxford University Press, 1992.

Kroll, Erwin. "Verbotene Musik." *Vierteljahreshefte für Zeitgeschichte* 7/3 (1959): 310–17.

Kühn, Volker. "Peter Kreuder." In *Die Musik in Geschichte und Gegenwart: Allgemeine Enzyklopädie der Musik*, ed. L. Finscher, vol. 10. Kassel: Bärenreiter, 692–95.

Leiser, Erwin. *Nazi Cinema*. Trans. G. Mander and D. Wilson. London: Secker and Warburg, 1974.

Levi, Erik. *Music in the Third Reich*. Basingstoke: Macmillan, 1994.

London, Kurt. *Film Music*. London: Faber & Faber, 1936.

Meyer, Michael. "The Nazi Musicologist as Myth Maker in the Third Reich." *Journal of Contemporary History* 10/4 (1975): 649–65.

———. *The Politics of Music in the Third Reich*. New York: Peter Lang, 1991.

Meyer, Sabine. "A Generation Led Astray: Community Singing as a Means of National Socialist Indoctrination of Youth." Ph.D. dissertation, Goldsmiths College, London, 1992.

Niedhart, Gottfried, and George Broderick, eds. *Lieder in Politik und Alltag des Nationalsozialismus*. Frankfurt am Main: Peter Lang, 1999.

Pacher, Maurus. "Franz Grothe: Ein Leben nach Noten." In *Franz Grothe Werkverzeichnis*, ed. L. von Berswordt. München: Franz Grothe-Stiftung, 1988, xv–xviii.

———. *Sehn Sie, das war Berlin: Weltstadt nach Noten*. Frankfurt am Main and Berlin: Ullstein, 1987.

Potter, Pamela M. *Most German of the Arts: Musicology and Society from the Weimar Republic to the End of Hitler's Reich*. New Haven, Conn.: Yale University Press, 1998.

———. "The Nazi Seizure of the Berlin Philharmonic, or the Decline of a Bourgeois Musical Institution." In *National Socialist Cultural Policy*, ed. G. R. Cuomo. New York: St. Martin's Press, 1995, 39–65.

Prieberg, Fred K. *Musik im NS-Staat*. Frankfurt am Main: Fischer Taschenbuch Verlag, 1982.

Riefenstahl, Leni. *Memoiren*. München and Hamburg: Albrecht Knaus, 1987.

Riemann Musiklexikon, ed. W. Gurlitt-Sachteil and H. H. Eggebrecht. Mainz: B. Schott's Söhne, 1972.

Riethmüller, Albrecht. "Komposition im Deutschen Reich um 1936." *Archiv für Musikwissenschaft* 38/4 (1981): 241–78.

Sarkowicz, Hans, ed. *Hitlers Künstler: die Kultur im Dienst des Nationalsozialismus*. Frankfurt am Main: Insel, 2004.

Siebert, Ulrich Eberhard. *Filmmusik in Theorie und Praxis: Eine Untersuchung der 20er und frühen 30er Jahre anhand des Werkes von Hans Erdmann*. Frankfurt am Main: Peter Lang, 1990.

Simeon, Ennio. "Giuseppe Becce." In *The New Grove Dictionary of Music and Musicians*, ed. Stanley Sadie. London: Macmillan, 2001, 3: 35.

Sington, Derrick, and Arthur Weidenfeld. *The Goebbels Experiment: A Study of the Nazi Propaganda Machine*. London: John Murray, 1942.

Stuckenschmidt, Hans-Heinz. "Musik unter Hitler." *Forum* (January 1963).

Taylor, Brandon, and Wilfried van der Will, eds. *The Nazification of Art: Art, Design, Music, Architecture and Film in the Third Reich*. Winchester: Winchester School of Arts Press, 1990.

Thiel, Wolfgang. *Filmmusik in Geschichte und Gegenwart*. Berlin (DDR): Henschelverlag, 1981.

Uhlenbrok, Katja, ed. *MusikSpektakelFilm: Musiktheater und Tanzkultur im deutschen Film 1922–1937*. München: CineGraph text + kritik, 1998.

Vogelsang, Konrad. *Filmmusik im Dritten Reich: eine Dokumentation*. Hamburg: Facta Oblita Verlag, 1990.

Volker, Reimar. *"Von oben sehr erwünscht": die Filmmusik Herbert Windts im NS-Propagandafilm*. Trier: WVT, Wissenschaftlicher Verlag, 2003.

Wulf, Joseph. *Musik im Dritten Reich. Eine Dokumentation*. Gütersloh: Sigbert Mohn, 1963.

Filmography (by composer)

COMPOSER	YEAR	FILM	DIRECTOR
Giuseppe Becce	1929	*Die weiße Hölle von Piz Palü* (The White Hell of Pitz Palu)	Arnold Fanck
	1930	*Der Sohn der weißen Berge* (Son of the White Mountain)	Luis Trenker
	1931	*Berge in Flammen* (Mountains on Fire)	Luis Trenker
	1932	*Das blaue Licht* (The Blue Light)	Leni Riefenstahl
	1933	*Der Rebell* (The Rebel)	Luis Trenker
	1933	*Gipfelstürmer* (Assault on the Summit)	Franz Wenzler
	1933	*Hans Westmar*	Franz Wenzler
	1935	*Hundert Tage* (Hundred Days)	Franz Wenzler
	1936	*Der Kaiser von Kalifornien* (The Emperor of California)	Luis Trenker
	1940	*Kampf um den Berg—Eine Hochtour vor 20 Jahren* (Battle for the Mountain)	Arnold Fanck
	1940	*Der Feuerteufel* (The Fire Devil)	Luis Trenker
	1945	*Monte Miracolo*	Luis Trenker
	1959	*Zauber der Dolomiten* (The Magic of the Dolomites)	Hans J. Gnamm
Werner Egk	1940	*Jungens* (Boys)	Robert A. Stemmle
	1948	*Der Herr vom anderen Stern* (The Gentleman from the Other Star)	Heinz Hilpert
Winfried Zillig	1934	*Der Schimmelreiter* (Rider on a White Horse)	Hans Deppe and Curt Oertel
	1957	*Jonas*	Ottomar Domnick
	1968	*Panamericana: Traumstraße der Welt* (Panamericana: Dream Road of the World)	Hans Domnick
Peter Kreuder	1931	*Peter Voss, der Millionendieb* (Peter Voss, the Man who Stole Millions)	E. A. Dupont
	1933	*Mazurka*	Willi Forst
	1935	*Das Mädchen Johanna*	Gustav Ucicky
	1935	*Tag der Freiheit: Unsere Wehrmacht* (Day of Freedom: Our Wehrmacht)	Leni Riefenstahl
Franz Grothe	1930	*L'Amour chante* (Love Songs)	Robert Florey
	1931	*Die große Attraktion* (The Big Attraction)	Max Reichmann
	1933	*La ragazza dal livido azzurro* (The Girl with a Bruise)	E. W. Emo

Herbert Windt's Film Music to *Triumph of the Will*: Ersatz-Wagner or Incidental Music to the Ultimate Nazi-Gesamtkunstwerk?

REIMAR VOLKER

When Leni Riefenstahl's *Triumph des Willens* (Triumph of the Will, 1935) was premiered, the Berlin correspondent of the *Observer* newspaper reported on 31 March 1935: "To the accompaniment of Wagnerian-like music, Hitler's Junker Plane is seen flying above summer clouds en route to Nuremberg." Critical literature on *Triumph des Willens* has continued this line of assessment. The Modern Museum of Art's sound and picture outline speaks of "Wagnerian marching music," "*Meistersinger*-music," and a "Siegfried-motif."[1] In an essay in the

Historical Journal of Film Radio and Television, the authors write that "the musical score by Herbert Windt is just the right mix of Wagner and Nazi marching songs for a film about how faith can move mountains," and that the sound track includes an "expectant orchestra theme reminiscent of Richard Wagner."[2] In her book on the film, Linda Deutschman states: "On the soundtrack the drone of the aircraft merges with the solemn orchestral theme from the overture to Wagner's *Meistersinger,*"[3] and, writing of a later moment in the film, that there is a "Wagnerian like theme sometimes attributed to Wagner's *Tristan und Isolde,* but actually composed by Windt in the manner of Wagner."[4] The German film scholar Peter Nowotny even goes as far as to suggest that the use of motifs and quotations from Wagner's operas in *Triumph des Willens* is deliberately intended to serve Hitler's personal preferences. He refers especially to the opening scenes of the film, where Nowotny identifies the Siegfried-Motif that accompanies Hitler's enthusiastically greeted arrival in the medieval city of Nuremberg. From the perspective of aesthetic reception and to those familiar with Wagner's work, this, according to Nowotny, is deliberately intended to provoke analogies between the original operatic settings elevating Hitler beyond the Führer myth to the status of a Hero.[5]

At a recent conference it was pointed out that the opening sequence of *Triumph des Willens* was accompanied by music frequently attributed to Bruckner. For Hitler's apotheosis—the moment when Hitler descends from the clouds like a god (the passage entitled "Ankunft des Führers" [Arrival of the Führer])—Herbert Windt was said to have composed, literally paraphrased, Brucknerian music.[6] It is interesting to note that Bruckner, too, was a personal favorite of Hitler. This had various reasons, less ideological (as in the case of Wagner) than personal. First of all, Hitler and Bruckner both came from the vicinity of Linz, Austria, where they grew up in modest middle-class households. It was in Linz that Hitler became determined to create a second kind of Bayreuth and a counterpoint to the decadence of Vienna, where both he and Bruckner had been rejected as young artists. In 1937, Hitler officially accepted his fellow Austrian Bruckner into the Pantheon of German artists at the Walhalla in Regensburg. The ceremony, which included speeches by many Nazi political and cultural functionaries, underlined the close connection between Austria and Germany. Bruckner was naturalized, just as Austria itself would be soon after its forceful assimilation into the German Reich.

Aesthetically, Bruckner remained high on the play list for Nazi events, with movements from his symphonies performed before cultural speeches at the Nuremberg rallies and fanfares appropriated especially for cultural events such as the infamous *Tag der deutschen Kunst* in 1937, where "pure" German art was presented in opposition to "degenerate art" of various kinds.[7] Hitler personally designated the slow movement of the Seventh Symphony to mark another event he considered to be of epic proportions: it followed the announcement of Hitler's *Heldentod* in April 1945 on what was left of German National Radio. The aesthetic reasons for Bruckner to be elevated to state composer may be found in his reliance on the fugue and the chorale, forms perceived to be archetypically German. He employed them in their purest forms, ones that preceded what Nazi musicology saw as their corruption in the Weimar Republic.[8] Reinhold Brinkmann has characterized the general susceptibility of nineteenth-century music to Nazi appropriation propaganda as a distortion of the sublime, a shift from subject to object. The sublime was no longer, as Kant defined it, in the eye of the beholder. It became the object itself, rendering the object sublime and not the sensation one might have in regarding it.[9] Symphonic music of the nineteenth century, with its heavy reliance on the concept of the sublime, was particularly vulnerable to distortion and appropriation. The tendency of early film music to use this musical vernacular made the music especially appropriate for Nazi propaganda film—or so it may seem at first glance.

The above-mentioned characterizations of Herbert Windt's music support this claim. None of these statements rest on the detailed musicological analysis of the music for *Triumph des Willens*. It is not my intention to question the authors' ability to describe accurately or distinguish between Wagner or Bruckner. There is, however, an obvious consensus in describing Windt's film music as either Wagnerian or Brucknerian, and a tendency to pinpoint certain Wagnerian motifs. A brief analysis of Windt's work and background in the context of the political and aesthetic climate of the 1930s will cast a somewhat different light on his music, releasing it from the overexposed Wagnerian interpretation that it has assumed in secondary literature. A closer, more contextual look at Herbert Windt's music reveals aspects of *Triumph des Willens* so far neglected by film scholarship.

Herbert Windt's score for *Triumph des Willens*

Windt composed seven consecutive sections of music for the first fifteen minutes of the film. One section, "Ankunft des Führers," is repeated, and a further section of original music, as Linda Deutschman notes, has often been attributed to *Tristan und Isolde;*[10] these are detailed in Table 2.1.[11]

Needless to say, the stylization of Hitler and the general setting of *Triumph des Willens* practically beg for Wagnerian music. Given the common perception of Nazi aesthetics, it might have been thought that the most obvious choice for the sound track would have been to use as much Wagner as possible, thus granting Hitler the lead role in his own personal Wagner opera. This would, moreover, have emphasized the persistently underlined and assumed master-disciple relationship between Wagner and Hitler.[12] There are, however, several reasons why appropriating Wagner in this way was not a serious option for film composers.

Table 2.1. Herbert Windt's music for *Triumph des Willens*, directed by Leni Riefenstahl, 1935

Time	Music	Image
0'00"	overture	black screen followed by
2'03"	illustration-music	brief historical introduction: captions commented by the music
2'52"	Horst-Wessel-Variation: variations on the theme of the Nazi-party anthem "Horst-Wessel-Lied"	Hitler's plane aproaching Nuremburg
5'12"	"Ankunft des Füher's": fanfares followed by two significant themes	touchdown of the aircraft
6'06"–10'27"	"Fahrt durch Nurnberg" / No. 4: succession and repetition of themes	drive through Nuremberg
13'23"–15'13"	"Wach' Auf"—Choir from Wagner's *Die Meistersinger* arranged for brass with a modified cadenza at the end	early morning Nuremburg
1:12'00–1:13'29	Theme often atributed to *Tristan und Isolde*	Hitler's motorcade driving to the central military parade in Nuremberg

First, the conservative Reichsmusikkammer (Reich Chamber of Music) considered "classical German" music sacrosanct. The use of snippets to accompany film was thought to denigrate the art form perceived and officially portrayed as the "most German" of all arts.[13] The Reichsmusikkammer's objections led them to develop a list of heritage pieces that were under no circumstances to be used as film music. For years a heated debate raged in daily papers and professional journals between film composers, affiliated with the more lenient and less dogmatic Reichsfilmkammer (Reich Chamber of Film), and the Reichsmusikkammer concerning the citation of "original" music.[14] Generally speaking, "serious" film composers, such as Herbert Windt, publicly rejected the practice of direct quotation. Hence they felt unjustly accused of adulterating German cultural heritage by tampering with masterworks. The Reichsmusikkammer's accusations were probably directed primarily at newsreel sound tracks, which were in fact compiled from archive recordings. As far as *Triumph des Willens* was concerned, one of the main artistic aims as stated by Riefenstahl and her employers was to transcend the newsreel style in cinematographic terms.[15] This would also have applied to the music, so that the direct quotation or paraphrasing of either Wagner or Bruckner was not a serious option.

Furthermore, Hitler and Goebbels's personal enthusiasm for Wagner and the opera used at official party rallies, *Die Meistersinger von Nürnberg*, was not necessarily shared by the majority of party members or the general public. If Albert Speer's memoirs are anything to go by, the 1933 party conference performance of *Die Meistersinger*, played by the Berliner Staatsoper under the direction of Wilhelm Furtwängler, was by no means a highlight for the invited party dignitaries. Hardly any of the seats had been taken when Hitler entered the opera house. Guards were sent out to round up anyone in uniform from nearby beer halls, wine bars, and residences, although even this did not lead to a capacity audience. In the following year—the year of *Triumph des Willens*—Hitler issued strict orders that party officials should attend the special performance. According to Speer, they seemed very bored, many fell sleep, and Hitler was infuriated by the meager applause and overt lack of interest. From 1935, tickets were sold to a more appreciative general public.[16]

As for the only genuine Wagner citation used by Windt, his sketches indicate that he had initially intended a composition of his own that would have built upon themes introduced in the overture. In an interview from the sixties, Riefenstahl claims to have had the idea of using what she referred to as "*Meistersinger* music" for images of early morning Nuremberg.[17] Direct intervention by Goebbels or other party officials overruling any artistic doubts on the part of the composer could have been just as likely, since the "Wach' Auf Chor" from the fifth scene in the third act of *Die Meistersinger*, in its appropriation as a kind of political wake-up call, had been a Nazi Party favorite since the movement began in the 1920s.

It seems clear that it was not the composer's first choice to use anything directly from *Die Meistersinger*. The brass arrangement replacing Wagner's original choir to some extent softens what might have seemed like a rather blunt visual and acoustic duplication of the Nuremberg awakening to the call of Wagner's "Wach' Auf, es nahet gen den Tag" (wake up, dawn is breaking); a direct quotation might well have seemed an artistic solution unworthy of any serious film composer, because it is too blatant. In fact, Windt even claims to have objected to the use of the "Horst-Wessel-Lied," the Nazi Party anthem—the other direct musical quotation in the film—because he considered it "too primitive" for use in film.[18] A further consideration relates to the propaganda value of the film; too many Wagner references audible and decipherable only by connoisseurs would have made the film elitist, thus undermining its mass-audience appeal.

The common denominator between Wagner's leitmotifs and certain motifs in Windt's score for *Triumph des Willens* may simply be the use of musical devices considered heroic ever since their first appearance and description in Ancient Greece: trumpet fanfares arpeggiating triads in simple modal harmony. The heroic connotations of these musical tropes would have been equally appealing to Wagner and to Windt; there may well, therefore, be far less intertextual congruence than appears at first sight. The wider context of Nazi cultural politics at the beginning of the Third Reich also serves as an interesting point of reference from which to gauge the impact and perception of Windt's music in its time. Alan Steinweis has explored the role of the Reichsmusikkammer from its conception in the 1920s as a self-governed institution established to safeguard musicians' interests in the especially difficult times of the Weimar Republic.[19] At the hands of the Nazis, the Reichsmusikkammer soon became a tool to deprive Jewish musicians of their livelihood as artists. Nazi propaganda aimed to re-purify German art from the "degenerate," "bourgeois," and "bolshevist" tendencies of the Weimar Republic that had corrupted all German art-forms, especially music. The hope was to clear the way for a genuine German art. Needless to say, the Reichsmusikkammer dismally failed to deliver, and artists in top positions were quickly replaced by bureaucrats. Herbert Windt's arrival into film music and the musical circuit falls into exactly this phase of early Nazi cultural politics. A closer look at Windt's biography and composition commitments prior to *Triumph des Willens* shifts the perspective from mere musical mimicry to cultural politics and the wider issue of Nazi aesthetics.

Herbert Windt, the Composer

Herbert Windt was born in 1894 in Senftenberg, a region in eastern Germany, now near the Polish border. He left school at sixteen for the renowned Sternsches Konservatorium in Berlin. Along with piano and conducting, Windt studied composition with Wilhelm Klatte, a pupil and assistant of Richard Strauss from his Weimar days. Upon the outbreak of the First World War, Windt immediately joined the army as a volunteer. He was badly wounded at Verdun and was taken to a hospital. Despite continuous treatment and plastic surgery, Windt was only released two years later, severely disfigured and permanently disabled. While still in the hospital he began writing chamber music and Lieder. His piano and conducting career now out of the question, Windt was forced to concentrate on composition.

In 1920 Windt was awarded a grant to join Franz Schreker's master class at the Berlin Academy of Music. Schreker was very supportive of Windt and suggested that he publish his chamber symphony *Andante Religioso*: "The piece is the most interesting and talented that has been written in my class in the last term," Schreker wrote to Universal Edition, where the work was subsequently published.[20] Theodor W. Adorno, who witnessed a performance of the piece in Frankfurt, was less impressed. He considered it unworthy of performance outside the inner circle of a composition class, characterizing it as perfunctory in its orchestration, amusing, at times even embarrassing in its naive imitation and illustrative appearance.[21]

Soon after, Windt left the class after a falling out with his teacher. The essay entitled "Die Atonalität bei Strauss," published in 1924, reveals Windt's artistic preferences. In it, Windt argues that Strauss, not Schoenberg, is the true father of atonality. He understood the dissolution of tonality as a process that started with Mozart, continued through Beethoven and Wagner, and culminated in Strauss. Windt distinguishes between thematic atonality, which he points to in *Ein Heldenleben* (Widersacherepisode), and harmonic atonality, as employed in *Also Sprach Zarathustra, Salome,* and *Elektra* which, according to Windt, all eventually lead to atonality.[22]

Although Windt received several prize grants, he could not sustain a living by composition alone. He gave private lessons and worked as an orchestrator for Universal Edition. A government grant enabled him to pursue a major opera project, and in 1932 *Andromache* was first performed at the Berlin State Opera under the baton of Erich Kleiber. It received a mixed response, but attracted the attention of a film producer from UFA who happened to be in the audience. Windt was asked to set the music to a new cycle of "heroic" and "nationalistic" films currently under production as a result of UFA's affiliation with ultra-nationalist and conservative political forces in the late Weimar Republic. The fact that Windt was also a card-carrying member of the Nazi Party surely added to his credentials.

Windt's first commission, *Morgenrot* (Vernon Sewell and Gustav Ucicky, 1933), is a nationalistic First World War drama about a submarine crew. The film reaches its dramatic climax when the main character exclaims, "We may not know how to live, but we Germans certainly know how to die," before committing suicide in order to save his comrades' lives. *Morgenrot*'s first performance in Essen coincided with the *Machtergreifung,* the Nazis' seizure of power. As a gesture toward the film industry, Hitler and his entire cabinet attended the Berlin opening on 2 February 1933.

Windt's effective and sparse sound track, subtly hinting at patriotic songs contrasting with dissonant fanfares, helped reestablish film in the eyes and ears of the attending Nazi functionaries. To the culturally conservative and reactionary Nazis, film, at least in its mainstream entertainment branch represented by the UFA corporation, was considered to be firmly in Jewish hands, hence a hedonistic and degenerate art form unworthy of any serious attention. Windt's score for *Morgenrot* seemed to prove that film music was capable of emphasizing a film's political and propagandistic intention, elevating it to an important political tool. *Morgenrot* established Windt as a specialist composer for "heroic" films, but also resulted in direct commissions from the new regime. He was asked to write a "Radio-kantate," a radio-play with a strong emphasis on choral and orchestral music for the Day of Potsdam, a ceremony held on 21 March 1933 in which Hitler laid claim to the Prussian lineage of Fredrick the Great and Bismarck in the historical setting of the Garrison church in Potsdam. Not surprisingly, the title of the radio play was "Das Reich ist unser" (The Reich is Ours).

Soon after, Windt was hired to compose music for the first official Nazi Party mass rally, the "Nationale Tag der Arbeit," on 1 May 1933, a Nazi appropriation of the traditional trade unions' Labour Day. Delegations from all over Germany marched to the Tempelhof airfield in central Berlin, where—as a precedent, if not even a trial run, to the Nuremberg rally later in the year—specific stalls were designed by Albert Speer and erected on the grounds. The various speeches and music performances ended with "Symphonie der Arbeit," which was performed at the main broadcasting house in Berlin, relayed to Tempelhof in real time, and broadcast live all over Germany. The next direct commission from the Nazi Party was for the first Riefenstahl party rally film *Sieg des Glaubens* (Victory of Faith, 1933). Due to the political ramifications of the Röhm purge in the summer of 1934, the film was removed from theaters.[23] Windt recycled most of the music for *Triumph des Willens*.

In 1934, Windt was commissioned to write music for a so-called *Thingspiel*. The Nazis revived the *Thing* in an attempt to at once establish and demonstrate a lineage to ancient Germanic culture. They added influences from passion and mystery plays that were recontextualized for Nazi purposes and served as the ersatz-religious aspect of Nazi ideology. Special amphitheater-style venues with especially designed amplification were built on purportedly "sacred" historical Germanic sites. The performances at the sites included musicians on Germanic brass-instruments such as the lure, choirs, bell ringing, and collective chanting. *Thingspiel* was the main attempt at creating an indigenous art form that the Nazis thought could best convey their aesthetic ideas in a collective mass-movement experience. The *Thing* movement was under especially rigorous scrutiny by the *Reichsdramaturg,* a sort of chief national theater director who personally made sure that the artistic and technical standards laid down by Nazi bureaucrats were kept. It is surely no coincidence that Windt was chosen to provide the music for the first ever *Thingspiel* to be performed at a specially constructed venue in Heidelberg, the "Deutsche Passion 1933" by Richard Euringer. One of the author's suggestions for the music to a section entitled the "ascension of the unknown soldier"—the character most obviously modeled on Hitler—reads: "Organ music from the heavens, sacred, rhythmically and harmonically wed to the worldly marching song."[24]

This striving toward a unique and distinct art form the Nazis could call their own was officially classified as *nationalsozialistische Feiergestaltung* (national-socialist celebration). It is interesting to note that apart from his continuous work in film, Windt was involved as a composer in all strands of *Feiergestaltung* from the outset: the first mass public rally "Symphonie der Arbeit" and its multi-media setting; the first radio cantata "Das Reich ist Unser"; and the very first *Thingspiel*, "Deutsche Passion 1933." *Feiergestaltung* made use of all the state-of-the-art media available at the time. The somewhat odd combination of modern media technology with archaic artistic forms and musical devices was very much in line with the Nazi perception of modernity: regression to a pre-modern condition in society and in the arts, using the most modern means.

In addition, it was a desperate attempt to fill the gaping hole in cultural life left after some of Germany's finest artists, composers, arrangers, and songwriters had been forced to emigrate. Many involved in film first went to France, then later to Hollywood.

There are musical devices common to all aspects of *nationalsozialistische Feiergestaltung.* From a musical-psychological point of view Windt chose a kind of *Überwältigungsästhetik,* an "aesthetics of awe." There are trumpet fanfares and short motifs connected in whole tone modulations, usually in the Dorian mode (often referred to by the postwar generation of German musicologists as "Nazi-Dorian"); archaic, plagal harmonic progressions; a very strong rhythmic foundation; and marked contrasts in orchestration. In short, the aesthetics of awe involved strong musical contrasts and stimuli, requiring a minimum attention span. This anti-intellectual, sensual, and very functional approach to music, which draws upon common and ancient perceptions of musical heroism, offered the most extreme counterpart to *l'art pour l'art* music the Nazis rejected as intellectual, elitist, effeminate, and degenerate. To them, such music was synonymous with the "decadence" of the Weimar Republic.

Shortly after the first performance of "Deutsche Passion 1933," Windt started work on the music to *Triumph des Willens.* I would like to propose that the commission for this film is in direct line with his work for *Feiergestaltung* and especially the *Thingspiel* movement. Musically, Windt underlines the pseudo-religious aspect of the film, already evident on a purely visual level. With the help of some aspects of Windt's music, the party rally in its cinematic treatment was set to be the ultimate, most genuine, Nazi festival and celebration, transcending and outperforming the actual event itself.

In *Triumph des Willens,* musical devices associated with *Thingspiel* and *Feiergestaltung* are balanced with the familiar and accessible nineteenth-century late-romantic sound world, in which Windt, due to his training, background, and personal preferences, was equally fluent. Thus the film music works on two levels. On a general level, the Wagner/Bruckner connotations of Windt's music—whether intentional or not—hint at the cultural and historical legitimization of the Nazi movement in general, and the party rallies in particular. In the context of film propaganda, mere connotation is more effective than direct quotation. Goebbels's philosophy of propaganda called for the utmost subtlety. He knew that the moment that propaganda reveals itself, it loses its effect. The specific quality of Windt's music is to point the hearer's attention in a particular direction. His music sets the boundaries for a very specific cultural space into which the events on screen can be projected. This is specifically the case with the overture and arrival of Hitler.

"Fahrt durch Nürnberg" / No. 4—which tends typically to be associated today with Wagnerian leitmotifs—could equally well have referred to *Thingspiel* and *Feiergestaltung* in the light of the context I have tried to outline. This is probably the most significant piece of music in the film. Windt connects and varies four motifs so as to highlight particular onscreen images. The motifs are mostly played by trumpets, such as the one transcribed in Musical Example 2.1, which evolves in an *aspera ad astra* style prologue. After the overture, the audience is presented with a brief history of Germany's *via dolorosa* before the redeeming arrival of Adolf Hitler. The four captions are accompanied by silent-film style music. First, there is a dissonant and muffled diminished chord, accompanying the caption "20 Jahre nach Ausbruch des Weltkriegs" (twenty years after the outbreak of the world war). It is followed by "16 Jahre nach dem Anfang des deutschen Leidens" (sixteen years after the beginning of German suffering—a reference to the Versailles Treaty). The music then slightly brightens with the appearance of "19 Monate nach Beginn der deutschen Wiedergeburt" (nineteen months after the beginning of the German renaissance—a reference to the Nazi seizure of power). With the caption "flog Adolf Hitler wiederum nach Nürnberg um Heerschau abzuhalten über seine Getreuen" (Adolf Hitler again flew to Nuremberg to visit the parade of his true followers), the audience hears the fanfare in Musical Example 2.1.[25]

Musical Example 2.1. Trumpet fanfare from the prologue. After sketches in the Windt estate (Sammlung Windt der Stiftung Deutsche Kinemathek).

In the later piece, "Fahrt durch Nürnberg / No.4," this fanfare is transposed, extended, and played by the orchestra in various instrumentations (Musical Example 2.2):

Musical Example 2.2. Extended fanfare motif from "Fahrt durch Nurnberg / No.4."

A further component of No. 4 is the plagal cadenza illustrated in Musical Example 2.3. This occurs at the same moment that a woman raises her hand for the Hitler salute after having broken free of the crowd. Her one arm holds a child, while her other presents the Führer with a bouquet of flowers.

Musical Example 2.3. Plagal cadenza from "Fahrt durch Nürnberg / No.4."

We should note the plagal progression from F minor to C major, a typically archaic trope. The above-stated motifs and themes hardly differ from any kind of "heroic" music and motifs past and present. The larger political and aesthetic context, however, makes them particularly effective in this setting. They accompany specific images, as is the case in Musical Example 2.3, and hence cannot be classified as leitmotifs in the normal sense. In a kind of acoustic iconology more in line with what Ponowfsky applied to the visual arts, the music highlights the passing images of Riefenstahl's rapid and fluid cinematography in the 1920s' tradition of "unchained camera" as pioneered by F. W. Murnau and his cinematographer Karl Freund.[26]

This specific technique of acoustically underlining specific images lends itself very well to the Nazi obsession with icons, flags, symbols, and so on. On a more theoretical level, the concept of *Anschauung* as defined and proposed by the Nazi Party's chief ideologist Alfred Rosenberg as early as 1929 is supported by Windt's specific application: "*Anschauung* was viewed and suggested as a means of combining all forms of art—specifically using signs, images and sounds—to generate a common cause and to underline the mythical aspects of Nazism."[27] To the contemporary spectator, the music may well have provided a link to other Nazi Party events, a link that stood in close connection with the aesthetic audio-visual demands of Alfred Rosenberg and his cronies.

The music of Windt must in its day have seemed autonomous and individual, not epigonic. He was distinctly recognized and in demand as a film composer of strictly classical work, music appreciated for its supposed seriousness (*Ernste Musik*) rather than its entertainment value (*Unterhaltungsmusik*).[28] Windt went on from *Triumph des Willens* to set the music to a further forty-six films during the Third Reich, the majority of which have been classified as propagandistic by German film scholars such as Gerd Albrecht,[29] and he remained in constant demand as a specialist for "heroic" films. His career was not quite as smooth as may seem, however. Although he joined the Nazi Party as early as 1931, he refused to serve any official party function whatsoever, had frequent fallings out with officials, and stopped working for long periods of time, resorting to the solitude of the North Sea Island of Sylt, only to return when in need of money. His opera *Andromache* was never performed again. Windt claimed that Alfred Rosenberg considered it "too modern."[30] Due to his disability and severe disfigurement, Windt could not serve as a trophy-artist for the Nazis, who fetishized the physical ideal. At official functions, Windt was often perceived as an embarrassment. After the war and denazification, Windt continued writing film music in the same style as before with moderate success until his death in 1964.

What became of the *Thingspiel* and *Feiergestalting* that had, I am claiming, such an influence on *Triumph des Willens*? The *Thingspiel* movement was officially dissolved in 1936 following a disastrous performance witnessed by an incredulous crowd of foreign visitors at the Berlin Olympics.[31] It was officially banned in 1937, and after the failure to produce and sustain anything of its own, Nazis resorted to the direct appropriation of the music of Wagner, Bruckner, and Beethoven for representational purposes. This shift in cultural politics is reflected in some of Windt's later film scores as well. The "Heroic Suite," composed of parts of the film music to *Triumph des Willens,* was recorded for radio, but never actually made it onto any of the official play lists for party functions, as may initially have been intended.

Until the very end, the demand for genuine, indigenous Nazi music was answered with dismally mediocre work. There were repeated attempts at reviving the arts scene and supporting contemporary opera. But as Hermann Goering, patron minister of the Berlin State Opera and one of the cultural antagonists to Goebbels, famously stated, it is easier to turn an artist into a Nazi than to turn a Nazi into an artist. By 1941, Goebbels himself filed a complaint and appealed to all party functionaries responsible for *Feiergestaltung* to be more creative in their choice of music for party festivities. One had the impression, Goebbels wrote, that the only music available for party functions was the *Rienzi* overture, the *Meistersinger* Vorspiel, Weber's *Freischütz* overture, and Richard Strauss's *Festliches Praeludium.* There follows a four-page list with alternative works ranging from baroque to contemporary, with quite a few modern composers represented. Interestingly, Windt is not included, although he extracted a "Heroic Suite" from his film music for *Triumph des Willens,* probably for the very purpose of usage outside film for party functions. This would also support the thesis that his film music was too closely tied to the *Thing* movement, which by 1941 had been out of favor for several years. Goebbels's list was personally approved by Hitler. Through his secretary, he told Goebbels that he was generally supportive of the idea and the list, but that he was unable to comment in detail on the individual pieces, since he was only familiar with a few.[32]

It seems apparent that Windt did not specifically answer to demands that he compose a certain kind of music. Nor did he deliberately compose in the manner of Wagner, Strauss, or Bruckner. His multi-functional and polysemantic style catered to a wide variety of political and propagandistic purposes, and comfortably blended in with many of the demands of a cultural bureaucracy desperate to deliver results. The film music to *Triumph des Willens*—with its *Feiergestaltung* legacy and demise—is a case in point.[33] Windt's style and musicianship, however, lent themselves to propagandistic purposes. The somewhat crude and blunt aspects of his style appealed to the concept of an aesthetic based on the least common denominator of musical stimulation. As Windt testified during his denazification trial, his style of composing was "very welcome by the powers that be."[34]

Notes

1. MoMA, *This Future.*
2. Loiperdinger and Culbert, "Leni Riefenstahl," 16.
3. Deutschmann, *Triumph of the Will,* 32.
4. Ibid., 75.
5. Nowotny, *Leni Riefenstahl,* 128.
6. Riethmüller, "Komposition," 229.
7. This dichotomy, propagandistically very successful in the visual arts, failed to have an impact in music. There was a degenerate music exhibition that failed to pinpoint degenerate aspects in music as it did in visual art. Dümling and Girth, *Entartete Musik.*
8. Gilliam, "The Annexation of Anton Bruckner."
9. Brinkmann, "The Distorted Sublime."
10. Deutschmann, *Triumph of the Will,* 75.
11. The times in the table refer to the print of *Triumph des Willens* available at the German National Filmarchive (Bundesarchiv-Filmarchiv Berlin), ref. 79 253.
12. Most recently so in Joachim Köhler's *Wagner's Hitler.*
13. This issue and its origin have been dealt with extensively in Pamela Potter's excellent book *Most German of the Arts.*
14. See Volker, *"Von oben sehr erwünscht,"* 26 ff.
15. Riefenstahl, *Hinter den Kulissen,* 11.
16. Speer, *Erinnerungen,* 71.
17. Delahaye, "Leni and the Wolf," 49.
18. Windt, Denazification File.
19. Steinweis, *Art, Ideology and Economics.* The initial concept of an organization by and for artists is supported by the first presidents of the chamber such as Richard Strauss and the nomination of Fritz Lang as president of the film chamber. Lang famously fled the country immediately after being called by Goebbels, as he sensed what he would have been in for. These early nominations also proved that the various chambers started out with very high hopes.
20. Schreker, Letter.
21. Adorno, *Gesammelte Schriften,* 25; text written in 1923.
22. Windt, "Richard Strauss," 646.
23. The events around the murder of Erich Röhm are referred to as the Röhm-purge; Röhm, a close associate of Hitler, had established the SA ("brown shirts") as a party-funded army and police force. By 1934 the position and future of the SA remained unclear and a constant cause of friction in the top echelons of the Nazi Party. Finally, rumors were circulated that Röhm was planning a coup against Hitler. This led not only to Röhm's execution, but also a general rounding up of further dissidents. The number of political murders by the Nazis upon this occasion ranges from 77 to as many as 401. For further information see Kershaw, *Hitler,* 499ff.
24. Vondung, *Magie und Manipulation,* 180. Very little research has been done into the *Thingspiel.* There are some references in Brenner, *Die Kunstpolitik,* 179ff.; Vondung, *Magie und Manipulation,* 180ff.; and Würrfel, "Hörspiel im Dritten Reich," 129. For more detailed information see Lurz, "Die Heidelberger Thingstätte."
25. Music samples transcribed and double-checked with sketches in the Windt estate: Sammlung Windt der Stiftung Deutsche Kinemathek (4.3.-87/13).
26. The art historian Panowsky developed the notion of a specific iconology inherent to a work of art. Its full appreciation could only be determined by the knowledge and specific

references to its cultural context. In the case of *Triumph des Willens,* Windt's motifs lead to specific connotations for the images on screen.

27. Brenner, *Die Kunstpolitik,* 276.

28. "E" standing for *Ernst* meaning "serious," as opposed to "U" standing for *Unterhaltungs* meaning entertainment music. See chapter 1 for a brief discussion of these terms.

29. Albrecht, *Nationalsozialistische Filmpolitik.*

30. Windt, Denazification File.

31. The *Thingspiel* was also performed in a specially built venue next to the Berlin Olympic Stadium, the Dietrich-Eckert-Bühne. Hitler considered Eckert one of his spiritual mentors from his days in Munich. The Dietrich-Eckert-Bühne was renamed to the more neutral and politically correct Waldbühne after the war, and is one of the most popular open-air venues in Berlin, with regular concerts by the Berlin Philharmonic, rock concerts, and opera performances.

32. See Bundesarchiv file NS 18/763—nationale Feiergestaltung.

33. In this context, it would also be interesting to establish if *Triumph des Willens* continued to be screened until the downfall of the Third Reich.

34. Windt, Denazification File.

References

Adorno, Theodor Wiesengrund. *Gesammelte Schriften,* vol. 19 (*Musikalische Schriften VI*), ed. R. Thiedemann. Frankfurt am Main: Suhrkamp, 1984.

Albrecht, Gerd. *Nationalsozialistische Filmpolitik.* Stuttgart: Enke, 1968.

Brenner, Hildegard. *Die Kunstpolitik des Nationalsozialismus.* Reinbek: Rowohlt, 1963.

Brinkmann, Reinhold. "The Distorted Sublime: Music and National Socialist Ideology: A Sketch." In *Music & Nazism: Art under Tyranny, 1933–45,* ed. M. Kater and A. Riethmüller. Laaber: Laaber Verlag, 2003, 43–63.

Delahaye, Michel. "Leni and the Wolf: Interview with Leni Riefenstahl." *Cahiers du Cinéma in English* 5 (1966): 49–55.

Deutschmann, Linda. *Triumph of the Will: The Image of the Third Reich.* Wakefield, N.H.: Longwood Academic, 1991.

Dümling, Albrecht, and Peter Girth. *Entartete Musik: Eine kommentierte Rekonstruktion.* Catalog for the 1988 Düsseldorf Exhibition.

Gilliam, Bryan. "The Annexation of Anton Bruckner: Nazi Revisionism and the Politics of appropriation." *Musical Quarterly* 78/3 (1994): 584–604.

Kater, Michael, and Albrecht Riethmüller. *Music & Nazism: Art under Tyranny, 1933–45.* Laaber: Laaber Verlag, 2003.

Kershaw, Ian. *Hitler: Hubris 1889–1936.* London: Allen Lane, 1998.

Köhler, Joachim. *Wagner's Hitler. The Prophet and his Disciple.* Cambridge: Polity Press; Walden, Mass.: Blackwell, 2000.

Loiperdinger, Martin, and David Culbert. "Leni Riefenstahl, the SA, and the Party Rally Films: Nuremberg 1933–34 *Sieg des Glaubens* and *Triumph des Willens.*" *Historical Journal of Film, Radio and Television* 8/1 (1988): 3–37.

Lurz, Meinold. *Die Heidelberger Thingstätte: Die Thingbewegung im Dritten Reich. Kunst als Mittel politischer Propaganda.* Heidelberg: Schutzgemeinschaft Heiligenberg e.V., 1975.

Museum of Modern Art (MOMA). *This Future Is Entirely Ours: The Sound and Picture Outline of Triumph of the Will.* New York: Museum of Modern Art, 1965.

Nowotny, Peter. *Leni Riefenstahls "Triumph des Willens."* Lollar: Prolit Buchvertrieb, 1981.

Potter, Pamela M. *Most German of the Arts. Musicology and Society from the Weimar Republic to the End of Hitler's Reich.* New Haven, Conn.: Yale University Press 1998.

Riefenstahl, Leni. *Hinter den Kulissen des Reichsparteitagsfilms.* München, 1935.

Riethmüller, Albrecht, ed. *Bruckner Probleme: Internationales Kolloquium 7.–9. Oktober in*

Berlin, Beihefte zum Archiv für Musikiwissenschaft, vol. 45. Stuttgart: Franz Steiner Verlag 1999.

Riethmüller, Albrecht. "Komposition im Deutschen Reich um 1936." *Archiv für Musikwissenschaft* 38/4 (1981): 241–78.

Schreker, Franz. Letter to Universal Edition dated 16.7.1921: UdK-Archiv, Bestand 1, Nr. 110.

Speer, Albert. *Erinnerungen.* Frankfurt am Main: Ullstein, 1969.

Steinweis, Alan. *Art, Ideology and Economics in Nazi Germany: The Reich Chamber of Music, Theater and the Visual Arts.* Chapel Hill: University of North Carolina Press, 1993.

Volker, Reimar. *"Von oben sehr erwünscht." Die Filmmusik Herbert Windts im NS-Propagandafilm.* Trier: WVT, 2003.

Vondung, Klaus. *Magie und Manipulation: Ideologischer Kult und politische Religion des Nationalsozialismus.* Göttingen: Vandenhoeck & Ruprecht, 1971.

Windt, Herbert. Denazification File (1949). Landesarchiv Berlin, EK 2272.

———. "Richard Strauss und die Atonalität." *Die Musik* 16/9 (1924): 642–53.

Würffel, Bodo. "Hörspiel im Dritten Reich." In *Kunst und Kultur im deutschen Faschismus,* ed. R. Schnell. Stuttgart: Metzler, 1978, 129–55.

Filmography

TRIUMPH DES WILLENS (**TRIUMPH OF THE WILL**)

release:	28 March 1935
duration:	114 mins
dir:	Leni Riefenstahl
prod:	Leni Riefenstahl
prod co:	Leni Riefenstahl-Produktion; NSDAP Reischpropaganda-leitung Hauptabt Film
camera:	Sepp Allgeier; Karl Attenberger; Werner Bohne; Werner Bundhausen; Walter Frentz; Hans Gottschalk; Herbert Kebelmann; Albert Kling; Franz Koch; Paul Lieberenz; Vlada Majic; Richard Nickel; Walter Riml; Arthur Schwertfeger; Károly Vass; Franz Weihmayr; Siegfried Weimann; Karl Wellert; Willy Zielke
music:	Herbert Windt
DVD:	Connoisseur/Meridian (18 August 2000), ASIN: B00004YA12
Synapse (17 April 2001), ASIN:	B00004WLXZ
Dd Home Entertainment, (31 August 2001), ASIN:	B00004YVEO
Synapse (28 March 2006), ASIN:	B000E41MRC

THREE

Alban Berg, *Lulu*, and the Silent Film

MARC A. WEINER

On 7 August 1930, Alban Berg penned an often-cited letter to his mentor, Arnold Schoenberg, in which he drew attention to a feature of his new opera, *Lulu*, that the composer explicitly described as essential to his project:

> You can see from the enclosed scenario that what is *separated* in Wedekind—after all there are *two* plays—is intentionally fused (by my IInd act). The orchestral Interlude, which in my version *bridges* the gap between the last act of *Erdgeist* and the first of *Die Büchse der Pandora*, is of course the central point of the whole tragedy. . . .[1]

As the letter spells out, Berg's plan for a three-act opera drew equally from two dramas, Frank Wedekind's *Earth Spirit* (1898) and *Pandora's Box* (1904), so that the middle of his second act constituted the point at which the opera moves from material in the first to that from the second of these works for the stage. Strangely, what Berg does not mention is the fact that the Interlude would be composed of a silent film with musical accompaniment, an aesthetic device intended to provide a narrative bridge between Wedekind's two dramas, filling in the gaps and making the machinations of the second half of the opera intelligible. Berg did not draw attention to his use of the relatively new medium of the film, emphasizing instead the music to the piece (hence his reference to the central point of the opera as an "Interlude"), and this omission may in part account for the relative lack of attention the use of a silent film in *Lulu* has received.[2] Indeed, given the fact that the work constitutes one of the most celebrated operas of the twentieth century, it is surprising just how little interest has been devoted to Berg's short film scenario. Those few critics who do mention it do so only in passing, and they limit their discussion to quoting the composer's notes for the cinematic scenario and to describing its music rather than asking why Berg wanted a film in his opera in the first place.[3] Nor have its ramifications for an understanding of the opera in which it appears engendered much interest, even by those scholars who do evince attention to Berg's connections with film. Thomas F. Ertelt, for example, in referring to Willi Reich's classical biography of the composer, claims it is "well known" that Berg was an avid moviegoer, and Reich informs us that Berg was interested in a number of projects that would have integrated music and film (Berg hoped, for example, that *Wozzeck* would be made into a movie), but neither Ertelt nor Reich subjects *Lulu*'s cinematic scenario to an extended investigation.[4] This is especially surprising, given the fact that the interconnections between film and opera have constituted an object of inquiry to which both musicologists and media specialists have devoted ever more attention in the recent past, so much so that one can perhaps even speak of a new sub-field of opera and film studies characterized by scholarly work from a variety of disciplines.[5] Nonetheless, there are many reasons for taking Berg's scenario seriously, if only for the importance he himself apparently accorded it. After all, it is well known that, from their initial conception, the composer imagined the overall plan of virtually all of his works in terms of their architectural organization, and his placement of a silent film at the center of *Lulu* itself therefore indicates that he regarded it as fundamental, or "central," to his project.[6]

In what follows, then, I should like to examine the makeup of the silent film in *Lulu*, first through an analysis of its function within the music drama, and second, within the context of early-twentieth-century discussions of the cinema. I hope to show that Berg based the scenario of his film on a wide range of tropes with which the early silent film was associated in the minds of European audiences in the early twentieth century, and that it served to evoke both a number of well-known examples of the genre in particular, and the institution of the cinema in general, an institution whose relationship to established theatrical traditions (both of the legitimate theater and opera) was hotly debated at the time Berg was developing his project. This will help to account for why Berg was drawn to use a film in his final opera, and I hope to show that consideration of the film helps us to appreciate much better the historical context in which this avant-garde operatic project unfolded.

Lulu tells the story of one of opera's most notorious femme fatales, an enigmatic, timeless, mythic figure who causes, or perhaps one should say witnesses, the demise of virtually every man who comes into contact with her as she climbs the social ladder—first, a professor of medicine, then a painter, followed by the newspaper mogul and businessman Dr. Ludwig Schön, and then his son, the composer Alwa (often seen as an autobiographical portrait of Alban Berg), until Lulu's fortune turns and she ends up a prostitute, dying in London at the hands of Jack the Ripper. In the middle of the three-act drama, Berg's plan calls for a short film (which lasts less than three minutes).[7] During the film the audience was to witness the schematic, visual narration of Lulu's arrest for the murder of Dr. Schön, her detention, trial (Figures 3.1 and 3.2), and imprisonment, followed by her ultimate escape from prison. She brings that escape about by switching undergarments (which have been infected with cholera) with her lesbian devotee, the Countess Geschwitz, and is then taken to the prison's hospital (Figure 3.3), where she and Geschwitz exchange clothes and Lulu escapes in disguise at the end of the film. Figures 3.1, 3.2, and 3.3 are from the original film, produced by Tempo, a firm of Hans Rudolf Meyer, for the first staging of *Lulu* in Zürich on 2 June 1937. While the stage director for the opera was Karl Schmid-Bloss, the film was directed by Heinz Rückert.[8]

Berg sketched a schematic depiction (Table 3.1) of his proposed film that emphasizes its many structural components.[9] One becomes aware of a symmetry in the dramatic content and its visual representation within Berg's film scenario, which functions at the opera's center as a fulcrum within a work organized around dramatic and musical correspondences that inform the entire piece. The first scene, depicting Lulu's arrest, has its counterpart in the final scene of her deliverance, and the second scene of Lulu's detention corresponds to the penultimate one spent in an isolation ward; the five witnesses of the trial correspond to the five helpers of the "medical consultation," and the judge and jury of the trial correspond to the doctors and students, the police van to the ambulance, revolver to stethoscope, legal paragraphs to medical guidelines, and so on. These correspondences within the film reveal a structural concept that informs the opera as a whole, such as those between Lulu's three husbands (the Professor of Medicine, the Painter, and Dr. Schön) in the first half of the opera, and her three clients as a prostitute (the Professor, the Negro, and Jack the Ripper) in its final scene, which are only the most obvious examples of many. Thus, the film may have been intended to draw attention to the formal or material makeup of the opera, and in this way to prepare the audience for its second half.

Through its many motivic correspondences and reversals the film reveals

Table 3.1. Lulu Film Music

(Act II, sc. 1, bars 651–722)

Bars		
	Arrest	**En Route to her final liberation**
	(The 3 participants)	(The 3 participants)
656	Alwa	Alwa 718
	Geschwitz	Geschwitz
	Schoolboy	Acrobat
661	Lulu in chains	Lulu at liberty (as Countess G) 712
	Detention pending trial	**Isolation ward**
	Nervous expectancy	Nervous expectancy
668	Dwindling hope	Growing hope 705
	Trial	**Medical consultation**
	Guilt	Illness
	Judge and jury	Doctor and students
677	The judgment	Rescue plan 696
	(the 5 witnesses)	(the 5 helpers)
	Her transfer in the police van to	Her transfer in the ambulance from
680	**Prison**	**Prison** 694
	The door shuts	The door opens
	Resignation	Awakening will to live
686	Her shadow on the wall (like the portrait)	Her image in the dustpan
		688

———————————→ —— One Year's Imprisonment —————→

Revolver	Stethoscope
Bullets	Phials
Law	Medicine
	Caduceus
Judge and jury	Doctor and students
Chains	Bandages
Prison Clothes	Hospital smock
Police	Nurse

an architectural model that informs the entire opera, which also falls into two halves that are replete with motivic, textual, and musical parallels. Berg emphasizes this point in his letter to Schoenberg when he continues the passage quoted above:

> The orchestral Interlude . . . is of course the central point for the whole tragedy and—after the ascent of the opening acts (or scenes)—the descent in the following scenes marks the beginning of the retrograde [or "reversal" = *die Umkehr*]. (Incidentally: the . . . men who visit Lulu in her attic room are to be portrayed in

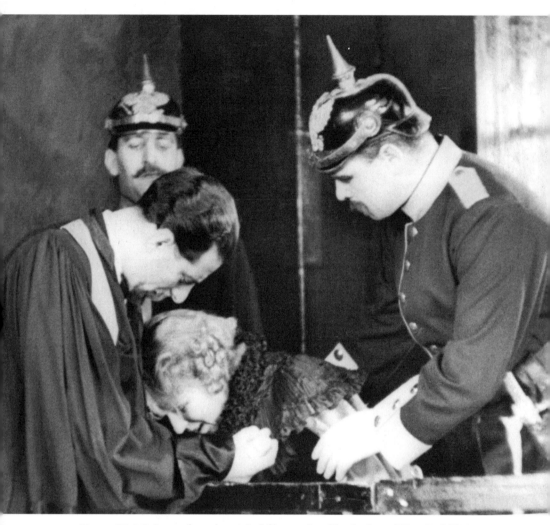

Figures 3.1–3.3. Images from the original film, produced by the firm of Hans Rudolf Meyer "Tempo," for the first staging of *Lulu* at the State Theatre in Zürich on 2 June 1937.

Figure 3.2.

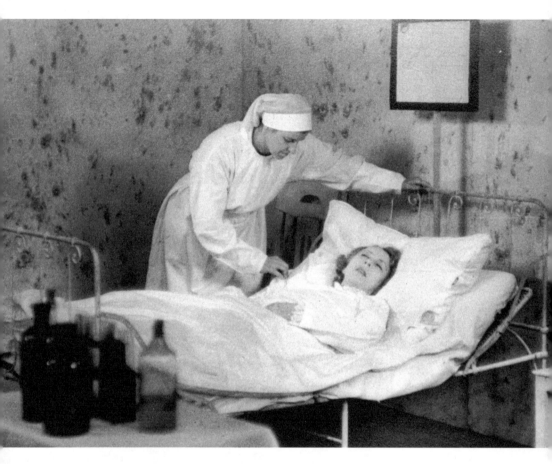

Figure 3.3.

the opera by the same singers who fall victim to her in the first half of the opera. In reverse order, however.)

That, I think, is the most interesting dramaturgical aspect I can tell you.[10]

In other words, immediately after he mentions the dramaturgical function of the musical structure of the film, Berg draws attention to the dramaturgical doublings of figures who appear in the first and the second half of the entire work. In this way, the film reveals the two central structural principles of the opera: a static doubling that suspends or transcends time, and the chronological, forward-moving development that constitutes Lulu's social and physiological ascent and descent. The film thereby assumes the function of a *mise en abyme:* a microcosmic mirror of the work as a whole.

George Perle has pointed out that the film's dramatic symmetry has its parallel in the structure of the music Berg wrote to accompany it, whereby material presented in forward motion in the first half has its counterpart in retrograde motion in the second, so that the film and its music unfold across a kind of pyramid, mirror, or palindromic shape which privileges its center.[11] One of the justifications for this structure is doubtless the fact that, as Douglas Jarman has ably argued, Berg consistently used the musical forms of the retrograde and palindrome "as a metaphor for negation or denial," and given this association, the drama of Lulu's decline would have made the implementation of such a musical structure at this point in the drama seem automatically appropriate in Berg's imagination.[12] Furthermore, this musical structure dovetailed with the film's ability to present a drama both in forward and reverse order (a feature that Berg's contemporary, Paul Hindemith, emphasized and exploited in his use of film in an opera, as described below).

But the musical structure is hardly as apparent to the average operagoer as that of the film's motivic make-up and plot development; the second half of the Interlude sounds rather different from the first, even though its underlying organizational structure and material reveal consistent correspondences. Of course, it is well known that Berg often chose to hide such technical features of his music from his audience, but here he draws attention to the musical form through the corresponding visual material of the film, and therefore one could say that the visual material has a complementary or even a corrective function to that of the acoustical, in so far as it reveals structure the way music—or this music—does not. It shows something that can be listened for (whether the listener untrained in dodecaphonic music can actually hear it is another matter), and thereby functions as an internal device that illuminates not only the unfolding plot, but the technical make-up of the work in which it appears. In this way, the cinematic project reverses the trope that would later usually be associated with the function of music in the movies, in which sounds are often thought of as accompanying or even subordinate to the visual material. In *Lulu* one might speak instead of a mutually enhancing relationship between the two, because the acoustical does not *serve* the visual, but unfolds loosely in accordance with it, as indicated by Berg's sketches.[13] The two art forms are complementary, neither more important than the other, but each exploiting features they alone exhibit in order to reveal those they have in common.[14]

There is an intriguing perception of a functional distinction between the genres of opera and film here. What up to this point had been a dramaturgically conventional chronological development in the opera is briefly suspended when the opera resorts to a foreign medium that is relied upon to provide concise, narrative information ostensibly necessary for an understanding of the second half of the drama. Following the film, the opera continues with its comparatively lyrical display of the feelings of the protagonists. In other words, the film narrates, and the opera emotes. According to Berg's statements to Schoenberg, the film was intended to "bridge the gulf" separating the two Wedekind plays, but he himself may have sensed that the short piece would be unable to fulfill this function, because in his libretto following the Interlude, he chose to retain a passage from Wedekind's *Die Büchse der Pandora* in which Lulu relates to Alwa virtually all of the events the short film had just portrayed to the audience:

> LULU: Oh, Countess Geschwitz arranged things very cleverly. You know that terrible outbreak of cholera this past summer in Hamburg? That gave her something to build her plans on—the plans for my escape. She took an emergency training course for nurses, and then went to Hamburg as a nurse for the cholera victims. At the first opportunity that came along, she put on some underwear belonging to one of the patients who had died. On that same morning she came back and visited me in prison. And in my cell, while the wardress was out of sight, we quickly changed underwear with each other.
> ALWA: So that was how you both felt sick with cholera on the very same day!
> LULU: Of course. Well, naturally they took her away from her apartment to the isolation wing attached to the city hospital, and they hadn't any other suitable place to put me either. The day before yesterday she was discharged, cured. And today, just now, she came back with the story that she'd left her watch behind by mistake. I put on her clothes, she slipped into my smock—the thing they make prisoners wear—and out I came. Now she's lying in there as the murderess of Dr. Schön.[15]

One could argue, of course, that Berg needed to preserve this text for diegetic purposes, in that while the audience may by this point be privy to the narrative information of the film, Alwa is not; but I would argue that there were other than simply narrative reasons for Berg's use of the film. After all, if the information concerning the trial, imprisonment, disease, and escape was so important, he could also have had a narrator intrude into the action to inform the audience of the events involved, something of a Brechtian device not unlike the use of the Circus Director in the Prologue, who speaks to the audience directly. And indeed, the performance history of the opera hardly suggests that the film

Berg planned was able to fulfill the function he claimed it was to serve. Reich informs us that, at the opera's premiere in Zürich in 1937, it became clear

> that the transitional music runs too quickly to allow for a clear perception of what transpires in the film [*daß die Verwandlungsmusik zu rasch abläuft, um ein genau wahrnehmbares Filmgeschehen zu ermöglichen*]. Therefore, in subsequent performances, the film was usually replaced by projected images showing the most important stages of the intervening action [*Zwischenhandlung*].[16]

In some cases in its subsequent performance history, any attempts at scenic realization have been abandoned altogether, and the Interlude has been played before a closed curtain, or before various tableaux formed by singers and dancers, rather than to slides or a film.[17] Apparently, the film does not prepare the audience for the second half of the drama as Berg had hoped it would; in his notes for the program to the work's premiere, Reich explained that Lulu's arrest and imprisonment would merely be "suggested" by the film (*was durch einen stummen Film mit Musik angedeutet wird*), further testimony to the film's impracticality.[18] Thus, Berg did not need to have a film for solely technical or narrative reasons. So if that was not its purpose, what was?

Berg's scenario constitutes a reference both to a body of images and to technical features in films with which he and his audience were familiar, and to an institution deemed foreign to the traditional Grand Opera, and I would argue that this was precisely part of the insurrectionary agenda that this revolutionary work—which shows an affinity with the contemporary new genre of the *Zeitoper* so critical of the traditional opera—was designed to further.[19] The schematic, hectic, abrupt transitions of the short film in *Lulu* recall the overall appearance of many films from the period, and thematically it draws upon the clichés of the early cinema associated with the hectic, dangerous life of the big city; the kind of motif found in *Metropolis* (Fritz Lang, 1926), *Berlin: die Symphonie einer Großstadt* (Berlin, Symphony of a Big City, Walther Ruttmann, 1927), and *M: Eine Stadt sucht einen Mörder* (M, Fritz Lang, 1931), as well as in a host of other works from the time.

Even its structure recalls the early cinema, for the film's ability to present a drama both in forward and reverse order and motion was one of the technical possibilities of the new medium that particularly fascinated the public at the time and that often appears, for example, in the work of Charlie Chaplin, whom Berg greatly admired. The composer emphasized the forward and retrograde movement of his film scenario when he stated, in an explanatory note, that the "sequence of the filmed events corresponding to the symmetrical course of the music is . . . to run in a quasi-forward and retrograde progression [*vorwärtsgehend und rückläufig*],"[20] and thus is directly comparable to the contemporary film, as well as to other operas also designed to evoke the cinema, such as Paul Hindemith's *Hin und Zurück: eine Zeitoper* from 1927, in which the dramatic movement of the short work replicates the forward and rewinding or backward movement of a film, and here, too, the plot concerns infidelity and murder.[21]

Through its employment of and reference to the new medium of the film, Berg's work can be compared to many others of the time that (more overtly and extensively) constituted a departure from the traditional opera. Both Berg and Hindemith's works, for example, are comparable to Max Brand's *Machinist Hopkins* of 1928, another attempt both to depict and to integrate the new technology of the age into the traditional opera.[22] Indeed, an early critic described Brand's libretto as "an extract from a film script in the best sense of the word,"[23] not only owing to the work's formal features, but also because it constituted "a mixture of crime and passion, high-tech fantasies, and social issues like the conflict of capital and labor,"[24] reminiscent of such silent films as the aforementioned *Metropolis* and, given its themes of urban life, *Berlin: die Symphonie einer Großstadt*. In the premiere of the Brand opera, a film projection was used, showing images celebrating the machine age accompanied by an off-stage speaking chorus which imitated the machine sounds. Other examples from this time of *Zeitoper* employing film are the sequence in Weill's *Royal Palace* (1927) and the film used in the final scene of George Antheil's *Transatlantic* (1930); both provide quasi-narrative information, and in Antheil's opera, the hero's dream, which is essential to understanding his action later in the opera, is filmed.[25] Nonetheless, in all these works (especially the Brand opera), a film is not used solely to provide narrative information, nor primarily to fulfill an essential dramatic function, but instead the operas are conceived in such a way that they are intended to evoke or even to replicate various features of the cinema. The social reference is as important as any technical innovation; or, to put it differently, the latter itself also already constitutes the former. This is especially the case with the film in *Lulu*, for as we have seen, its narrative function is little more than a gesture to cinematic convention; Berg himself realized that it does not work as a narrative device.

However, *Lulu* is normally not regarded as a *Zeitoper*. It is well known that Berg made no comments on the new genre, but as Jarman has suggested, Berg's silence can be interpreted as his reluctance to be estranged from his teacher and mentor Schoenberg, who attacked the new genre, rather than as his disapproval of the *Zeitoper* per se. In typical *Zeitopern*, the aural and visual contemporaneity and the celebration of modern life and technology appear in much more aggressive ways than in *Lulu*: for example, the on-stage appearance of loudspeakers and also, in lavish productions, real cars and trains in Ernst Krenek's *Jonny spielt auf* of 1927; the use of twelve typewriters in the office scene in Hindemith's *Neues vom Tage* of 1929, which function as on-stage percussion instruments; and the employment of the gramophone as a stage prop in the seduction scene in Weill's *Der Zar lässt sich photographieren* of 1928. To some minds, *Lulu*'s story is too dark and tragic to be a *Zeitoper*, which is commonly characterized as cheerful, light, and comic. And Lulu is both a primordial, archetypal figure and a representative of a precisely defined historical time. Moreover, and perhaps most decisively, the opera's overall musical language is too elitist, in no small part because of its reliance on the twelve-tone technique.[26]

Nonetheless, in spite of the prevalent musicological view that excludes *Lulu* from the repertoire of the *Zeitoper,* Berg's opera certainly suggests some affinity with the genre, which can be demonstrated through attention to a host of features that constitute allusions to contemporary operatic innovations. For example, its use of an alto saxophone, especially in the Canzonetta in Act I, Scene 1; the employment of the on-stage jazz band, and, perhaps, the use of a violin solo in the Wedekind cabaret song (the *Lautenlied*), both of which evoke Krenek's and Weill's recognition of a violin as a legitimate dance band instrument;[27] its occasional (although feeble) hints at popular musical idioms in such numbers as the circus music of the Prologue and the Ragtime; its visual/aural/narrative references to the modern world (the Stock Exchange, the cabaret theater, the telephone, etc.); and most blatantly, the use of film. Berg's desire to expand the parameters of the opera helps to account for his transplantation of Wedekind's dramas set in the fin-de-siècle to the contemporary world of the 1930s. For this shift in temporal setting allowed him to introduce a variety of new, contemporary art forms, such as the circus, variety shows, and jazz, into Grand Opera; they called its elitist institutional status into question. All these art forms were associated in the minds of Berg's more conservative contemporaries with America, and were viewed by them as socially inferior and non-European art. Berg's use of film fits right into this social context, and it was such associations, perhaps even more than its technical possibilities, that made the film scenario seem appropriate to him.

His film comes at a time shortly after the introduction of sound into cinema, but as a film without song or dialogue—only, so to speak, with extradiegetic musical accompaniment—and thus, it evokes both the silent film up to 1927 (the year of the *Jazz Singer*) and the talkies; that is, it evokes the institution of the cinema per se. The melodramatic elements of Berg's film are typical of the kind of cinematic material that Siegfried Kracauer, one of the great theoreticians of the Weimar cinema, associated with the new institution of the movie houses of the 1920s and 1930s, which were frequented, as he stated in his famous sociological essay, "Die kleinen Ladenmädchen gehen ins Kino" ("The Little Shopgirls go to the Movies"), by a new demographic of thrill seekers from a wide social spectrum, rather different from those who traditionally went to the theater.[28] When Berg's student, Theodor Adorno, and Walter Benjamin engaged in their famous debate about film in the 1930s, the one thing they both agreed on was its association with a wide, lower-class audience unskilled in the aesthetic tropes presupposed by more esoteric art works, such as opera, intended for a middle- and upper-class public.[29]

A passage from an anonymous essay, "Die Karriere des Kinematographen" (The Career of the Cinematograph), published in the journal *Lichtbild-Bühne* in 1910, characterizes the silent film and the modern cinema in Berlin in the early twentieth century by using social epithets that could easily have been meant to describe the music and the scenario Berg later wrote for his silent film, itself intended for a different kind of audience than that usually associated with the Opera. The anonymous critic writes of:

> nervous impatience . . . rapid developments: extracts, condensations, 3-minute novels. . . . [One is jolted] out of a state of complacency into a feverish ecstasy of the most amazing mobility. . . . It celebrates its championship for the moment in the aesthetics of fever.[30]

The text clearly evinces trepidation, or even fear and amazement at the new artistic medium, and in this respect it resembles a similar description of the modern film by an acquaintance of Berg's, the polymath and actor Egon Friedell (who had a small role in the first performance of *Pandora's Box*).[31] In 1912 Friedell published a treatise entitled "Prolog vor dem Film" (Prologue before the Film), in which he stated that the new medium "is short, rapid, at the same time coded, and it does not stop for anything. There is something concise, precise, military about it."[32] These passages could describe Berg's music, with its "rapid developments," compressed, "condens[ed]" manner, and compact, evocative sounds aptly characterized as programmatic, as illustrating a "3-minute novel." And Friedell's observation that "there is something concise, precise, military about it" would seem to go hand in hand with the way Berg's piece evokes, incorporates, and organizes violence. At the same time, the art is deemed a highly technical accomplishment, something difficult to fathom; if it is not intended solely for specialists, then at least for a clearly defined and apparently rather foreign or threatening audience, and therefore it is "coded." It is an intimidating, bewildering, and undeniably powerful art.

It makes sense that these various, typical observations from German critics could be applied to Berg's scenario and music, for the film in *Lulu* evokes the new subject matter of social dissolution, violence, and calculated timing and effect, all attributes of many silent films from the 1920s, and even of the institution of the cinema itself in the minds of the more conservative critics writing in the early twentieth century, who feared that the new art form would threaten the hallowed traditions of German theatrical culture, and that meant not only the legitimate theater, but opera. The reaction of a figure such as Hans Pfitzner to the efforts of Berg, Krenek, and others shows what these artists were up against and underscores just how shocking their works were to the more traditional, bourgeois sensibilities of the time. Pfitzner and equally nostalgic and elitist conservatives of the time thought of the cinema as something non-German, products of a cultural pollution brought to Germany by the American

victors following World War I. Indeed, he saw the cinema as rightfully belonging solely to the working, uneducated, and uncultured masses, with whom he
also associated a host of other cultural activities he thought of as specifically
American, such as radio, golf, boxing, horse races, the circus, variety shows,
and jazz.[33] In his notorious foreword from 1926 to his essay *Die neue Ästhetik
der musikalischen Impotenz* (The New Aesthetic of Musical Impotence) of 1920,
directed against the music critic Paul Bekker, Pfitzner decried precisely this
influx of foreign art:

> He who has a genuine perception of this time of *battle against German nationalism*
> [*Deutschtum*] unclouded by a fear of the truth, he will understand that my attacks
> carried out in this book are not offenses, but defenses. Those who do not notice the
> decay of all German culture and art and act with indifference or even promote em-
> pathy, also promote the demise of all European culture, whose uppermost source
> and refuge has always been Germany, and help to transplant onto our solid land
> the international lack of spirit, pseudo- or a-national Americanism. A portion of
> European and German mankind feels quite good about this; the other is horrified
> at the thought that in the foreseeable future—perhaps in no more than two or three
> decades—Beethoven's symphonies and Wagnerian operas and other symbols of
> our art will not be played at all. . . . Now I see this world vanishing completely and
> the other one surfacing—yes, it is already here and begins its triumphant march
> through Europe, grinding everything—the American tanks of the spiritual battle
> against European culture![34]

These pronouncements typify Pfitzner's reaction to the cinema as well, and thus
it is no coincidence that he engaged in a highly public polemical exchange with
Berg concerning the development of modern music, carried out in this essay
and in Berg's response to it, *Die musikalische Impotenz der "Neuen Ästhetik"
Hans Pfitzners* (The Musical Impotence of Hans Pfitzner's "New Aesthetic").[35]
As *Lulu* demonstrates, they were on opposite ends of an aesthetic debate regarding the exclusion or the integration of "das Neue," and that included film, into
the legacy of the German operatic tradition.

It is precisely such associations that are at the heart of Berg's project and
that help to account for his use of film in *Lulu,* for it is no coincidence that the
last three of the aesthetic pursuits listed above, all despised by Pfitzner, appear
in Berg's opera. This suggests that, at the time, much of the work evoked for his
audience a culture that was decidedly non-German, non-Austrian, non-aristocratic, and clearly American, and that is how many would have viewed the film
in *Lulu.* These associations also explain why G. W. Pabst chose to employ not
a German, but an American actress, Louise Brooks, to play Lulu in his 1928
film, *Die Büchse der Pandora,* based on Wedekind's dramas. We do not know
whether Berg ever saw the Pabst film from 1928 based on Wedekind's dramas,
though there is evidence that his student, Theodor W. Adorno, wrote to Berg
about it.[36]

In all these works, a European aristocracy is shown in decline, socially and even physiologically threatened by forces represented by a bewildering array of non-classical art forms. Thus, while the aristocracy is portrayed as both licentious and effete, as hypersexual and, at the same time, as destroyed through excessive engagement in extra-marital sexual pursuits, it is surrounded by nationally foreign forces incarnated in non-aristocratic art forms, in the athlete and the circus trainer, both of them artists brimming over with sexual potency and danger. The film, with it social attributes as a low-class art for the masses, fits right in to the work's insurrectionary aesthetics.

These social distinctions are thematized in the work itself. The juxtaposition in Berg's and Wedekind's works of such renowned and pseudo-aristocratic figures as painters, composers, and literati with artists socially a world removed from them could hardly be overlooked. Certainly the subject matter of Berg's film concerns a threat to the established social order, depicting the escape from prison of a convicted murderess, her bisexuality in her exchange of clothes with the Countess Geschwitz, and the strategic spread of cholera, a motif that often appears in early-twentieth-century German discourse as representing homosexuality and social dissolution, not only in the works of Thomas Mann, but in the medical writings of the time as well. Indeed, the crowning foreign force par excellence, of course, is Lulu herself, the being who, symbolically, brings about the dissolution of the European aristocratic order, and of its artistic pursuits. Berg's opera depicts a refined opera composer, Alwa, who writes an opera about Lulu, and the athlete hates it. He says: "You've written a horrible opera in which my wife's thighs are the leading roles and which no Court Theater will ever perform!"[37] And that is the point: no "Court Theater," for Alwa's composition is clearly a microcosmic mirror of Berg's *Lulu,* which is not intended for traditional operagoers, whose tastes are implied as decidedly aristocratic.

Lulu is sexually ill-defined and associated with a spectrum of artistic pursuits located on the outskirts of the socially acceptable, and that means, through Berg's innovative experimentation, with the silent film as well. Thus, it is no surprise that, in *Lulu,* the opera relinquishes its own devices of narration to a foreign aesthetic medium at an ideologically key point, at the moment in which the protagonist is associated with disease and deviant sexuality. As previously stated, the film narrates and the opera is suffused with the traditionally operatic effulgence of emotion, and it is the content of that narration that underscores the connection between film and specific motifs of the time; sexual transgression, social decline, and the threat of fatal disease and murder are the stuff of film, both in Berg's work and in his world. Therefore, it simply makes sense, within the cultural vocabulary of the period, that Lulu becomes ill and evinces behavior evocative of or bordering on bisexuality not within the context of opera, but on film.

Berg clearly longed for a heterogeneous audience, comprised both of cognoscenti and the uninitiated, and one reason his film is so much shorter than the allusions to the cinema found in other contemporary *Zeitoper* may be the fact that he attempted not to completely reject the tradition in which he was working, but to transform it. And that transformation brought with it social ramifications. It is not for nothing that Kurt Weill regarded *Wozzeck* as "the grandiose conclusion" of the Wagnerian music drama,[38] and as Jarman has rightly argued, "[*Lulu*'s] being couched in the conventions of traditional opera is a vital part of its subversive tactics, and it exploits not only the musical but also the social conventions of opera."[39] Peter Burkholder has explained the aesthetic repercussions of this desire to expand or transform the tradition of opera from within:

> Berg achieves what Haydn and Mozart achieved, the complete integration of surface rhetoric and inner structure, so that the connoisseur and the lay audience hear the same things in his work, differing only in their level of penetration. This is why Berg's music appeals to both kinds of listener. . . . Berg revitalized the familiar, writing atonal music that constantly invokes tonal expectations, music that preserves and intensifies the emotional expressivity of the common romantic heritage.[40]

It is not for nothing that Pierre Boulez, the conductor of the first performance of the work in its complete, three-act version, claims that *Lulu* represents "the intrusion of opera into the modern world . . . at the very last moment when 'modern' opera could be a valid quest within a form taken directly from tradition."[41] In *Lulu,* the operatic material has come dangerously close to being entrapped as a prisoner of the ivory tower of aesthetic modernism; and thus it seeks to break out of its impasse, like its diseased female protagonist, by resorting to the inclusion of the new and, by the 1930s, increasingly popular genre of the film without abandoning the tradition—and the audience—from which it emerged. A kind of early-twentieth-century, modernist Quentin Tarantino, Berg seeks out shocking, socially dangerous, salacious material, and diverse, new, and foreign aesthetic media, because, he feels, these speak to a wider audience than the late-romantic musical idiom and historically removed or mythic dramatic themes of a Franz Schreker, Richard Strauss, or Hans Pfitzner. One could even claim that *Lulu* exemplifies Peter Bürger's classical interpretation of the avant-garde as an example of that moment in the development of art as an institution at which it grows critical of itself.[42] For if we think of Berg's cinematic scenario in *Lulu* as the integration of film into the twentieth-century manifestation of the Wagnerian tradition of the music drama, its *institutional,* self-critical function becomes manifest, clearly demonstrated by the consternation it and other, more obvious examples of the *Zeitoper* caused in the more traditionally minded members of the audience of its time.

Thus, though its cinematic component has been relatively ignored, it is worth remembering that *Lulu* can be seen as part of a widespread experimental trend in early-twentieth-century opera that attempted to integrate the new medium of the film into long-standing musical dramatic conventions. How strange, then, that the short filmic Interlude—the feature of the work that so typified its modernity—should have been so seldom realized in the recent past, an age in which the technical problems it once posed could so readily be addressed (to say nothing of the fact that current audiences would be far more receptive to the rapid scenario and its attendant quickly cut pace than would have been the case with an audience of Berg's time). *Lulu*'s film is a key to our understanding of the work, if not of its machinations (as Berg had originally intended), then certainly of its place in the early-twentieth-century cultural scene. It, as much as the opera's dodecaphonic musical vocabulary and dramatic subject of sexual license, makes it a crowning example of the modernist avant-garde, of a moment that is past, to be sure, but that—to cite a cliché—has been captured on, and has always been associated with, film.[43]

Notes

1. Berg, *Berg-Schoenberg Correspondence,* 405–6, here 406 (emphasis in original); I have slightly modified this translation, which renders "der zentrale Punkt" as "focal point" rather than "the central point"; original German taken from Berg, *Lulu: Alban Berg,* 18.

2. Another reason may lie in the fact that, as George Perle has pointed out, due to an editorial oversight that was only corrected with the publication of the three-act version completed by Friedrich Cerha, the version of the orchestral score hitherto available to scholars omitted the dramaturgical details from the film scenario that Berg had included in his *Particell.* See Perle, "The Film Interlude of *Lulu,*" 3; for the complete, three-act orchestral score, see Berg, *Lulu,* 499–527. Berg used two terms to refer to this piece, *Zwischenspiel* and *Interludium,* the latter found in a note contained in material related to the genesis of the opera. See Ertelt, *Alban Berg's "Lulu,"* 172.

3. See Reich, *Alban Berg,* 93–94, 160–61; Seehaus, *Frank Wedekind,* 378–80; Neumann, "Wedekind and Berg's *Lulu,*" 47–57; Jarman, *Alban Berg,* 20; Floros, *Alban Berg,* 319–21; Perle, *The Operas,* 48–49, 149–57; Scherliess, *Alban Berg,* 19, 121. Bryan R. Simms has argued persuasively that Berg's film scenario was influenced by the production of the Wedekind plays mounted at the Munich Kammerspiele by Otto Falkenberg, but here, too, the discussion concerns Falkenberg far more than Berg. See Simms, "Berg's *Lulu,*" 153–57. In his discussion of the figure of Lulu, Sander Gilman mentions the fact that both G. W. Pabst's film and Berg's opera focus on the trial (which falls between the Wedekind plays), but he does not mention that Berg used a film in his opera. See Gilman, "The Nietzsche Murder Case," 68. For a discussion of just how silent the "silent" film was, see Altman, "The Silence of the Silents."

4. See Ertelt, *Alban Berg's "Lulu,"* 180n18. On *Wozzeck* as film, see Reich, *Alban Berg,* 93–94.

5. The increasing number of opera and film studies that have appeared over the past fifteen years or so make it clear that scholars have tended to favor or to focus on the use of the former in the latter, on film when examining the admixture of the two arts, and accordingly much more attention has been devoted to the diversified history of the role opera has played in the cinema than to the aesthetic reverse. Some examples that ably represent the heterogeneity of the new field of study include the following: Tambling, *A Night in at the Opera;* Miller, "*Farinelli's* Electronic Hermaphrodite"; Citron, *Opera on Screen;* and Joe and Theresa, *Between Opera and Cinema.* A study of a more recent incorporation of film into opera, or perhaps one should say, more precisely, of the making of an opera out of a film, is Joe, "The Cinematic Body." An exception to the pervasive interest in opera within film can be found in an intrigu-

ing investigation of the early impact of opera on the silent film, Grover-Friedlander, "'*The Phantom of the Opera*'."

6. See Jarman, *Alban Berg*, 56–57. For this reason, the rhetorical ambiguity in Berg's letter to Schoenberg is ultimately insignificant; by "the central point of the entire tragedy" ("der zentrale Punkt der ganzen Tragödie") Berg might have meant solely the *place* ("Punkt") located within the structural middle of the entire work as he then envisioned it (which he himself, of course, never completed), or he could also have been speaking metaphorically, meaning that, in a general sense, the Interlude is the *most important* part of the work. The distinction is insignificant because Berg was so preoccupied with the structural makeup of his works, so that placing the film in the middle automatically indicated its privileged status for him.

7. Berg originally intended to have a much longer film, but abandoned that project. See Ertelt, *Alban Berg's "Lulu,"* 171–80.

8. Reich, *Alban Berg*, 175. Images from the program to the premiere are used here with the kind permission of Stadtarchiv Zürich. I would like to take this opportunity to express my gratitude to Christiane Arndt for her invaluable assistance in locating images from this original film. An excellent rendition of the film may be found in a video from a 1996 production of the opera at Glyndebourne, directed by Graham Vick, which takes some liberties with the scenario, but is nonetheless, all in all, quite faithful to Berg's stated intentions.

9. The sketch is reproduced in Reich, *Alban Berg*, 161; and Perle, *The Operas*, 152.

10. Berg, *The Berg-Schoenberg Correspondence*, 406.

11. See Perle, *The Operas*, 48–49, 149–57, esp. 152. This is not to say that the second half of the music is simply the first half reversed, because Berg also uses it to effect an atmospheric transition, but it does have structural elements within it that are based on the palindromic mirroring of formal details.

12. Jarman, "Secret Programmes," 169. Jarman even argues, in a discussion of the Lyric Suite, that "the large-scale palindromic structure of the second movement represents Mathilde's [Schoenberg's wife's] decline into illness after leaving [her lover, the painter Richard] Gerstl in 1908 and returning to Schoenberg" (170). If so, that would suggest that the association of the palindrome and "decline into illness" following the separation from a lover also links this piece with the drama of *Lulu*.

13. By "mutually enhancing" I am, of course, evoking and recognizing a debt to Claudia Gorbman's insight concerning the "mutual implication" of cinematic image and sound, whereby the audience "automatically imposes meaning on [their] combinations," because each—image and sound—affects the signification of the other at any given moment. See Gorbman, *Unheard Melodies*, 15.

14. It is worth noting, however, that the relationship between sound and image here is decidedly not what Michel Chion has described as *synchresis,* in which there appears to be "an immediate and necessary relationship" between what is seen and what is heard. That relationship is not a set of one-to-one correspondences; the acoustical and the visual do not unfold in a manner of mutual illumination. Instead, it is what Chion would call one of "counterpoint" or even "dissonant harmony," whereby "sound and image . . . constitute two parallel and loosely connected tracks, neither dependent on the other." See Chion, *Audio-Vision*, xviii–xix, 62–63; and Chion, *The Voice in Cinema*, 172.

15. Berg, *Lulu*, 53.

16. Reich, *Alban Berg*, 161; Reich, *Alban Berg* (trans.), 229n18. I have modified this translation. Karen Monson makes a similar claim: "Rueckert provided proof that it is difficult if not impossible to include all the visual images Berg wanted within the time span of the music he provided." Monson, *Alban Berg*, 341.

17. See Reich, *Alban Berg*, 160n1.

18. Reich, *Lulu*, 7.

19. On *Lulu* as a *Zeitoper* see Jarman, *Alban Berg*, *"Lulu,"* 91–101.

20. Cited in Perle, *The Operas*, 152; see also Reich, *Alban Berg*, 161.

21. On the Hindemith work see Eisinger, *Hindemith.*

22. See Mehring, "Welcome to the Machine."

23. Waldemar Weber, *Musikblätter des Anbruch* 11 (1929): 223–25, cited in ibid., 162n10.

24. Mehring, "Welcome to the Machine," 160.

25. Like Berg, Weill also used a film to portray the progress of his heroine in his opera *Royal Palace* (1927). See Drew, "Musical Theatre," 193.

26. Though the question as to whether the twelve-tone system and the *Zeitoper* are mutually exclusive is still debatable: Schoenberg parodied the "new opera" in his *Von Heute auf Morgen* of 1930, but unlike *Lulu,* its story is comic, clearly evoking *Neues vom Tage.* See Jarman, *Alban Berg,* 95.

27. As the most eclectic of the Second Viennese School, Berg even produced *Der Wein* (1929), the only jazzy piece produced by the twelve-tone composers around that time. Anthony Pople writes that in "*Der Wein* . . . Berg deploys tonalistic configurations almost ostentatiously, both melodically and harmonically, at one and the same time depicting symbolically a world of sleaze and sensation, reveling in it, and perhaps gaining a certain satisfaction from using Schoenberg's serial technique to compose a work that comes closer to the tonality of the *Seven Early Songs* than anything he had written since those sections of *Wozzeck* that were borrowed from his student piano pieces." See Pople, "In the Orbit of *Lulu,*" 215.

28. Kracauer, "Die kleinen Ladenmädchen."

29. See Benjamin, "The Work of Art"; Adorno, *Berg,* 486; Adorno, "Rede über Alban Bergs Lulu," 649.

30. Anonymous, "Die Karriere des Kinamotographen," *Lichtbild-Bühne* 124 (December 10, 1910): 5, cited in Kaes, "The Debate About Cinema," 12–13.

31. Barker, "Battles of the Mind," 26, 30.

32. Egon Friedell, "Prolog vor dem Film," *Blätter des deutschen Theaters* 2 (1912): 509ff., cited in Kaes, "The Debate About Cinema," 13.

33. See Pfitzner, *Reden, Schriften, Briefe,* 132; Pfitzner, "Vorwort zur dritten Auflage"; on Pfitzner's xenophobia and its implications for his aesthetics, see also Weiner, *Undertones,* 35–71.

34. Pfitzner, "Vorwort zur dritten Auflage," 113, 116.

35. Berg's essay first appeared in *Anbruch* 2.11–12 (June 1920): 399–408; for an English version, see Reich, *Alban Berg,* 205–18.

36. Ertelt, *Alban Berg's "Lulu,"* 180n18. See also Csampai and Holland, *Lulu,* 302.

37. Berg, *Lulu: Libretto,* 48. My translation; Jacobs incorrectly renders "Schauderoper" as "melodrama" and "Hoftheater" as "decent theatre"; see 49.

38. Weill, "New Opera," 465.

39. Jarman, *Alban Berg: "Lulu,"* 99.

40. Burkholder, "Berg and the Possibility of the Popular," 53.

41. Boulez, "*Lulu,*" 5.

42. See Bürger, *Theorie der Avantgarde.*

43. An earlier version of this paper was presented at a conference on "Music and Film" sponsored by the Royal Musical Association in Southampton, England, on 19 April 2001. I would like to thank Jeongwon Joe for discussing this project with me and for providing me with invaluable suggestions. Of course, any egregious errors and/or infelicities of interpretation are entirely my fault, not hers.

References

Adorno, Theodor W. *Berg: Der Meister des kleinsten Übergangs.* In *Die musikalischen Monografien.* Frankfurt am Main: Suhrkamp, 1986, 321–494.

———. "Rede über Alban Bergs Lulu." *Gesammelte Schriften* 18 (*Musikalische Schriften* V), ed. R. Tiedemann and K. Schultz. Frankfurt am Main: Suhrkamp, 1984, 645–49.

Altman, Rick. "The Silence of the Silents." *Musical Quarterly* 80/4 (1997): 648–718.

Barker, Andrew. "Battles of the Mind: Berg and the Cultural Politics of Vienna 1900." In *The Cambridge Companion to Berg*, ed. A. Pople. Cambridge: Cambridge University Press, 1997, 24–37.

Benjamin, Walter. "The Work of Art in the Age of Mechanical Reproduction." In *Illuminations*, ed. H. Arendt, trans. H. Zohn. New York: Schocken, 1969, 217–51.

Berg, Alban. *The Berg-Schoenberg Correspondence: Selected Letters*. Ed. J. Brand, C. Hailey, and D. Harris. New York: Norton, 1987.

———. *Lulu: Alban Berg*. Ed. W. Willaschek and M. Leinart. Program to a new production of *Lulu* at the Deutsche Oper am Rhein, Düsseldorf. Duisburg: WAK-Druck, 2000.

———. *Lulu: Libretto in German and English*. Trans. A. Jacobs. Vienna: Universal Edition, 1977.

———. *Lulu: Oper nach Frank Wedekinds Tragödien* Erdgeist *und* Büchse der Pandora; *Partitur (I. und II. Akt)*. Vienna: Universal Edition, 1985.

Boulez, Pierre. "*Lulu:* The Second Opera." Trans. P. Griffiths. In *Alban Berg: Lulu*. Booklet accompanying the Deutsche Grammophon recording, ed. M. Karallus. Polydor International, 1979, pp. 4–5.

Bürger, Peter. *Theorie der Avantgarde*. Frankfurt am Main: Suhrkamp, 1974. Trans. M. Shaw as *Theory of the Avant-garde*. Minneapolis: University of Minnesota Press, 1984.

Burkholder, J. Peter. "Berg and the Possibility of the Popular." In *Alban Berg: Historical and Analytical Perspectives*, ed. D. Gable and R. P. Morgan. Oxford: Clarendon, 1991, 25–53.

Chion, Michel. *Audio-Vision: Sound on Screen*. Ed. and trans. C. Gorbman. New York: Columbia University Press, 1994.

———. *The Voice in Cinema*. Trans. C. Gorbman. New York: Columbia University Press, 1999.

Citron, Marcia J. *Opera on Screen*. New Haven, Conn.: Yale University Press, 2000.

Csampai, Attila, and Dietmar Holland. *Lulu: Texte, Materialien, Kommentare*. Reinbek: Rowohlt, 1985.

Drew, David. "Musical Theatre in the Weimar Republic." *Proceedings of the Royal Musical Association* 88 (1962): 193.

Eisinger, Ralf. *Hindemith,* Hin und Zurück/*Martinç,* Komödie auf der Brücke/*Rossini,* Der Heiratswechsel (*Nationaltheater Mannheim, Programmheft 8*). Darmstadt: Mykenae Verlag, 1992.

Ertelt, Thomas F. *Alban Berg's "Lulu": Quellenstudien und Beiträge zur Analyse*. Alban Berg Studien 3. Vienna: Universal Edition, 1993.

Floros, Constantin. *Alban Berg: Musik als Autobiographie*. Wiesbaden-Leipzig: Breitkopf & Härtel, 1992.

Gilman, Sander L. "The Nietzsche Murder Case; or, What Makes Dangerous Philosophies Dangerous." In *Difference and Pathology: Stereotypes of Sexuality, Race, and Madness*. Ithaca, N.Y.: Cornell University Press, 1985, 59–75.

Gorbman, Claudia. *Unheard Melodies: Narrative Film Music*. Bloomington: Indiana University Press, 1987.

Grover-Friedlander, Michal. "'*The Phantom of the Opera*': The Lost Voice of Opera in Silent Film." *Cambridge Opera Journal* 11/2 (1999): 179–92.

Jarman, Douglas. *Alban Berg: "Lulu."* Cambridge: Cambridge University Press, 1991.

———. "Secret Programmes." *The Cambridge Companion to Berg*, ed. A. Pople. Cambridge: Cambridge University Press, 1997, 167–79.

Joe, Jeongwon. "The Cinematic Body in the Operatic Theater: Philip Glass's *La Belle et la Bête*." In *Between Opera and Cinema*, ed. J. Joe and R. Theresa. New York: Routledge, 2002, 59–73.

Joe, Jeongwon, and Rose Theresa, eds. *Between Opera and Cinema*. New York: Routledge, 2002.

Kaes, Anton. "The Debate About Cinema: Charting a Controversy (1909–1929)." *New German Critique* 40 (1987): 7–33. Expanded version of the introduction to Kaes, *Kino-Debatte: Texte zum Verhältnis von Literatur und Film 1909–1929*. Tübingen: Max Niemeyer Verlag, 1978.

Kracauer, Siegfried. "Die kleinen Ladenmädchen gehen ins Kino." In *Das Ornament der Masse: Essays*. Frankfurt am Main: Suhrkamp, 1977, 279–94.

Mehring, Frank. "Welcome to the Machine! The Representation of Technology in *Zeitopern*." *Cambridge Opera Journal* 11/2 (1999): 159–77.

Miller, Felicia. *"Farinelli's* Electronic Hermaphrodite and the Contralto Tradition." In *The Work of Opera: Genre, Nationhood, and Sexual Difference,* ed. R. Dellamora and D. Fischlin. New York: University of Columbia Press, 1997, 73–92.

Monson, Karen. *Alban Berg.* Boston: Houghton Mifflin, 1979.

Neumann, Karl. "Wedekind and Berg's *Lulu.*" *Music Review* 35 (1975): 47–57.

Perle, George. "The Film Interlude of *Lulu.*" *The International Alban Berg Society Newsletter* 11 (1982): 3–8.

———. *The Operas of Alban Berg,* vol. II *Lulu.* Berkeley: University of California Press, 1985.

Pfitzner, Hans. *Reden, Schriften, Briefe: Unveröffentlichtes und bisher Verstreutes.* Ed. W. Abendroth. Berlin: H. Luchterhand, 1955.

———. "Vorwort zur dritten Auflage." *Die neue Ästhetik der musikalischen Impotenz: Ein Verwesungssymtom?* in *Gesammelte Schriften,* vol. 2. Augsburg: Benno Filser-Verlag, 1926, 115–18.

Pople, Anthony. "In the Orbit of *Lulu:* The Late Works." In *The Cambridge Companion to Berg,* ed. A. Pople. Cambridge: Cambridge University Press, 1997, 204–26.

Reich, Willi. *Alban Berg: Leben und Werk.* Zürich: Atlantis, 1963. Trans. C. Cardew. New York: Harcourt, Brace & World, 1965.

Scherliess, Volker. *Alban Berg in Selbstzeugnissen und Bilddokumenten.* Reinbek bei Hamburg: Rowohlt, 1975.

Seehaus, Günter. *Frank Wedekind und das Theater.* München: Laokoon-Verlag, 1964.

Simms, Bryan R. "Berg's *Lulu* and the Theatre of the 1920s." *Cambridge Opera Journal* 6/2 (1994): 147–58.

Tambling, Jeremy, ed. *A Night in the Opera: Media Representations of Opera.* London: John Libbey & Co., 1994.

Weill, Kurt. "New Opera." In Kim Kowalke, *Kurt Weill in Europe.* Ann Arbor: University of Michigan Press, 1979, 464–67.

Weiner, Marc. *Undertones of Insurrection: Music, Politics, and the Social Sphere in the Modern German Narrative.* Lincoln: University of Nebraska Press, 1993.

Filmography

FILM INTERLUDE OF LULU

release:	2 June 1937, Zürich
duration:	approx. 3 minutes
dir:	Heinz Rückert
prod:	Hans Rudolf Meyer
prod co:	Tempo
actors:	Bahrija Nuri-Hadzic (Lulu); Asger Stig (Dr. Schön); Peter Baxevanos (Alwa)
camera:	Hans Rudolf Meyer
music:	Alban Berg

FOUR

From Revolution to Mystic Mountains: Edmund Meisel and the Politics of Modernism

CHRISTOPHER MORRIS

In his influential *From Caligari to Hitler,* Siegfried Kracauer cites a passage from James R. Ullman's adventure novel *The White Tower* in which a Swiss guide compares national attitudes to climbing: "We Swiss—yes, and the English and French and Americans too—we climb mountains for sport. But the Germans, no. What it is they climb for I do not know. Only it is not for sport."[1] The quotation appears in the context of a discussion of the *Bergfilm* (mountain film), one of the most successful German film genres or the twenties and thirties. Writing in exile in the United States after the war, Kracauer saw a very tangible link between the mountain films with their apparent fetishization of struggle, vitalism, and heroic endeavor, and the ideal heroic Volk projected by National Socialism. For Kracauer, the mountain films embodied a whole series of proto-fascist tendencies: the regressive nature cult, the power and militaristic implications of the ability to dominate peaks, the ecstatic experience of the anti-rational, the celebration of the athletic body.[2] Certainly the German cult of the body and nature is deeply intertwined with the emergence of National Socialism, and the *Bergfilm* seems to be an important celebration of that cult. The pervasive presence in these films of the young Leni Riefenstahl only makes the connections all the more tangible.

Until the late twenties the genre was practically synonymous with Arnold Fanck, a geologist, photographer, and documentary film maker whose still and film photography of the Alps had already earned him a national reputation before he began directing and producing narrative film.[3] Like many of Fanck's films, *Der heilige Berg* features a melodramatic plot: two mountaineers find themselves competing for the affections of the dancer Diotima, played by Riefenstahl, here appearing in her first acting role. Filmed on location (Fanck's trademark), *Der heilige Berg* sets this love triangle against the backdrop of the real stars, the Alps. Fanck admitted to having little interest in the music for his films, but his Freiburg studio had recently been acquired by UFA (Universum Film AG), the giant German film conglomerate. UFA financed and distributed *Der heilige Berg,* and was probably responsible for commissioning the orchestral score, something that was still very much the exception in German cinema. Orchestras were employed in some of the larger houses in the UFA chain, and its flagship cinema, the UFA-Palast in Berlin, included a seventy-eight-piece ensemble, the largest of any cinema in Germany. It is a mark of the seriousness with which they viewed *Der heilige Berg* that it was earmarked for a gala premiere on the 17 December 1926 in the Ufa-Palast, replete with a full-length score for large orchestra.

The commission went to Edmund Meisel, a Berlin theater composer who was at the time riding a wave of acclaim (or at least notoriety) for his score for *Bronenosets Potyomkin* (Battleship Potemkin, Sergei Eisenstein, 1925). The fact that the conservative UFA had refused to allow the cinemas in its network to screen *Bronenosets Potyomkin* would not have prevented the company from seeing the value of commissioning a composer who was much in the spotlight.[4] Meisel's situation is more puzzling. This is a composer who, for a number of years, had been involved almost exclusively in the political theater of the Left: he had written music for a number of Piscator productions, and he was deeply committed to revolutionary socialism, to the idea of artist collectives and to the desire to unite artists and proletariat in a political-aesthetic resistance to the bourgeois, consumerist forces of mainstream popular culture. Perhaps tempted by the resources and distribution potential offered by UFA, he now accepted a commission from a big business conglomerate with notoriously conservative sympathies, and to score, of all things, a *Bergfilm*.

Yet, as Eric Rentschler has shown, contemporary perspectives complicate the picture and undermine the attempt to align its values exclusively with reactionary, nationalistic politics. The critic for the Social Democrat *Vorwärts* (19 December 1926) extolled *Der heilige Berg* as "impart[ing] to millions, both in Germany and throughout the entire world, visual delight and a heightened feeling for nature's vast and demonic powers,"[5] while the Communist Party organ *Die rote Fahne* (19 November 1929) praised another Fanck film as "undoubtedly one of the best German films ever," singling out its "stirring images" and "outstanding achievements of inordinate beauty and gripping suspense."[6] The writer and film theorist Béla Balázs saw no contradiction between his enthusiastic embrace of Fanck's films and his own commitment to the Left. Why, he asks in "Der Fall Dr. Fanck" (1931), should the "feeling for nature" be monopolized by those who use it as mere "diversion and opium"? Those who are committed to the "social struggle," he adds, have no more reason to abandon nature to the conservatives "than they would music."[7] Fanck's films, it seems, were embraced by a wide political spectrum, and it becomes difficult to align it with any particular political persuasion.

But a political reading of the *Bergfilm* need not be confined to this explicit left-right reading: Meisel's involvement with *Der heilige Berg* is politically charged, but in many subtle ways, some of which might seem apolitical. Two issues in particular concern me here. One is what I would like to call the politics of urban experience, the perception that the foundations of modern culture are to be found in the city. For the composer, this implies an opposition to the nineteenth-century, and specifically Romantic, tendency to gravitate toward the representation of nature, whether this be in nostalgic, idyllic, or sublime forms. A political dimension emerges here in the establishment of identities against the perceived opposition of rural and urban, conservative and progressive, static and dynamic. How does a composer whose music speaks so vividly of contemporary urban experience react to the neo-romantic world of Fanck's films? A second issue is what I would call the politics of autonomy, the sense in which modernism foregrounds the need for legitimization according to still influential values of aesthetic creativity, uniqueness, and authorship. How does the self-consciously modernist artist justify involvement in a populist medium or genre, and is it even possible for the film music composer to carve out a traditional authorial space in this industrially produced modern medium? These are the questions I intend to address, reading Meisel's score against an essay on the music written in 1927 for the UFA house magazine.[8]

Masochistic Enthusiasm

One of the recurring themes of "Wie schreibt man Filmmusik?" (How is film music written?) is what Meisel calls "the rhythm of our times." He writes enthusiastically of "modern nerve-stimulating rhythms" and of the need for music to correspond to the "nervous pulse of our era."[9] This squares with the Meisel familiar from *Bronenosets Potyomkin,* from *Berlin: Die Sinfonie der Großstadt* (Berlin: A Symphony of a Big City, Walter Ruttmann, 1927), and from much of his stage work, and it points toward his almost industrial use of percussion, experiments with combinations of music and noise, and his development of a noise machine.[10] Reporting on these experiments, Fritz Zielesch argued that Meisel truly reflected what he called an "era ruled by motor and machine."[11] He goes on to say that "for the musical illustration of spinning flywheels, clattering crane arms, racing spindles, and the whole inferno of the modern factory, the musical means of romantic and idyllic eras can not suffice."[12] What is suggested here is not merely the need to reflect one's own times and social conditions, but an adaptation to technology that borders on a kind of technological determinism. Critical questions about the effects of technology and the means to control it seem to take a backseat to an enthusiastic adaptation to the motors and machines.

For Peter Sloterdijk, the kind of accommodation suggested by the *neue Sachlichkeit,* that "matter of factness" of later Weimar culture, is always double because it represents what he calls a "masochistic enthusiasm" for technology. He writes: "The philosophy of the new 'matter-of-factness', insofar as it is engineers' philosophy, tries out a hectic embracing of the new discomfort."[13] Sloterdijk's Weimar subject embraces technology but grimaces at the same time. But I suspect that Meisel's attitude, the attitude of his music, lacks much of that discomfort and embraces much more enthusiastically what Raymond Williams calls "a streamlined technological mass-modernity."[14] The percussive representation of the ship's engines in *Bronenosets Potyomkin* or the train in *Sinfonie der Großstadt* is not presented as alienating, even discomforting, but a dynamic, irresistibly progressive way into a new era. And this is the attitude that comes through in Meisel's article: his reference to the "nervous pulse of our time" is very telling, because his machine music lends an almost organic quality to the cityscape. It is as if that constant pounding and clattering of machine and motor represented a life substance throbbing through the urban environment, suggesting a city that is alive with an uncanny, and unstoppable, heartbeat.

Meisel's claim to modernity rests precisely on his embrace of the urban soundscape. But *Der heilige Berg* confronts him with the very kind of regressive nature representation that had played such a prominent role in high art's claims to a supposedly ahistorical and apolitical transcendence. And this nostalgic allegiance to Romantic values summons the legacy of nineteenth-century music with its metaphysical baggage and its intimate associations with nature. Perhaps no cultural form in the nineteenth century had been more intimately aligned with the irrational and the timeless, with the kinds of sublime experiences embodied within the concept of nature. How, in this context, can Meisel write of the "rhythm of our times" and of the need to reflect the "nervous pulse of our era"? Part of the answer lies in his adoption, in at least two scenes, of precisely the urban, "nerve-stimulating" style with which he was associated: one is a ski-race—Meisel called this the "most rewarding part of the score"[15]—and the other is the ascent by the rival suitors of the holy mountain's dangerous north face. These are scenes that involve a very explicit interaction between nature and technology (skiing and modern climbing techniques turn mountains into sporting grounds), and the fact that Meisel here draws on his music of motors and machines seems to reinforce that technological spirit. Certainly the scenes support his claim in the article to have pursued what he calls "exact conformity" between music and film: "Right down to the smallest detail," he writes, "there in images, here in tones."[16] The ascent scene becomes a literal ascent in the music, a chromatic five-minute crescendo with increasingly raucous orchestration. Equally chromatic, the ski-race touches on more familiar territory, its strongly gestural musical patter suggesting the Keystone Cops and the classic tradition of "chase" music.

Haunted Immediacy

Both scenes seem to embrace nature from an entirely modern perspective. They remind us that the *Bergfilm* as a genre is more than a retreat into a timeless nature, that the genre constructs a dialectic between nature and technology. Technology is openly thematicized in the diegesis (modern climbing equipment, skis, automobiles, and aircraft), and it lies behind the filmic process: Fanck invested heavily in the very latest cameras, lenses, and film. At the same time, there is an investment in preserving, emphasizing, and constructing a sublime quality in the images of the mountains: for every encroachment by technology, the images compensate by recharging the aura of the mountains (something made possible precisely by the technology of the image). Following Elsaesser, we might configure this nature-technology dialectic in a different way. Expanding on Lotte Eisner's characterization of Weimar cinema as a repository of "Romantic fancies," Elsaesser wonders if the Romantic cult of inwardness, which offered the subject a foil against the political and compensated for the subject's alienation from nature with an immediacy of experience, might not find new energy in Weimar cinema:

> The Romantic project of arming the subject against political experience through inwardness, and transforming inwardness into the sensuous perception of immediacy has found its "realization" in the cinema, but with a vengeance. Nature returns in the form of the uncanny and the fantastic, because Romanticism wedded to technology produces a reified and thoroughly mediated form of immediacy.[17]

That is, cinema's immediacy led to a renewed investment in the uncanny surplus that exceeds it, hence Weimar's fantastic cinema with its obsessive return to Romantic themes. But this should not be reduced, Elsaesser stresses, to the banal idea of Romantic influence. What interests Elsaesser is the possibility that Weimar cinema knowingly adopts, plays upon, even parodies these "Romantic fancies." The neo-Romantic tone of Weimar cinema is not, in other words, a historicist gesture, but a reworking in the light of new upheavals and new experiences of alienation. Viewed from this angle, the "reified and thoroughly mediated" immediacy also has a positive aspect, in that it mobilizes new experiences and opens up new perspectives. Here, Elsaesser argues, the stress is on the "sensuous presence of the commodity," on "images and surface-effects" that announce the birth of the modern consumer.[18] This sensuous commodification demands critical scrutiny, but no more so than the notions it seems to have challenged and threatened: notions of depth, authenticity, spirituality, or the fetishistic "aura" that Benjamin would identify in "The Work of Art in the Age of Mechanical Reproduction."

Fanck's mountain films vividly embody this dialectic in that the uncanny return of nature (here the mystic, hypnotizing lure of the mountains) is met with a thoroughly modern experience and representation of the mountains. As Rentschler has shown, Fanck's films draw equally on the imagery of Romantic landscape painting and the abstracted play of geometric shapes characteristic of the *neue Sachlichkeit*.[19] An iconography of sublime nature oscillates with an ornamental play of lines and patterns: images reminiscent of Caspar David Friedrich give way to a nocturnal torchlit rescue party whose play of light exemplifies Kracauer's concept of the Weimar "mass ornament."[20] Meanwhile, operatic melodrama oscillates with documentary. *Der heilige Berg* represents the Alps in the matter-of-fact marketing style of a travelogue, and the "sports and leisure" atmosphere of Fanck's earlier documentary features is still very much in evidence. For all Fanck's skill with shots of moody, cloud-piercing peaks, the Alps come across above all as a tourist paradise. Yet all this frames a melodramatic kernel that becomes increasingly unworldly and uncanny as the narrative unfolds. On the brink of death, the heroic climber dreams of a marriage ceremony with Diotima in a giant gothic ice-temple inside the holy mountain. Summoning some of the strangest imaginings of Romantic opera and painting, this phantasmagoria seems to embody Elsaesser's notion of an uncanny surplus that rises up in response to filmic immediacy. Beneath the tourist paradise and the playful patterns of ski-trails, the film seems to suggest, lies a realm accessible only in dreams—and yet of course this too is represented with cinematic immediacy.

Music, particularly German art music, is no stranger to this dialectic between immediacy and the uncanny. Nineteenth-century aesthetic ideology had granted music a privileged capacity to bridge nature and the inner subject, a capacity that often hinged on metaphysics. Music was understood to penetrate to the inner essence of the natural world and reveal it to the suitably receptive subject. More than any other medium, music seemed to suggest that access to (external) nature depended on inwardness. Yet all this idealism rested on the development of a set of representational conventions, musical signifiers that had accumulated considerable cliché value by the end of the century. Meisel demonstrates an awareness of this tradition; his score draws on a range of very familiar musical nature tropes: posthorn themes, string tremolos, stern, mystical brass chords. In a sense these are Meisel's "Romantic fancies," and just as Fanck's *Naturmystik* confronts modern technology and experience, so Meisel's nature music dialectically confronts the "machine" music that plays such an important role in his other film scores. The musical signifiers of nature inherited from the nineteenth century are so often about a circular motion—motion that is at the same time static—and this carries with it an impression of timelessness, as though the cyclical temporality of nature resisted the linearity of the human and rational. Typical musical features include ostinati, a constant flow of sound, circular motion, what Meisel calls "self-perpetuating sequences."[21] But these are all features of his machine music as well. Circularity, repetition, and a loss of goal orientation are the very characteristics with which Meisel constructs the "rhythm of our times." It is not far, then, from the spinning flywheel to the rushing stream, as though the millwheel, that archetypal Romantic image of the engagement between nature and technology, still cast a shadow over modernism long after its function had been rendered obsolete by the factory. The perpetual motion of Schubert's mill is never far away, and the "rhythm of our times" adapts quite comfortably to what Meisel calls the "mysterious, majestic natural rhythm of the mountains."[22]

"Exact conformity"

But we can take this dialectical reading further. Meisel's "rhythm of our times" needs to be understood in relation not merely to the score as self-sufficient entity, but to its interaction with the visual track of the film. The arrangement of his music follows the rhythm of the film's editing almost parasitically. The music intercuts itself very frequently and at an often frenetic pace: again and again a new shot is taken as a cue to switch gears musically. In "How is film music written?" Meisel calls for a conception of film and film music in which one without the other would represent a half-entity.[23] Yet this idea of a meeting of equals, while perhaps relevant to Meisel's Eisenstein collaborations, hardly applies to the slavish parallelism of *Der heilige Berg*. Although there are illustrative moments in *Bronenosets Potyomkin*, Meisel's score for that project tends to shun direct synchronicity with the film's montage technique in favor of the "contrapuntal" approach that Eisenstein would later champion in his theoretical writings. *Der heilige Berg* seems to stand almost at the extreme opposite pole: it takes the idea of parallelism to an extreme.

Yet it lacks a feature that will become a characteristic of popular cinema and a cornerstone of Hollywood practice. In those traditions music is crucially called upon to smooth over edits, to camouflage and soften the supposedly jarring effect of the editing technique, to enhance (ideally) the sense of coherence or structure of a given sequence. If anything, Meisel's music can be interpreted as highlighting the edits by forming itself "around" rather than "through" them. Meisel's approach is easily dismissed as a naive prototype of film scoring technique, one which would be improved upon. His practice in *Der heilige Berg* often comes uncomfortably close to an orchestral version of a poor cinema pianist, who reacts to each shot with the first musical idea that pops into his/her head. But it complicates the synchronized vs. contrapuntal binary that would soon preoccupy film music theory, resituating aspects of so-called synchronized scoring (associated above all with Hollywood practice) as gestures toward music-film counterpoint. It reminds us, that is, that the careful musical transitions, segues, and dove-tails in classic practice, while formative of a broader filmic totality and wholeness, in fact work in tension with the often fragmentary visual and narrative impression of even supposedly "smoothly" edited sequences. At the same time, Meisel's parallelism anticipates some of the "reforms" Adorno and Eisler propose in the name of a more contrapuntal film-music practice. They argue, for example, that only avantgarde music is able to accommodate the "immediate juxtaposition of themes,"[24] yet Meisel's score achieves something like a musical montage using traditional, tonal material. Equally, their suggestion that gradual musical conclusions and fades might be replaced by "abrupt" breaks to coincide with a change of scene is in some ways realized by Meisel's score with its jagged musical splices arranged to shadow shot sequences or scene changes.

Meisel's insistence on conformity might also respond to some of the reservations expressed by Béla Balázs in his *Der sichtbare Mensch* (1924), a pioneering work of film theory in the silent era. Balázs welcomed what he called the "programmatic" scores now beginning to be written for film, but he worried that any music written for film would tend to carve out its own meanings as distinct from the visual track, that the "gestural mood" and the "musical mood" would "demand their own completely distinct duration and tempo."[25] What is particularly striking about Balázs's argument is that, in stark contrast to the still-potent legacy of German music aesthetics, he worries not about music's lack of meaning or indeterminacy, but about the potency of its signifying potential. In an era in which musical absolutism had gained a new lease of life in the guise of abstraction and objectivity, Balázs wonders how film can avoid being overwhelmed by music's flood of meaning. From this perspective, synchronicity, as such, is unachievable. Perhaps, then, Meisel's claim of "exact conformity" amounts to an announcement of a challenge met. He has brought his music into line with Fanck's film, a process that implies not so much propping it up or filling it out with filmic signification (as though this is where music would find meaning and coherence), but of taming its semantic energies and carefully shaping its formal outlines to match the film's edited structure.

The effect of this close parallelism on the *film* is to create a disjointed, episodic quality, further accentuating its melodramatic character. The effect on the *music* is actually to give each cue a soundbite quality and stifle any sense of its own momentum or unfolding. The score becomes a series of sound images, snapshots in music that have the effect of a musical slideshow. Just as each musical image appears, it is supplanted by the next musical block. Any sense of dynamism is generated not within each image but by their succession, by the almost Stravinsky-like way the musical blocks are arranged in sequence. The "rhythm of our times" turns out to be the rhythm of cinematic editing. By contrast, Meisel's strident industrial style, the style with which he is most closely associated, tends to be given ample space to unfold. It depends on its very persistence, on the cumulative effect of its repetition, to represent that "nervous pulse" of the city and construct a machine age that courses with life.

In Meisel's hands, then, nature becomes ironically inert, inorganic—and also transparently artificial. Nature here becomes a kind of pastiche of stereotyped stock images that revolve past us rather mechanically and transparently. One of the effects is to direct attention to the very means of representation, to the technologies we use to represent nature. Those musical signifiers of nature were always technologies of representation; they simply became naturalized, and without necessarily intending to do so, Meisel can be seen to highlight their artificiality. His strangely alienated, picture-postcard construction bestows upon nature a technified rhythm that was supposed to be alien to its unrepresentable organic form. Our idea of nature is critically revealed in all its artificiality and convention. *Der heilige Berg* is situated somewhere between the city and the mountains, a testament to the tension between a sublime of nature and a technological sublime.

Silent Film Speaks

There is another nineteenth-century technology lurking behind all this, and this leads me to my second modern struggle, the politics of autonomy. Meisel's article returns repeatedly to the question of the conformity between music and film. What is needed, he writes, is a conception of film and film music in which one without the other would represent a half-entity. "In this way," he adds, "I construct a new style in my music: filmic music drama."[26] And so the *Gesamtkunstwerk* raises its head, unexpectedly for a composer who has repeatedly called for a new music for new times. In fact there is an unresolved tension in the article: in the very next sentence he calls for freedom from the shackles of tradition. And it is precisely the tradition represented by the *Gesamtkunstwerk*, with its goal of totalizing immediacy and synthesis, that is the target of the theatrical circles in which Meisel worked. Self-reflexiveness, irony, parody, and counterpoint were the buzzwords of Piscator's theater. In the program booklet for Piscator's 1927 staging of Ernst Toller's *Hoppla, wir leben!*, Meisel, composer of the music for the production, issued something of a personal manifesto: "Modern music for the masses! Away with outmoded, bourgeois, pedantically constructed music written only for the individual! For the masses an articulation of events in the spirit of recent times!"[27] However, in "Wie schreibt man Filmmusik?" Meisel analyses *Der heilige Berg* in terms familiar from the very traditions he claims to reject. The leitmotifs of the score, he tells us, allow him to reconstruct faithfully in music the tragic configuration of the plot and its characters . He also discusses the need to underscore operatically certain exchanges between characters, such as Diotima's first encounter with the mountaineer. "If the film includes a lyrical dialogue," he writes, "it can only be reinforced as lyrical. The intensive impression of speech must be called forth."[28]

Underlying Meisel's call for an intimate connection between music and film is a desire to make silent cinema speak, to compensate for its muteness with a total artwork in which music can substitute for the limitations of technology, an idea that recalls Nietzsche's remark that in Wagner, nothing wanted to be silent, everything had to speak. On a literal level, Meisel's experiments with orchestral noise and noise machines "envoice" events that silent film mutes. In *Der heilige Berg*, for example, percussion is used to imitate the sounds of waves crashing and avalanches. In fact, in *Der Geist des Films* (1930), Balázs singles out Meisel as a composer whose experiments had anticipated sound film.[29] But at issue here also is the less literal sense in which silent film scores allowed (forced?) the filmic object to speak its language. In *Theory of the Film*, Balázs questioned whether silent film had ever really lacked speech:

> Its silence was not mute; it was given a voice in the background music, and landscapes and men and the objects surrounding them were shown on the screen against this common musical background. This made them speak a common silent language and we could feel their irrational conversation in the music which was common to them all.[30]

It is as though the silence of the images onscreen opened a space in which music might ventriloquize, drawing everything together into its language. Again the totalizing effect of the *Gesamtkunstwerk* casts a shadow, reminding us of Wagner's famous definition of music drama as "deeds of music made visible."[31]

Yet Meisel is interested in more than this envoicing of mute visual images. In an article published in the film periodical *Licht-Bild-Bühne*, he seems to articulate the corollary of Wagner's definition, stressing the need for the film music composer to focus on the "invisible" of the film and of his/her ability to "bridge all the gaps over which the director has to leap."[32] By this he means not smoothing over the edits but filling in semantic and narrative gaps. So, for example, the music might foreshadow later developments, even where the film still seems innocent of events to come. Here we see a Wagnerian additive dimension in which the total film covers every possibility thanks to its complementary components. Complete and whole in itself, the *Gesamtkunstwerk* knows nothing outside of itself and "naturalizes" its totality by means of its overwhelming scope and scale. Meisel seems to be calling for a cinema that would not acknowledge its limitations or gaps but would seek to create its own fully coherent, self-sufficient world, and music, he implies, is critical to its effect and power.

Distraction and Drapery

How can all this be reconciled with the composer who wants to sweep away a moribund past? A crucial point to consider here is the nature of the audiences to which UFA marketed its films: these were not Meisel's ideal proletariat masses hungry for revolutionary art, but rather a seemingly broad social and economic cross-section centered on what Meisel would have seen as middle-of-the-road tastes, tastes more comfortable with melodrama, popular fiction, and operetta than political theater, avant-garde music, and experiments with noise. In this respect the appeal to filmic music drama might represent a concession to more familiar, less avant-garde territory. The trouble is that Meisel's practice in the score leans further toward popular culture than a term like "filmic music drama" might suggest: his score is not really at all Wagnerian or operatic, but actually quite often alludes—sometimes playfully, sometimes seemingly straight-faced—to operetta, popular song, and dance music. So why the reference in Meisel's article to high art in the bourgeois tradition that he supposedly despises?

One answer surely lies in the need for the film composer to carve out a space among a critical establishment suspicious of cinema and the aesthetic values of film music. Meisel makes this clear in other articles when he reacts very defensively to negative press from just these kinds of critics. Crucial here is the strategy of distancing his music from past film music practices, and that is how he opens "How is Film Music Written?": he denounces the tradition of stock accompaniments and arrangements as "stylistic nonsense" and dismisses many of the original compositions for film that he has heard.[33] Here he echoes Béla Balázs's call in *Der sichtbare Mensch* for an end to the practice of accompanying films with pre-composed music, a practice, Balázs complains, which "transplants us to a completely different atmosphere that has nothing more to do with the film."[34] The sort of values to which Meisel appeals—originality, unity, formal coherence—seek to "redeem" film music from its suspect origins. And yet the pastiche quality we observed in the nature music suggests precisely the sort of practices he condemned. Meisel in fact seems to draw from a whole range of languages here, as though he were choosing appropriate selections from a film accompaniment catalogue.

And there is another value associated with high culture to which Meisel refers: authorship, that is, the traditional notion of the aesthetic creator to whom the work of art is traced. Film music composers, he complains, are not taken seriously enough because they are merely part of an industrial process, consigned to the shadow of the director. Meisel finishes the article by looking forward to his next project (*Berlin: Die Sinfonie der Großstadt*) in which "for the first time film and music, in ideal fashion, will go hand in hand from the outset, and a work will originate from the combined efforts of director and composer."[35] This is the real meaning for Meisel of the "filmic music drama" in which film and music without each other are half entities. The composer becomes a joint *auteur,* a creative figure worthy of mention alongside the director. This anticipation of a bright future beginning with his next film hardly flatters *Der heilige Berg,* and yet it might be said that if Meisel implies that his contribution to the film was merely an afterthought, he was in part the victim of his own demand for "exact conformity." In the case of a true working partnership with the director, this phrase would imply a collaborative process, but in the real-world conditions of cinematic production, it condemns the composer to a potentially ungrateful post-production role in which he parasitically responds to the image track—and this role hardly squares with the demand for *auteur* status.

That Meisel should appeal to traditional high culture with his emphasis on authorship and a unified totality comes as something of a surprise. A proponent of the artist collective should be happy to dismiss these notions, while a populist film like *Der heilige Berg* surely ought not to be hidebound to such remnants of high-art ideology. But Meisel, still partly loyal to the older concepts of the "artist," looks over his shoulder at the arbiters of aesthetic value. As Elsaesser suggests, popular film in Weimar Germany may have challenged such values and even mimicked them subversively, but there was also a lingering need for critical affirmation from an influential "conservative-taste elite."[36] In his essay "Cult of Distraction," written only a few months before the premiere of *Der heilige Berg,* Kracauer picked up on this issue. Anticipating several features of Walter Benjamin's celebrated "The Work of Art in the Age of Mechanical Reproduction" (1936), Kracauer takes an affirmative view of the "distraction" culture that he detects in the lavish cinemas of Berlin, with their fabulous interiors, elaborate pre-screening light-shows, and, Kracauer adds, orchestras:

> The interior design of movie theaters serves one sole purpose: to rivet the viewers' attention to the peripheral, so that they will not sink into the abyss. The stimulations of the senses succeed one another with such rapidity that there is no room left between them for even the slightest contemplation. Like *life buoys,* the refractions of the spotlights and the musical accompaniment keep the spectator above water.[37]

The result of this distraction (Kracauer refers to it as a "*Gesamtkunstwerk* of effects") is an externality that is authentic to its cultural and historical situation. Traditional arts have lost their relevance, he insists, because they continue to peddle outdated concepts such as "inwardness" and "tragedy."[38] Cinema has the potential to allow the audience to "encounter itself" because its externality mirrors the audience's own fragmented existence. But Kracauer adds an important qualification: this potential is rarely realized because cinema insists on clothing itself in the garb of traditional aesthetic values. The grandiose interiors mimic their high-culture counterparts, while the program of events that compose a cinematic evening aspire to an "aesthetic totality" that is whole and organic in the spirit of traditional cultural values. "Distraction," he concludes, is "festooned with drapery."[39]

Modernism and the Masses

Der heilige Berg seems haunted by these tensions between tradition and progress, high art and popular culture. Meisel seeks to define the identity of his music (modern, dynamic, urban) against the weight of a now moribund inheritance (Romantic, static, rural). At the same time, though, he draws on that tradition's ideology to support his stance, while his music seems uncertain whether to parody or absorb it. Meisel's music, like the film as a whole, seems to occupy the disputed territory between modernism and modern "mass culture," between the individualized, heroicized notion of the artist on the one hand and mass production and consumption on the other. But the term "mass culture" needs to be scrutinized and historicized. Arguably already problematic when it first entered critical discourse, it has become a buzzword of twentieth-century cultural history and criticism, popularized in part by its adoption by Frankfurt School theorists to denote the debased nature of popular culture.

When Meisel calls for "modern music for the masses" his language comes directly out of a left-wing tradition committed to the "politicization of the masses." Yet this mobilization of the concept of "mass" (as proletariat) differs in important ways from the less explicitly political, and much more critical, concept of mass culture (*Massenkultur*). The latter can be traced in part to the emergent cultural theory of Weimar Germany, and it inevitably carries with it pejorative connotations of the rise of new faceless hordes whose numbers and tastes will have a leveling, perhaps degenerative, effect on cultural production. Kracauer can hardly be accused of adopting paranoid attitudes toward *Massenkultur,* yet even as his essay "Cult of Distraction" affirms the new developments, it betrays a certain negativity. While he derides the "so-called educated classes"[40] for their pomposity, Kracauer declares them an anachronism: "They are being absorbed by the masses, a process that creates the *homogeneous cosmopolitan audience* in which everyone has the *same* responses, from the bank director to the sales clerk, from the diva to the stenographer."[41] Those who lament the passing of the old culture, he adds, need to recognize the drastic social transformations that have made it irrelevant. Yet there is a sense of loss in Kracauer's language, as though this absorption into the masses were the only acceptable choice in the face of overwhelming social pressure.

The final sentence of the essay is similarly tinged with regret. Kracauer characterizes Berlin as "home of the masses—who so easily allow themselves to be stupefied only because they are so close to the truth."[42] This strategy of affirming the truth-value of the "stupefied" masses comes at a price: the insight of the masses into contemporary reality is achieved without their awareness. They become little more than pawns in a cultural-historical process of critical revelation, tools in Kracauer's critical arsenal. Absorbed into his critique of a by-now debased individualism, Kracauer's cinema spectators disappear as subjects, their agency erased. And this is the critical distinction between the masses of Marxist ideology and those of *Massenkultur*. For all their collectivity, the Marxist proletariat are envisaged as agents of their own political destiny: they act and choose—collectively, to be sure, but actively nonetheless. In *The Political Theater* (1929) Piscator quotes a review of *Revue Roter Rummel*, his agit-prop piece (with music by Meisel) staged for the German Communist Party's 1924 election campaign: "The effect of the scenes on the expectant and excited audiences is without parallel. Such mass appreciation—indeed mass participation—is found in no other theater."[43] The point is not whether Piscator's political theater is actually more participatory (the review is from *Die rote Fahne* and so its enthusiasm is predictable), but the reading of "mass" as a positive and active entity. It was Balázs's hope, indeed, that cinema would transform the representation of the mass, displacing the sense of the individual's disappearance in the "dull, amorphous crowd," and highlighting the reflection of the spirit of the mass in the individual's face.[44]

Massenkultur, on the other hand, suggests manipulation at the hands of the "culture industry," a debased and commodified fusion of art and entertainment whose "subjects" are blindly stimulated and persuaded as a passive and obedient throng. The question is whether the audiences for a film like *Der heilige Berg* might be read in the active terms that political theater sought for its audience. From this perspective the film's ambiguities—its oscillations between the domains of popular culture and high art, between celebrations of individual heroic achievement and the community spirit represented by the "mass ornament" of the torchlit nocturnal rescue party—would be more than signs of ideological confusion or bad conscience; they would open up spaces for multiple readings, some more ironic or critical than others. Although Meisel champions the notion of the single-authored film score, the heterogeneity of the musical language in *Der heilige Berg* suggests precisely the sort of intertextual combinations and collisions that Balázs associated with the use of pre-composed music in film. And if Balázs worried that these practices risked a kind of semantic anarchy, *Der heilige Berg* celebrates this plurality in an almost postmodern fashion, anticipating more recent filmic practices with their ironic, playful manipulation of pre-composed music and their assumption of a knowing audience alive to the potential layers of meaning that this generates.

And what of modernism, the other term in this traditional binary? Meisel's call for "modern music for the masses" might assume a commitment to the avant-garde, and there is little question that he sought to push the frontiers of musical experience in new directions. But this is not to say that he drew a line between modernism and popular culture. In fact his commitment to popular music is clearly demonstrated in the montage-like interweaving of multiple traditions (popular song, dance-band numbers, political anthems) in all his theater and film projects. That this fluid mixture was intended to subvert traditional cultural associations and distinctions between high and low seems to be confirmed by reports of a project left unfinished when Meisel died in 1930 at the age of thirty-six. He had been commissioned to write the score for *Stürme über dem Montblanc* (Storm Over Mont Blanc, 1930), Fanck's first sound film. Casting aside the traditional German art-music signifiers of sublime nature (and as the title indicates, sublime nature was to feature heavily in the film), Meisel planned something along the lines of his most recent film project, *Goluboy Ekspress* (The Blue Express,1929, Ilya Trauberg). For this Soviet adventure film he had recorded music with the Lewis Ruth Band, the jazz combo featured in the premiere of Kurt Weill's *Die Dreigroschenoper.*[45] When even critic Kurt London, a professed admirer of Meisel's work, expressed doubts about the use of jazz in a *Bergfilm,* he probably spoke for many: "I have it on good authority that before his death Meisel was planning to have the *Montblanc* music performed by a jazz orchestra à la *Blue Express.* Such a combination doesn't bear thinking about."[46] Replacing distant horns with an up-tempo dance number was, it seems, a step too far.

Notes

1. Kracauer, *From Caligari to Hitler*, 111n11.

2. Ibid., 110–12. Kracauer had originally reviewed *Der heilige Berg* (The Holy Mountain, Arnold Fanck, 1926) for the *Frankfurter Zeitung* (4 March 1927) and was no more impressed then. He mocked what he saw as a "misty brew of vague sentimentality" (Kracauer, *Von Caligari zu Hitler*, 399–400).

3. *Bergfilm* titles directed by Fanck include *Der Berg des Schicksals* (Mountain of Destiny, 1924), *Die weiße Hölle vom Piz Palü* (The White Hell of Pitz Palu, 1928), and *Der weiße Rausch: Neue Wunder des Schneeschuhs* (The White Flame, 1931). Paul Hindemith wrote an ambitious orchestral score for Fanck's early documentary *Im Kampf mit dem Berge: 1. Teil: In Sturm und Eis. Eine Alpensymphonie in Bildern* (1921), but it was never performed at the film's screenings.

4. Letter from Richard Pfeiffer to Sergei Eisenstein (1 June 1926), in *Sowjetischer Film.* UFA was shortly to come under the control of the conservative nationalist Alfred Hugenberg, who would shape the company's political sympathies in his own image, but in Kracauer's view it had pursued a right-wing, nationalist agenda from its very origins as a producer of propaganda in the First World War (Kracauer, *From Caligari to Hitler*, 36–37). For more on UFA see Kreimeier, *The UFA Story*, and Elsaesser, *Weimar Cinema and After* (especially chapter 4). One of the most intriguing aspects of the reception of *Bronenosets Potyomkin* in Ger-

many is the suggestion that Meisel's score was banned from screenings of the film in certain jurisdictions. Meisel himself claimed as much in an unpublished article addressed to the Moscow press. There is, however, no evidence that state-sanctioned prohibition was ever enforced, although temporary, local bans may have been put in place. The nearest we come is a letter from Foreign Minister Gustav Stresemann to Prussian prime minister Otto Braun, in which Stresemann claims that the latter's decision not to support a ban on the film may be due to his having viewed it without Meisel's score (Bernhard, *Gustav Stresemann*, 408). *Kinematograph,* a film periodical belonging to Hugenberg's Scherl publishing group, stirred the pot when it claimed in 1926 that "a good deal of the effect of the film has to be credited to the musical arrangement. The film would immediately prove irreproachable if it were to be seen without the inflammatory music" (Sudendorf, *Der Stummfilmmusiker Edmund Meisel,* 18).

5. Rentschler, "Mountains and Modernity," 143.

6. Ibid.

7. Balázs, *Der sichtbare Mensch,* 90–91.

8. My research is based on detailed comparisons of Meisel's score as reconstructed, conducted, and recorded by Helmut Imig (Edel 0029062) and a version of the film released on video by the Friedrich Wilhelm Murnau Stiftung (Kino Video K307). Since the two versions were independently reconstructed, there is no consistent synchronization between them. Imig's score appears to have been based on a shorter version of the film, and, as always with reconstructions of scores for silent films, the problem of projection speed looms large. There are, however, enough plausible correspondences and cues to gain an impression of the interaction of music and image.

9. Meisel, "Wie schreibt man Filmmusik?" 60.

10. How familiar Meisel was with the music/noise experiments of the Italian and Soviet futurists is not clear. A characteristic feature of the circles in which Meisel worked, however, was an intensive cultural exchange with the Soviet Union, and it seems likely that his own experiments owed something to Soviet models.

11. Zielesch, "Beim Schöpfer der Geräuschmusik," 61.

12. Ibid.

13. Sloterdijk, *Critique of Cynical Reason,* 449.

14. Williams, *The Politics of Modernism,* 18.

15. Meisel, "Wie schreibt man Filmmusik?" 59.

16. Ibid., 60.

17. Elsaesser, *Weimar Cinema,* 97.

18. Ibid.

19. Rentschler, "Mountains and Modernity," 147–48.

20. Kracauer, *The Mass Ornament.*

21. Meisel, "Wie schreibt man Filmmusik?" 59.

22. Ibid., 58.

23. Ibid., 60.

24. Adorno and Eisler, *Composing for the Films,* 40. For some critical perspectives on the "counterpoint" idea in film music theory, see Chion, *Audio-Vision,* 37–38, and Cook, *Analyzing Musical Multimedia,* 114–15.

25. Balázs, *Der sichtbare Mensch,* 99.

26. Meisel, "Wie schreibt man Filmmusik?" 60.

27. Sudendorf, *Der Stummfilmmusiker,* 8. One of the leading directors in Berlin during the Weimar period, Piscator (1893–1966) had begun his theatrical career in the immediate postwar period with modest revues and agit-prop in support of a range of left-wing organizations. By the end of the twenties he was staging large-scale productions, including an innovative use of film and the simultaneous staging of multiple scenes. Meisel was involved with seven Piscator productions.

28. Meisel, "Wie schreibt man Filmmusik?" 58.

29. Balázs, *Schriften zum Film,* 172–73.

30. Balázs, *Theory of the Film*, 32.
31. Wagner, "Über die Benennung 'Musikdrama,'" 306.
32. Meisel, "Subjective und objective Filmmusik," 67.
33. Meisel, "Wie schreibt man Filmmusik?" 58.
34. Balázs, *Der sichtbare Mensch*, 98.
35. Meisel, "Wie schreibt man Filmmusik?" 60.
36. Elsaesser, *Weimar Cinema*, 42–43.
37. Kracauer, *The Mass Ornament*, 326; author's emphasis.
38. Ibid., 327.
39. Ibid., 328.
40. Ibid., 325.
41. Ibid.; author's emphasis.
42. Ibid., 328.
43. Piscator, *The Political Theatre*, 83.
44. Balázs, *Schriften zum Film*, 109.
45. Meisel's music was recorded on phonographs for synchronized replay during screenings, a method that was about to give way to the new technology of recording sound directly onto the film strip.
46. London, "Paul Dessaus Musik," 27. Ernst Krenek's *Jonny spielt auf* (1927) critically highlights the musical gap between nature and the city when he juxtaposes representations of a glacier (pompous, austere modalism for full orchestra) with the dance-band sound world of the metropolis. Joseph Auner argues, however, that the opera's celebration of popular music is not all it seems to be (see Auner, "'Soulless Machines'").

References

Adorno, Theodor, and Hanns Eisler. *Composing for the Films*. London: Athlone Press, 1994.
Auner, Joseph. "'Soulless Machines' and Steppenwolves: Renegotiating Masculinity in Krenek's *Jonny spielt auf.*" In *Siren Songs: Representations of Gender and Sexuality in Opera*, ed. M. A. Smart. Princeton: Princeton University Press, 2000, 222–36.
Balázs, Béla. *Béla Balázs: Schriften zum Film*, vol. 2. Ed. H. H. Diederichs and W. Gersch. München: Carl Hanser, 1984.
———. *Der sichtbare Mensch oder die Kultur des Films*. Frankfurt: Suhrkamp Taschenbuch, 2001.
———. *Theory of the Film: Character and Growth of a New Art*. Trans. E. Bone. New York: Dover, 1970.
Benjamin, Walter. "The Work of Art in the Age of Mechanical Reproduction" (1936). In *Illuminations*, ed. H. Arendt, trans. H. Zohn. New York: Schocken, 1968.
Bernhard, Henri, ed. *Gustav Stresemann: Vermächtnis. Der Nachlaß in drei Bänden*. Berlin: Ullstein, 1932.
Chion, Michel. *Audio-Vision: Sound on Screen*. Trans. Claudia Gorbman. New York: Columbia University Press, 1994.
Cook, Nicholas. *Analyzing Musical Multimedia*. Oxford: Oxford University Press, 1998.
Elsaesser, Thomas. *Weimar Cinema and After: Germany's Historical Imaginary*. London: Routledge, 2000.
Kracauer, Siegfried. *From Caligari to Hitler: A Psychological History of the German Film*. Princeton: Princeton University Press, 1947.
———. *The Mass Ornament*. Trans. and ed. T. Y. Levin. Cambridge, Mass.: Harvard University Press, 1995.
———. *Von Caligari zu Hitler: Eine psychologische Geschichte des deutschem Films*. Frankfurt: Suhrkamp Taschenbuch, 1984.
Kreimeier, Klaus. *The UFA Story: A History of Germany's Greatest Film Company, 1918–1945*. Trans. R. and R. Kimber. Berkeley: University of California Press, 2000.

London, Kurt. "Paul Dessaus Musik: *Stürme über dem Montblanc.*" *Der Film* 6 (7 February 1931): [pagination unknown]. Reprinted in "Paul Dessaus Musik" (*Filmmaterialien* 6), ed. Hans-Michael Bock and Wolfgang Jacobsen. Hamburg: Cinegraph, 1994. http://www.cinegraph.de/filmmat/fm6/fm6_17.html.

Meisel, Edmund. "Subjective und objective Filmmusik." *Licht-Bild-Bühne* 21/133 (2 June 1928): [pagination unknown]. Reprinted in *Der Stummfilmmusiker Edmund Meisel* (Kinematograph 1), ed. W. Sudendorf. Frankfurt: Deutsche Filmmuseum, 1984, 67–68.

———. "Wie schreibt man Filmmusik?" *Ufa-Magazin* 2/14 (April 1927): [pagination unknown]. Reprinted in facsimile in *Der Stummfilmmusiker Edmund Meisel* (Kinematograph 1), ed. W. Sudendorf. Frankfurt: Deutsche Filmmuseum, 1984, 58–60.

Piscator, Erwin. *The Political Theatre*. Trans. H. Rorrison. London: Methuen, 1980.

Rentschler, Eric. "Mountains and Modernity: Relocating the *Bergfilm.*" *New German Critique* 51 (1990): 137–61.

Sloterdijk, Peter. *Critique of Cynical Reason*. Trans. M. Eldred. London: Verso, 1988.

Sowjetischer Film in Deutschland 1922–1932. Filmwissentschaftliche Mitteilungen 8/3 (1967).

Sudendorf, Werner, ed. *Der Stummfilmmusiker Edmund Meisel* (Kinematograph 1). Frankfurt: Deutsche Filmmuseum, 1984.

Wagner, Richard. "Über die Benennung 'Musikdrama'" (1872). In *Sämtliche Schriften und Dichtungen*. 16 vols. Ed. Richard Sternfeld and Hans von Wolzogen. Leipzig: Breitkopf und Härtel, 1916, 9: 302–08.

Williams, Raymond. *The Politics of Modernism: Against the New Conformists*. Ed. Tony Pinkney. London: Verso, 1989.

Zielesch, Fritz. "Beim Schöpfer der Geräuschmusik." *Berliner Volks-Zeitung* 76:97 (26 February 1928). Reprinted in facsimile in W. Sudendorf, *Der Stummfilmmusiker Edmund Meisel* (Kinematograph 1). Frankfurt: Deutsche Filmmuseum, 1984, 61–62.

Filmography

DER HEILIGE BERG

release:	17 December 1926 (Berlin)
duration:	100 mins (106 mins restored version)
dir:	Arnold Fanck
prod:	Harry R. Sokal
prod co:	Berg und Sportfilm; Universum Film A.G. (UFA)
actors:	Leni Riefenstahl (Diotima); Luis Trenker (Karl); Ernst Petersen (Vigo); Frida Richard (Mother); Friedrich Schneider (Colli); Hannes Schneider (Mountain Guide)
camera:	Sepp Allgeier; Albert Benitz; Helmar Lerski; Hans Schneeberger
music:	Edmund Meisel
DVD:	Kino; 12 August 2003; ASIN: B00009XN90
CD:	Sound Track Factory; 19 September 2000; ASIN: B00000811E (with *Bronenosets Potyomkin*)

FIVE

New Technologies and Old Rites: Dissonance between Picture and Music in Readings of Joris Ivens's Rain

ED HUGHES

In 2001 I was invited by the UK Bath International Music Festival to arrange a concert based around two screenings of the film *Regen* (1929, hereafter *Rain*) by Dutch director Joris Ivens. The first screening was accompanied by the 1941 score *Vierzehn Arten den Regen zu beschreiben,* or *Fourteen Ways of Describing Rain,* by Hanns Eisler; the second by my own 2001 score, entitled *Light Cuts Through Dark Skies* in response to an effect of light in a panoramic scene halfway through the film.

The two scores inhabit different aesthetics. Eisler's score was written using the avant-garde composing methods of his teacher Arnold Schoenberg, and emphasized continuity and development to the exclusion of silence. My own score was composed in the post-minimal era, and used repetitive and cellular rhythmic techniques, fused with polyphony of texture and line; it contained and exploited discontinuity, abrupt change, and silence. Whereas Eisler's score was concerned with concision, short forms, and the uncompromising foregrounding of music in the perception, my own score had longer time spans and permitted momentary disappearance of music from the perceptual foreground; occasionally images dissolve the music.

Since the performances in Bath, I have completed a number of live music to film performance projects, and have had time to reflect on some of the issues that this form of artistic engagement raises. Very often my thoughts were drawn back to the memory of this first project, precisely because the very different musical styles used in this experiment highlighted the possibility of alternative models for that creative friction between media which informs an active cinematic experience. Specifically, the following questions persisted:

Did the film *Rain* welcome or resist musical scoring?
Could the musical notions of consonance and dissonance be
    extended to discussions of music and picture interactions?
Could musical forms find their analogy in visual domains, and vice
    versa; would forms in different media collide or merge?

In any discussion of such questions, one must return to Eisler's own account of the process of conceiving his retrospective score for *Rain,* contained in *Composing for the Films,* written with Theodor Adorno and published in the United States in 1947, the first significant attempt to form a sociological critique of film music.[1] Eisler's work on his score for *Rain* was written in a highly reactive atmosphere. Composed in the course of extensive research into the possibilities for a reformed music practice in a mass medium, the score constituted an explicit rejection of what he and Adorno regarded as outmoded ways of working. These ways of working made manifest Adorno's concept of "pseudo-individualization,"[2] or the pretense that a product was new, when in fact it was merely a manufactured variant on a known formula. They argued that, in cinema, pseudo-individualization found its counterpart in musical "standardization," a performance style in which all types of musical expression and articulation were exaggerated, so that they became merely shallow signifiers of emotion, or faint, de-contextualized echoes of a past and now redundant musical language. An extension of this, they argued, was found in the standardization of the studio orchestra, which uncritically employed a routine ensemble derived from the nineteenth-century western tradition, in a way that tended to "standardize the sound itself."[3] Eisler and Adorno suggested that the ensemble might be reinvented for the microphone, using smaller forces and some of the delicate colors pioneered in the "genuine chamber ensemble"[4] of such a piece as Arnold Schoenberg's *Pierrot Lunaire* (1912).

Eisler's score for *Rain* should be heard and understood in the context of this manifesto for a reformed film music. He consciously adopted a number of novel procedures:

- use of an unusually small instrumental ensemble (flute, clarinet, violin doubling viola, cello, piano), inspired by the instrumentation of *Pierrot Lunaire* (but without a singer);
- use of a "complex composing technique"[5] (the twelve-tone method) to match the advanced visual resources of Joris Ivens's *Rain;*
- conscious rejection of "coarse" symphonic formal models, or the adoption of "means of contrast more subtle than the allegro followed by the adagio."[6]

But Eisler's work was also more than a protest against the banal formulations of studio cinema music. His "Report on the Film Music Project," which appeared as an appendix to *Composing for the Films,* ended in a criticism of the montage ideas of no less a person than the Soviet film director Sergei Eisenstein, who was accused of exaggerating the value of the music for his film *Aleksandr Nevskiy* (Alexander Nevsky, 1938), scored by Sergei Prokofiev. Eisler asserted the progressive value of avant-garde musical resources by critiquing the film-music ideas of an avant-garde film director. Although such a dissonance between avant-garde musical conceptions of picture and avant-garde visual conceptions of sound might seem paradoxical, it dates back to the beginning of the twentieth century, and points to the persistence of a mismatch between aspirations in the audio and visual domains. Eisenstein's own theoretical starting point had been the sound-color ideas of the visual artist Wassily Kandinsky.

Kandinsky, unlike Schoenberg with whom he corresponded, was a "spontaneous synaesthete"; when he listened to *Lohengrin,* he said, vivid colors "stood before my eyes."[7] Kandinsky's synaesthesia led him to theorize the association of sound with color, placing this absolute association at the apex of spiritual experience. His theory was attacked by Eisenstein in *The Film Sense.* Eisenstein mocked the painter's metaphysical union of sound and color. For Eisenstein, different media established a relationship through shared emotional qualities, but through collision rather than equivalence. He insisted that though certain qualities might be shared, the fundamental properties of different media were unlike. Quoting Diderot, Eisenstein wrote that the madman "'holds a blade of shiny yellow straw in his hand and shouts that he has caught a sunbeam.' . . . This madman was an ultra-formalist, seeing as he did only the *form* of the sunbeam and the *yellowness* of the colour, seeing only *line* and *color.*"[8] Eisenstein's rejection of Kandinsky's synaesthesia was driven by his own research into music synchronization in the sound film of the 1930s. His self-positioning as an anti-formalist was expressed in his commitment to the didactic qualities of narrative, and the establishment, on a case-by-case basis, of systems of meaning and association.[9] In turn, shared narrative qualities articulated, or brought into relief, the separate laws of individual media. Part IV of *The Film Sense* analyzed a sequence from his collaboration with Prokofiev in *Aleksandr Nevskiy* in order to demonstrate picture and music in the service of narrative.

In this crucial piece of theory, Eisenstein considered types of audio-visual correspondence. He first rejected formulaic musical responses to stock situations, caricatured in the image of the silent cinema pianist providing cues for such situations as courage, sadness, inspiration, or love. This tended to lead, Eisenstein argued, to "visualizations of a most platitudinous character."[10] Instead, Eisenstein aimed for a higher form of montage, rooted in landscape and movement. Referring to *Aleksandr Nevskiy*'s iconic scene on the ice, he perceived "an organic binding" in the movement of the shots' plastic compositions which corresponded with "musical movement,"[11] so that, for example, the craggy outline of vertiginous rock, which drew the eye downward, was embodied in a slowly descending cello arpeggio.

This analysis attracted the criticism of Adorno and Eisler, who argued in *Composing for the Films* that Eisenstein was himself in danger of committing formalist errors. Associating graphic outline with musical movement (descending pitch, in this case) was itself a move, they argued, in the direction of "absolute equivalence."[12]

Adorno and Eisler also argued that Eisenstein's definition of movement, in both musical and visual terms, was vague. And, indeed, Eisenstein's conception of movement was figurative and painterly. Musical movement, being grounded in divisions of time through the action of pulse, is by contrast "real." Eisenstein extended painting's static, two-dimensional, and figurative evocation of movement and rhythm into the arena of sound and music, in order to suggest a form of correspondence which was to prove problematic. But perhaps Eisenstein's painterly perspective was more subtle than is sometimes allowed. If Eisenstein argued that the complex array of figurative and real rhythms generated by the collision of a moving picture sequence and music could work together to create a plausible audio-visual synchrony, then it seems reasonable to suggest that, in the scene of the vertiginous rockface in *Aleksandr Nevskiy,* the separate elements of graphic and aural "descent" were combined in order to magnify the theme of anxiety over possible defeat. By pointing abstract elements toward a kind of synthesis or resolution in narrative, one might, in some cases, find a way out of circular arguments concerning formalism.

Eisler's further criticisms of Eisenstein's *Aleksandr Nevskiy* analysis reflected both his specialist insights as a musician and his critical agenda as co-author of *Composing for the Films*. The comments were forensic; but they were not entirely free from prejudice. For example, Eisler asserted, first, that Prokofiev's music was "so inconsequential that it might relate to anything or nothing at all. . . . The motif should be at least so clear that no doubt is left concerning the relation between music and picture."[13] This comment recorded Eisler's disapproval of any musical imprecision or subordination to picture. But, in context, Prokofiev's music *fits itself* (primarily through its spare textures) to the stillness of the scene and the themes of waiting and anxiety.

Second, Eisler wrote that "the picture moves on while the music marks time";[14] again, the themes of waiting, building tension, and anxiety are arguably best matched *in* music by properties exclusive *to* music. In music, repetition *is* potentially meaningful. But Eisler's musical modernism insisted upon progressive, developmental (therefore non-repetitive), and advanced (therefore non-tonal) techniques.

Third, Eisler said that the true nature of Prokofiev's "neo-classical" musical style was "impassivity" and that Eisenstein attributed too much significance to a "harmless piece" of music.[15] However, the allegedly regressive "neo-classical" two-bar patterns of Prokofiev's music actually contributed to the groundedness of the passage through which tension and anxiety were built. The stable two-bar patterns, anathema to Eisler, functioned *like a ground* (in the musical sense), over which the themes (which were largely visual, and not musical) were built.

The act of separating out Eisler's antipathy toward Prokofiev's "neo-classicism" exposes the self-limiting nature of strategies employed by Eisler in composing a new score for his special sound print of *Rain*. The score was "the richest and most complete of all those written under the auspices of the project"[16] and therefore should be understood as enshrining the composer's key research discoveries as well as his doctrines for the new film music. Eisler's strategies could reasonably be tested against, first, his synchronization of *Fourteen Ways* with *Rain* and, second, the parallel experience of alternate musical readings of the same film.

Rain

The film itself was conceived and shot by Joris Ivens and Mannus Franken over several months in 1928, and depicted the city of Amsterdam in a shower of rain. Featuring handheld shots in low-lighting conditions, highly experimental for the time, there were many scenes of considerable beauty. Elements of the documentary and the poetic were combined in a classic and condensed instance of the city-symphony-poem.[17]

For the Bath 2001 project I used the British Film Institute's 16 mm print of *Rain*.[18] This has 155 shots, and is a reasonably complete version. With a running speed of twenty-four frames per second, each shot lasts between one and ten seconds; shot lengths of three to five seconds are typical. On first viewing, the cutting seems rapid because contrasting images are mounted in quick succession. For this reason, the film's form seems elusive on initial presentation. However, the film is by no means "static,"[19] as Eisler argued; it is characterized by subtle modulations of tempo, conveyed both through cutting and varying degrees of activity within frames. The shots are carefully constructed and edited to create formal balance and symmetry. In this way, the filmic rhythm resembles musical phrasing. Thus both the organization of shots and their relative durations sometimes suggest slowing down, or coming to rest, or, sometimes, acceleration.

The film opens with two views of sunlight dappling the canal water. It then cuts to a cityscape of houses, followed by a succession of images of boats and barges passing. All the key visual elements of the film are condensed into the first thirty seconds. These are water, light, reflection, movement (motion), and the forms of the city. As rain visibly begins to fall, the light fades, increasing luminosity of movement. Then, in a sequence striking for its rapidity of cutting, the focus moves rhythmically to the city: birds in flight over water, a gutter flowing, an umbrella opening, and a roof window closing. The sequence discloses one of the typical forms of the film: the standardized black umbrella, aestheticized throughout in close up and *en masse,* from ground to overhead shots, at times creating visual patterns which could be called (in the sense of harmonious correlation of parts) rhythmic, both across the frame and in movement. Visual rhythm in film can define or support periodic cutting and large-scale structure; but it can also be understood as the phenomenon of movement within the frame. Onscreen movement clearly has an impact, because shots without such movement may seem (or indeed be) longer. Both rhythmic construction of sequences and shots capturing various kinds of movement are found in *Rain.*

As effects of light and shadow intensify, a long sequence intercuts reflection and inversion with various types of city movement (people, cars, and horses; see Figure 5.1). A tree is reflected in the canal as the rain falls. A person is reflected in the water collecting on the stone cobbles. A moving bicyclist is seen first from above, and then, reflected, in the pools of water on the road. These studies of light and movement verge on the abstract. Next comes a sequence of views from on board a moving tram. The handheld shots through windows record the tram's motion as it follows the sometimes curving tracks. As the camera continues to survey traffic, there is a brief shot from above, documenting the intersection of trams, pedestrians, and bicycles.

A number of analogous musical processes suggest themselves. As already discussed, rhythm might be interpreted in a number of ways. For reflection, one could imagine musical inversion (the exactly opposite replication of one line's musical intervals in another—as one line rises, the other falls). For a moment of intersection, with independent yet simultaneous trajectories, one could imagine musical polyphony (music made from layered voices).

Figure 5.1. Joris Ivens. View on the Valverstraat in Amsterdam, still from *Rain*, The Netherlands 1929 © *European Foundations Joris Ivens / Joris Ivens Archive.*

The viability of inversion as a principle of correspondence between musical and visual domains is doubtful because it relies upon acute and conscious tracking of melodic shapes. On the other hand, contrasting textures of sound and vision are instantly perceivable because they do not rely upon heavy mental processing or tracking. Thus a connection between a polyphonic musical texture and diverse visual linear movements may establish itself quickly enough to be perceptually recognized. Musical Example 5.1 is an extract from the score *Light Cuts* corresponding to the shot at the street intersection in *Rain*. The use of layered lines and pulses enlivens the visual texture, because its counterpoint is invested with musical rhythm and directionality. The sense is that the connection between music and picture is not created by some notionally equivalent

Table 5.1. Table of shots 95 to 129, *Rain*

Shot Description	Eisler	Hughes
'Vergunning'	No. 8 (Intermezzo), 88 bpm	[End] Section No. 4, 104 bpm
Umbrella		
Man with Umbrella		
Umbrella—3 people—side view		
Same, rear view		
Water surface		*silence*
Umbrellas from above		Section 5, 50 pbm
Umbrellas from rear		
Umbrellas from front		
Umbrellas from rear		
Dark Clouds		
Roof tops		
Radio mast	No. 10 (presto Etüde), 132 bpm	
Bridge		*silence*
Tiles through window (focus pull)		
Tiles		
Tiles (close up)		
Window (tiles out of focus)		
Blind		
Window (tiles out of focus)		
Downpipe		
Window pane		
Cobbles		
Curb		
Curb (water gushing)		
Dog	No. 11 (Überleitung), 132 bpm	
Water surface		
(View from) Tram		
Clouds		
(View from) Tram		
Barges on water		*silence*
Canal and bridges		*silence*
Houses (pan up)		*silence*
Dark skies (cut by light)		*silence*
Pavement (with flock of sparrows)		Section No. 6, 92 bpm

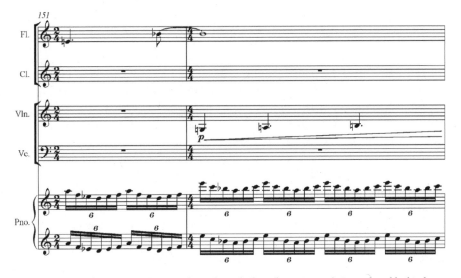

Musical Example 5.1. Light Cuts Through Dark Skies (bars 151–154). *Reproduced by kind permission of University of York Music Press.*

formal device, but by the extension of the sense of motion, generated by the vivid interaction of two separate media.

But care still needs to taken to avoid the criticism of mere duplication at an exclusively formal level. For, as Nicholas Cook writes, one must be wary of being trapped by a language "predicated on similarity."[20] Some sort of synthesis is required, which the combined energy of a city intersection and an instrumental polyphony may begin to address. However, film music theory and practice is still haunted by the difficulty of theorizing purely abstract principles of correspondence.

Media Dissonance

This difficulty makes one wonder whether Eisler's methodology in scoring *Rain* produced unintended dissonance between images and music. Or, at least, that Eisler's connection between advanced musical resources and the experimental character of *Rain* may have resulted in the mapping of a set of musical structures onto a different, and unrelated, visual conception. In their advocacy of advanced musical resources, Adorno and Eisler made a virtue of musical modernism's short forms, and its rejection of tonal diatonicism. In a key argument, they argued that such features were particularly suitable to movie music:

> Most motion pictures use short musical forms. The length of a musical form is determined by its relation to the musical material. Tonal music of the last two and a

half centuries favoured relatively long, developed forms. Consciousness of a tonal centre can be achieved only by parallel episodes, developments and repetitions that require a certain amount of time.[21]

There are two problems here. First, diatonic tonality in both short and repetitious fashion was applied in a surrealist context by composer Erik Satie in his score for the film *Entr'acte* (1924) by René Clair. Satie achieved a new form of film music, based on fragmentation, by entering imaginatively into the particular needs of the surrealist encounter in which he was engaged. He thus anticipated the fact that the motion picture would favor networks of musical meaning based upon discontinuity. To exclude *a priori* diatonic tonality from participation in a new film music language seems premature. Second, the argument that short musical forms were ideally suited to the mobile, fast-paced surfaces of the moving image in contemporary film is a syllogism: most motion pictures use short forms; modern music uses short forms; therefore motion pictures and modern music are compatible. As a principle, the idea of the concentrated short musical form being matched to fast-paced visuals failed to take into account the nature and construction of images in any one specific film, or indeed moment. And indeed, the concept of matching length and form exactly is itself formalistic, in this instance serving to highlight disjunction and media dissonance. Longer or offset forms might provide the necessary dovetailing to facilitate the illusion of a more fluid, but nevertheless meaningful, interaction between picture and music.

As an example, the start of Eisler's No. 4 (Scherzando) in *Fourteen Ways* was synchronized with a rapid sequence of images already described (a bird in flight; rain at the curbside; an umbrella opening; a roof window closing; a water surface). The concentration and breathless rapidity of the music in his synchronization weakens the effect of the equally rapid montage because one is overloaded with information from both domains. My own score, *Light Cuts,* is, at this point, silent, in order to allow the snappy film cutting to take its effect on its own uncompromising rhythmic terms.

Not only did Eisler exclude the possibility of tonality and repetition from his musical resources, but he also ruled out using any slow tempos:

> A slow tempo was out of place in the newly composed music to Joris Ivens's *Rain,* not because it was necessary to illustrate the falling of the rain, but because the music's task was to push forward this plotless and therefore static motion picture.[22]

Eisler's decision to compose music both continuous and fast contributes to the sense of an unremitting and relentless energy. This contradicts rhythmic and temporal signals in the filmic construction at certain points. For while "new differentiations,"[23] which resist "sham collectivity" based upon non-alignment and music's refusal to "intoxicate,"[24] are desirable as a general principle, Eisler's observation that *Rain* is "plotless and therefore static"[25] seems an oversimplified reading of this specific film. The decision to rule out slow tempos, and to adhere strictly to developmental and non-repetitive structures, was driven by ideology and not by reflective analysis upon the particular requirements of the picture.

To illustrate the significance of tempo differentiation and the issue of continuity versus discontinuity, Table 5.1 is a table of *Rain's* shots 95 to 129, beginning at approximately 6'25." This sequence moves from city forms to landscape, and then back to city forms. There are three aspects to the perception of movement in visual terms: the first is relative duration of shots; the second is movement within the shots; and the third is montage of shots.

During this sequence there is a transition from medium-length shots, to long shots, back to medium-length shots; and from onscreen movement to near stillness to onscreen movement. Throughout, the montage construction in groups of four shots is confirmed by temporal consistency of shot-length within each group.

Eisler had excluded the possibility of a slow tempo; my reading of this sequence is that it represents a critical shift from movement to stasis and back to movement, and that the emotional center of the film is located in the "adagio" landscape section. For whereas Eisler denounced symphonic form as regressive, one of the notable aspects of early musical modernism in the late nineteenth and early twentieth century was its elision, not liquidation, of sections of symphonic movements. This was one path initially pursued by composers such as Liszt, Richard Strauss, and Schoenberg to achieve greater fluidity and internal structural complexity. As an analogy with Joris Ivens's achievement here, in visual terms, this seems more apt than the model of developmental variation based on short forms. In this case, the transition to a reflective landscape phase compels a transformative musical reading with a slower metronome mark. Although this mapping is perhaps predictable and no doubt imbued with a problematic subjectivity, it is motivated by the form of the visual material itself and clarifies the montage patterns of the picture. In addition, the insertion of silence permits a kind of aural cleansing through fragmentation. The active coexistence of different languages (aural and visual) is acknowledged, without the one dominating the other.

In this essay I have focused on specific aspects of Eisler's composition process in relation to his score for *Rain* which seem to invite debate. In particular, I have questioned his assumption that advanced musical resources necessarily correspond with advanced visual resources. For while the modernism of Ivens and Eisler is not in doubt, what seems increasingly clear is that modernism in one is not equivalent to modernism in the other. Filmic modernism is concerned with clarity, motion, and the aestheticization of everyday objects (such as the umbrella); musical modernism, on the other hand, is concerned with the development of an opaque, baroque, and self-referential language. As a result, it is possible that Eisler's score to Ivens's short film generated a dissonant friction; a friction symptomatic, perhaps, of larger issues of mismatch between the worlds of music and visual arts.

Nevertheless, Eisler's agenda for change was visionary and remains relevant, which is extraordinary in a document that is now sixty years old. It is unfair to characterize Adorno and Eisler's investigation as "testy and relatively valueless."[26] Many ideas spring out of the pages of *Composing for the Films* and claim attention today. For example, their discussion of the industry's pursuit of "technification" over aesthetic development in cinema; their analysis of "pseudo-individualization"; their recommendation to use streamlined small ensembles and to deploy new electronic sounds instead of formulaic large ensembles. These and other observations are still pertinent to the development of new film music languages. In his pursuit of a new language for film music in the 1940s, Hanns Eisler was both idealistic and exemplary; and if his commitment to an avant-garde language of advanced musical resources created some blind-spots in his response to the picture, then this was no doubt in part a function of necessarily different negotiations of modernity between the new technologies of film and the older art of music. If a dissonance between musical and visual languages is embodied in the intriguing 1941 synchronization of Eisler's music to Ivens's picture, then the negotiation required to resolve it was neatly envisaged by Adorno and Eisler in their closing remarks: "Cinema music should sparkle and glisten. It should attain the quick pace of the casual listening imposed by the picture, and not be left behind."[27]

Notes

1. Adorno and Eisler, *Composing for the Films.*
2. Ibid., 19.
3. Ibid., 106.
4. Ibid., 108.
5. Ibid., 148.
6. Ibid., 101.
7. Cook, *Analysing Musical Multimedia,* 49 (quoting from Hahl-Koch, *Arnold Schoenberg,* 149).
8. Eisenstein, *The Film Sense,* 138; his emphasis.
9. For Eisenstein (color) tones evade "absolute" values; they are instead "dependent only upon the general system of imagery that has been decided upon for the particular film" (ibid., 151).
10. Ibid., 161.
11. Ibid., 174.
12. Adorno and Eisler, *Composing for the Films,* 67; although Eisler uses descending pitch very effectively in bars 263 to 266 of *Fourteen Ways,* which, in the new reconstruction of *Rain* by the musicologist Johannes Gall, clearly equates with the onset of darkness (fade to black).
13. Ibid., 154.
14. Ibid.
15. Ibid., 155–56.
16. Ibid., 148.
17. Other, longer examples include *Berlin: Die Sinfonie der Großstadt* (Berlin: Symphony

of a City, Ruttmann, 1927), *Chelovek s kino-apparatom* (Man with a Movie Camera, Vertov, 1929), and *People on Sunday* (Siodmak, 1930)

18. Copy A, derived from the London Film Society's print. Thanks to Andrew Youdell, BFI.

19. Adorno and Eisler, *Composing for the Films*, 101.

20. Cook, *Analysing Musical Multimedia*, 65.

21. Adorno and Eisler, *Composing for the Films*, 38.

22. Ibid., 101,

23. Ibid.

24. Ibid., 23–24. Eisler's oppositional use of music works to profound effect in other films, such as *Kuhle Wampe: oder: Wem gehört die Welt?* (To Whom Does the World Belong?, Dudow, 1932) and *Nuit et brouillard* (Night and Fog, Resnais, 1955), where the character of Eisler's music is deliberately antithetical to the human misery depicted in the images, in order to arouse resistance and an active response in the viewer.

25. Ibid., 101.

26. Prendergast, *Film Music*, 3.

27. Adorno and Eisler, *Composing for the Films*, 133.

References

Adorno, Theodor, and Hanns Eisler. *Composing for the Films*. Oxford: Oxford University Press, 1947.

Cook, Nicholas. *Analysing Musical Multimedia*. Oxford: Oxford University Press, 1998.

Eisenstein, Sergei. *The Film Sense*. Trans. J. Leyda. New York: Harcourt, Brace, 1947.

Hahl-Koch, Jelena, ed. *Arnold Schoenberg-Wassily Kandinsky: Letters, Pictures and Documents*. Trans. J. Crawford. London: Faber, 1984.

Prendergast, Roy M. *Film Music: A Neglected Art*. New York: Norton, 1992.

Filmography

REGEN (RAIN)

release:	14 December 1929, Netherlands
duration:	12 mins
dir:	Joris Ivens; Mannus Franken
prod co:	Capi-Holland
camera:	Joris Ivens
music:	Lou Lichtveld (1929); Hanns Eisler (1941); Ed Hughes (2001)

SIX

"Composition with Film": Mauricio Kagel as Filmmaker

BJÖRN HEILE

In his late article "Filmtransparente," Theodor W. Adorno mentions the film *Antithese* by the Argentine-German composer Mauricio Kagel as one of the most powerful examples for his thesis that the most fruitful potential for film is to be found in influences from other media, in this case music.[1] A relatively obscure production for West Germany's third television channel was thereby elevated to one of very few positive examples in the text, which is a darker, but also arguably more poignant, analysis of the medium than Adorno's earlier and better known collaboration with Hanns Eisler.[2] Although it would be simplistic to regard Kagel's cinematographic approach as a practical realization of Adorno's aesthetics, it may be illuminating to see what the philosopher found in the composer's work. Where both agree is on the critique of what Adorno calls the "reactionary nature of any aesthetic realism today,"[3] which the vast majority of films adhered to, then and now, resulting in a growing divergence from the most progressive tendencies in the visual arts. For the avant-gardist Kagel, bringing film to a similar level of artistic development as exhibited by the other arts could only be achieved through a radical questioning of the conventions of the genre, notably filmic illusion. As an outsider to the industry, he was particularly well placed to critique habitual practices, and he was independent enough to be able to ignore them.

In a sense, Kagel's filmic work rests on taking cinema's claim to represent a multimedia art form literally. Consequently, his films are audio-visual compositions in which sound and image are independent but interrelated elements, which contribute equally to the overall effect. Whereas the intersection of composition and film is conventionally film music, or music film, in Kagel's case the film *is* the music.

Depending on definition, Kagel has produced some twenty-one mostly short films (see the filmography at the end of this chapter). The majority of them are music films, that is, television productions of pre-existing stage works. After some fifteen years of filmmaking, Kagel also reluctantly agreed to compose "proper" film music, namely for Buñuel's and Dalí's *Un chien andalou* (An Andalusian Dog, 1929), the synchronized version of which was produced and distributed by Swiss Television (DRS) in 1983. Although Kagel's achievements in either category are noteworthy (in particular, his score for *Un chien andalou* unquestionably adds a whole new dimension to the film), I want to concentrate on those works where the film *is* the composition. By this I mean that they are autonomous productions not directly connected to pre-existing music, and that there is no primacy of either visual or sonic element. The films which arguably show Kagel's most creative reconceptualization of the medium in this sense are *Antithese* (1965), *Solo* (1967), *Duo* (1968), and *Ludwig van* (1969).[4] The musical perspective Kagel brings to cinema in these works is not confined to "rhythmic" cuts or developing structural proportions in accordance with musical forms. Rather, his explorations are founded on the principles that film is hardly ever silent, just as music is not an exclusively acoustic phenomenon. His cinematographic approach is therefore not characterized by simply combining music and film, but by making artistic use of diegetic (or seemingly diegetic) sound as well as the visual elements of music.

The Search for a Visual Music

Kagel's interest in film dates back to his early years in Buenos Aires. In a recently published interview, he talked about pestering staff at the film studio in his immediate neighborhood until being admitted to observe the work, and finally to participate as an extra (alongside one of the principal actresses, one Ev[it]a Duarte, later Perón). During the shortages of World War II and its aftermath, Kagel was involved in restoring films that had been destined for recycling into raw material for the chemical industry.[5] The restored films were to act as the stock of the Cinémathèque Argentine, of which Kagel was a founding member. He also claims to have been the first to synchronize René Clair's *Entr'acte* with Satie's music for the film.[6] In 1954, he wrote the music to Alejandro Sanderman's *Muertos de Buenos Aires* on Jorge Luis Borges's poem of the same title (now in the Museum of Modern Art, New York); the film was duly banned by the censors for showing people searching for food on a landfill (that Borges was *persona non grata* may also have played a role). Shortly after that, Kagel himself directed another film which featured empty buildings; this was accompanied by "acoustical loops" from a chamber ensemble, thus introducing the deliberate non-synchronicity which would become a hallmark of his later films. His interest in visual media also led him to work as cinema and photography editor for the journal *nueva visión,* which was edited by one of his university lecturers, none other than Borges.

As a composer, Kagel was essentially self-taught, since he had failed the entrance exam to the conservatoire. Nevertheless, his close association with the Agrupación Nueva Música and his work as rehearsal pianist and assistant conductor at the Teatro Colón, the Buenos Aires opera house, made him a familiar figure in the bustling musical life of the Argentine capital.[7] Acting on the advice of Pierre Boulez, Kagel applied for a scholarship to work at Karlheinz Stockhausen's and Herbert Eimert's electronic studio in Cologne.[8] According to him it was only after winning the grant and settling in Germany (where he has lived ever since) in 1957 that Kagel finally decided to concentrate on composition.[9]

Given this background, it is not surprising that a significant part of his work explores the interrelations between the visual and sonic spheres, and, as a consequence, the development of a "visual music." His cinematographic works are important milestones in this respect. His understanding of film as a musical genre is evident when he describes "composition with film [as] the only possible continuation of opera"—which did not stop him from writing operas.[10] This reveals a holistic concept of music which by far transcends the conventional meaning of the word, and according to which—similar, if in many ways diametrically opposed to, John Cage—everything can be or become music, including non-sounding material.

For an understanding of these ideas, it is best to turn to Kagel's most celebrated innovation with respect to the integration of sight and sound, the "instrumental theater," since its development predates his filmic works and provides some of the fundamental artistic discoveries later also employed in the films.[11] The instrumental theater is based on the visual associations of music and the kinetic qualities of music making, which are normally suppressed in concert music. Thus, the dramatic potential and corporeal properties of music making are emphasized to a point where sound *production* and the sound *produced* are amalgamated into one integral music-theatrical action. Conversely, a primarily scenic action may focus on sound production as an activity, so that the sound produced cannot be regarded as a purely narrative and accidental event as in conventional theater. Either way, the performance often verges on the boundary between ordinary musical performances and diegetic music in some kind of fictional play, resulting in a dream-like, surreal atmosphere.

In this way, visual processes can be conceptualized as rhythmicized motion, while conversely music can be understood as the result of a potentially theatrical, kinetic action, a principle also applied in Kagel's films. This is what Kagel must have had in mind when he claimed that one can compose with "sounding and non-sounding objects, [such as] actors, cups, tables, omnibuses and oboes, and finally . . . film."[12] To give a short example: in *Pas de cinq* (1965) five actors walk across the stage in specified patterns outlining a pentagon. Their steps are scored in precise rhythmic notation, and they also use walking sticks for additional rhythmic complexity. The stage setting consists of ramps of different materials, producing variations in pitch, timbre, and resonance. Here, the visual and sonic spheres have been integrally linked to one another in a non-hierarchical way: it makes little sense to suggest either that the sounds produced are just accidental by-products of the action (as in conventional theater or film), or that the stage action is just a way to realize the musical rhythms (as in standard music performances).

A similar effect is at work in one of Kagel's earliest films, *Solo,* which is a distant adaptation of *Visible Music II* (later to be called *nostalgie,* 1962) by Kagel's friend and fellow composer Dieter Schnebel. At the beginning of the film, a conductor is wandering around in a room full of elaborate *art nouveau* decorations. The sound of the conductor's steps precedes his visual appearance by about a minute; hence the sound is "acousmatic."[13] Their acousmatic nature enables us to hear the sounds as forming a musical rhythm, something diegetic noise discourages since the immediate connection to the visible source renders the sounds as such perceptually opaque (this is one reason for Kagel's critique of diegetic sound). Nevertheless, the possibility of hearing the footsteps as music remains intact even after their source is revealed and they are connected diegetically to the image track. The modesty of means notwithstanding, this re-evaluation of the audiovisual process of walking challenges the accepted hierarchy between image and sound: not only does the sound of the footsteps appear as equally important as the image of the walking conductor, but we are also encouraged to hear them aesthetically, not purely semantically. In this way, Kagel draws the consequences from the overcoming of the distinction between noise and music in the twentieth century: noise track and underscore become one—or at least their rigid separation in classical film practice is undermined through a mutual rapprochement. In this audiovisual composition, the camera movement, with its slow pans, plays an important part: rather than simply capturing the protagonist, it seems to have a life of its own, and the steadiness of its rhythm makes it appear like a part in an audiovisual polyphony.

Film as Multimedia Art Form

This blurring of the boundary between noise and music and the resulting new combinations between the visual and sonic spheres are already well advanced in Kagel's first film in Europe, the aforementioned *Antithese* ("antithesis"). In the film, an engineer's grappling with an enormous pile of malfunctioning technology is coupled with electronic music, making it almost impossible to separate the noise coming from the assembled gadgetry and the underscore.[14] This anti-illusionist effect is reconfirmed by *Antithese*'s constant play with the diegetic connection between image and sound. This hardly ever accords to expectations (or if it does, it is hardly less surprising), but is out of synch or slightly mismatched, when, for instance, the engineer's shooting with a handgun is combined with the belated sound of machine gun fire. In this, as in most, cases, the "original" sound has been replaced by a different sound from the same semantic field. In instances such as this, Kagel is using the surrealists' techniques of association by connecting objects through overlapping semantic fields, physical likeness, or—more innovative on Kagel's part—similar sound.[15]

This slight mismatch calls attention to the strict conformity between sight and accompanying diegetic noise in conventional narrative cinema. At the same time, it underlines the content of the film, which consists of an eerily comical version of the old tale of the battle between man and machine. In *Antithese,* the mysterious relations between visual events and noise production depict a world with strange unknowable rules. This accords with the engineer's perception; he is unable to control the machinery, since it seems to function according to laws he cannot fathom. Another occasion of what Adeline Mueller calls "false diegesis" shows the engineer joining two hoses together producing the sound of running water, although it is clearly visible that no water is flowing.[16] He then combines two smaller hoses producing a higher-pitched sound. A little later, the sound suddenly stops, after which the engineer puts a small pipe loosely into a big hose, both of which lie on the ground unconnected, thus enabling the water to flow again—acoustically, that is. Here, the combination between image and sound appears strangely natural, although it is totally illogical: we can unmistakably see that the hoses do not contain water, and that there is no reason why it should flow or stop flowing. Nevertheless, the mental associations tube-noise-running water and smaller tube-higher pitch are so ingrained that the scene seems to "make sense," if in a rather surreal way. The undermining of supposedly natural diegesis, which goes almost unquestioned in mainstream illusionist cinema, leads to a liberation of sound from its subservient role as the accompanying shadow of screen action, and consequently enables the treatment of image and sound as independent categories, which can be correlated according to artistic criteria.

In order to clarify the image-sound relations established by Kagel, it may be useful to refer to the theories of Michel Chion, which arguably offer the most sophisticated account of the cinematic use of sound. Chion is at pains to point out that diegetic sound is not simply natural, but deliberately produced for specific artistic effects. Nonetheless, his theories never challenge the principle of cinematic illusion and the primacy of the visual. Even the most complex image-sound relation he describes, "synchresis,"[17] in which image and sound are welded together without any rational basis, is apparently meant to create perceptual fusion in that the sound—although objectively unrelated—is to be reduced to its visible source by the recipient. By contrast, Kagel deliberately tries to drive a wedge between seeing and hearing, causing the audience to question their senses. Interestingly, though, not just any image-sound relation will do: *Antithese* starts with only slight desynchronization of diegetic sounds, and later relations, such as the one between handgun and machine gun, while obviously incommensurable, are also clearly semantically related. Thus, the noise track does not simply double the image track, but adds a completely different level of meaning which demands interpretation. In contrast to the illusionist apparatus of conventional cinema, which bypasses conscious perception, thereby also opening the doors to ideological manipulation, this approach engages the audience's intellect. Kagel lets the puppets dance, but he makes sure that the strings are visible. It is Kagel's implicit critique of cinematic realism and its capacity to blind the audience which must have attracted Adorno, since—as so often with Adorno—his remark that any aesthetic realism is reactionary has to be understood ideologically as well as aesthetically.

More than Chion's theories, Sergei Eisenstein's idea of audiovisual montage may offer a way into Kagel's approach to audiovisual composition. Eisenstein based his concept of "vertical montage"[18] on the same principles as purely visual montages ("horizontal montages," as it were, although Eisenstein does not employ this term), the latter being defined as the process whereby *"two film pieces of any kind, placed together, inevitably combine into a new concept, arising out of that juxtaposition."*[19] If vertical montages work in the same way, the acoustic component must be thought of as an independent element that plays an equal role in forming the synthetic concept. In other words, its function and meaning is not necessarily pre-determined by the image (as it is in Chion's work). Indeed, Eisenstein makes clear that image-sound relations do not have to be harmonious, but can be based on dissonance, syncopation, or "rhythmical counterpoint";[20] in any case, they have to be *compositionally controlled.*[21] This idea of a compositional control of potentially heterogeneous image-sound relations makes Eisenstein's concept of vertical montage relevant for a discus-

Table 6.1. Relations between image and sound according to Kagel

Image	Sound
A) Instrumental Action	1. Silence (silent movie)
	2. Full Synchronicity: same rhythm and instrument
	3. Rhythmic Synchronicity: same rhythm, different instrument
	4. Asynchronicity: same rhythm and instrument, but out of synch with image
	5. Rhythmic Asynchronicity: same rhythm, different instrument, out of synch
	6. Parallelism: different rhythm, same instrument
	7. No relation: different rhythm, different instrument
B) Ordinary action with sounding materials	1. Silence (silent movie)
	2. Synchronicity
	3. Asynchronicity
	4. No relation between image and sound
	[N.B.: Kagel's practice explores more relations in analogy to A]
C) Diverse	1. Silence (silent movie)
	2. Background sound: 'mood music,' 'atmosphere'

sion of Kagel's work, despite Eisenstein's famously questionable talk of correspondences in his own audio-visual analysis of a sequence from his *Alexander Nevsky,* which falls short of his theoretical insights.[22]

The most far-reaching realizations in Kagel's work of the techniques discussed so far is *Duo* (1968), which is loosely based on Schnebel's *Visible Music I* (1960–62). Table 6.1 shows Kagel's own conceptualization (which I have translated and edited) of the different relations between image and sound—different types of vertical montages, to employ Eisenstein's terminology—in *Duo,* as quoted by Schnebel from Kagel's program note for a presentation of the film at the Donaueschinger Musiktage (Kagel's sketches for the later *Ludwig van* contain a similar table).[23] In the example, Kagel focuses on the depiction of music making (category A), but it is clear that the relations between other objects or actions and noise (category B) can be described in the same way, leading to the same seven options, which also accords with Kagel's artistic practice in *Duo.*

What is striking here is that category C, the underscore, is "under-theorized," and it is true that Kagel at that time (i.e., before his music for *Un chien andalou*) was more concerned with diegesis or its undermining. All the music heard in *Duo* can in some way be regarded as diegetic. This is connected with the premise of the film which consists of manifold transformations of two characters, one a tramp who has stolen an exotic plucked instrument and keeps popping up in unlikely places playing unusual string instruments, and the other an immaculately groomed shopkeeper who pursues him. (In the manner of chains of associations I mention above, the transformations become more and more abstract until they bear little relation to the original characters, retaining only the basic structure of two men pursuing one another.) However, in order to interpret the music as diegetic, one often has to assume that an instrumental action seen earlier carries on in the background, even where this is not quite possible, as for instance during a subway ride. Conversely, the "source" of the music heard for some time is often only revealed several scenes later, when, as in one instance, the camera pans to one of the characters who is playing in a window pane quite far away (which would clearly be inaudible in a real-life situation).

The first rapid sequence of scenes in *Duo* presents a variety of relations between image and sounds according to Kagel's own table (Table 6.1), the most consistently used being "rhythmic synchronicity" in category B, meaning that the sounding object is different from the one shown but the rhythm is the same and in synch—a *trompe l'oreille* effect that Kagel particular loves. The sequence begins after the titles with the first character (A), the tramp, entering a music shop.[24] While crossing the street, he appears to cause a car crash which we hear but do not see (which makes one wonder why such discrepancy between image and sound is not exploited more often, since it is obviously consistent with verisimilitude). Although the (apparently desynchronized) shop bell announces his entry, he has to alert the second character (B), the shopkeeper, and gestures him to demonstrate a guitar, proceeding to "conduct" him with his gestures (which is an element from Schnebel's composition). In a humorously illogical connection between image and sound, the striking of a string seems to start a car outside which can be heard driving away. While the shopkeeper busies himself on the guitar, the tramp snatches another instrument and runs out, quickly followed by the shopkeeper. They then chase one another around a monument (the Bismarck memorial in Hamburg). While running, the tramp picks up a wreath which he rolls with the help of a stick like a children's toy. The sound produced by this is often slightly different from what we see, while belonging to the same semantic category. For instance, the wreath appears to be a laurel wreath (although this is hard to see in black and white), but sounds as if it were made out of bronze. When it falls from a wall onto the concrete it produces a sound as from an object thrown into water; due to the similar physical appearance one is reminded of a life preserver. Since the wreath on the ground

Table 6.2. Analysis of first sequence of *Duo*

Time	Image	Sound
0:00	Titles in shop window (some moving from left to right), in the background passing cars	Diegetic (atmosphere)
0:25	A comes running (seen in the shop window)	Continued
0:35	On reaching door, camera pans sideways on door and A	Car crash
0:40	A enters shop	Shop bell (desynchronized?)
0:45	B decorates shop (and A)	Diegetic
1:15	A knocks on guitar, gestures to B to demonstrate it	Diegetic (guitar plus atmosphere
1:17	B strikes string	String sound transforms into starting car
1:20	A conducts B	Diegetic
1:35	A grabs another instrument, runs out, quickly followed by B	Continued
1:45	Both can be seen through the shop window running away	Continued
1:55	Cut to Bismark memorial, A takes laurel wreath, rolls it, wreath rolls in the path of B	Brass metal (bronze?) on ground
2:05	A rolls wreath again	Continued
2:13	A lies next to wreath on ground	Atmosphere
2:15	Camera glides down monument to memorial ribbon	Continued
2:25	A jumps from wall	Percussion entry
2:30	A rolls rubber tire	Wooden hoop
2:40	Camera pans to head of monument	Atmosphere
2:45	Both characters run, rolling wreaths	Continued
3:00	Both characters run around monument, camera turns over sideways; when both change direction, camera turns over sideways in other direction	Continued
3:10	Camera pans to head of monument, zooming to include whole monument; end of sequence	Continued

looks funereal, we next see the tramp lying next to it, as if dead. However, in this instance the associative links have only temporarily overridden the actual plot, and the chase soon goes on. Shortly afterward, in the manner of a chain of associations, the wreath transforms into a rubber tire which produces the sound of a wooden hoop. There are also cartoon effects such as a downward-moving percussion figure when the tramp jumps from a wall. (Table 6.2 gives an overview of the relations between images and sounds in this sequence.)

The systematic replacement of the expected sound with one produced by objects of similar shape but different material in the chase scene creates a discrepancy between the aural and the visual sides of the story, not unlike the invisible car crash and the starting car earlier, or, for that matter, the handgun scene in *Antithese*. Led by habit to mainstream narrative cinema, we might regard the images as telling the "right" story and some of the noises to be replaced by "false" ones. However, that would mean to disregard Kagel's challenge to the traditional hierarchy between image and sound. For *Duo* rests on the premise that there is nothing natural about diegetic noise, and that this is only one of a variety of combinations between image and noise tracks. The film demonstrates that different types of vertical montage can be used to great (in this instance mostly comical) effect and thus enrich cinema.

In the course of *Duo,* there are also more disparate combinations of image and sound than the rhythmic synchronicity discussed earlier. For instance, on some occasions the noise track undoubtedly bears what little there is of a narrative thread, whereas the image has been replaced (the exact opposite of "rhythmic synchronicity"), as when the sound of a toilet flush—an essential part of the story here—is coupled with footage of Niagara Falls, which has no direct connection with the narrative. Another instance sees the music "illustrating" a painting in an antique shop, which depicts music making in the Bach household, by using the same instruments as seen; the music enters exactly when these come into view. There are also mock-baroque elements, although the music is extremely dissonant like the rest of the sound track; and, as mentioned, the diegetic function of the playing of instruments onscreen also becomes more and more complex throughout the film.

The Legacy of Integral Serialism and Its Influence on Conceptions of Multimedia

The intentional systematization evident from Table 6.1 and the independence accorded to image and sound points to a rather unexpected influence from the musical postwar avant-garde: integral serialism. It appears as if Kagel treats image and sound as parameters which can be controlled independently of one another, but also correlated according to artistic criteria, replacing the uncritical acceptance of the conformance of the two in mainstream narrative cinema. Schnebel goes so far as to suggest that Kagel's use of film techniques such as cut, camera angle, perspective, and camera movement is also governed by serialist principles, and Kagel himself has spoken about the use of number series for determining cut sequences and decoration in *Antithese*.[25] Although the prominence and perceptual validity of such numerical rows is questionable, the positing of correlatable independent parameters—a more fundamental principle of integral serialism—is clearly in evidence, and proves fruitful for a reconceptualization of the relations between image and sound.

The richest and most varied interactions between noise, music, and screen action take place in *Ludwig van*, which, at some hundred minutes, is also the only full-length of Kagel's films (albeit a television production). In fact, as far as the types of vertical montage employed are concerned, it is a synthesis of the three earlier films already mentioned. The focus in *Antithese* on asynchronicity, false diegesis, and generally bridging the gap between noise track and underscore, the concentration in *Solo* on the musical use of diegetic noise, the exploration in *Duo* of rhythmic synchronicity in Kagel's sense (i.e., sound from a different source than shown), and the experimental employment of diegetic music: all are combined in *Ludwig van*.

The film was produced for the bicentenary of Beethoven's birth, and, predictably, created a huge scandal. The first part shows Beethoven, personified by the camera (his shoes and gloved hands appear from time to time), arriving by train in Bonn and visiting his (imaginary) "home" (the rooms have been designed by the notable visual artists Diter Roth, Robert Filiou, Ursula Burghardt, Stefan Wewerka, and Joseph Beuys) before making a trip on the Rhine aboard a steamer. The latter part of the film acts as a caricature of the Beethoven cult, consisting of a confusing conglomeration of scenes, loosely held together by their common relation to Beethoven and the history of his reception. This is presented as a satire on television, in that deliberately unprofessional presenters appear from time to time, as if to introduce the following scenes, which, however, have little to do with the announcements. Some of these scenes are also modeled on popular programs of the time, particularly a discussion round with Kagel and some music critics for which Kagel managed to enlist the moderator and the set of a widely watched political program.

All the music in the film is by Beethoven, but arranged by Kagel for a rather ill-balanced ensemble and played "scratchily," thus producing a "damaged" collage of the original music. The relations between image and sound are based on the same principles outlined by Table 6.1; but what is unique about *Ludwig van* is the way Kagel uses all imaginable relations and degrees between the two spheres, and the subtlety of his playing with the boundary between diegetic and non-diegetic music, as well as diegetic and non-diegetic noise. The sound track appears to be underscore, but every now and then music is played on screen, often without breaking the continuity of the sound track. This happens, for instance, on the steamer where Beethoven from time to time catches glimpses of musicians who always disappear before he can really observe them play. Such diegetic music making may not conform to the music heard, but it can be out of synch, consist of the wrong instruments, and so forth.

Another possible interpretation is that the underscore represents Beethoven's imagination. which is plausible given that we see part of the film through his eyes. This is what Gorbman seems to refer to as "metadiegetic" music—music which is not actually heard on the scene but imagined by one of the characters.[26] However, this illusion is also occasionally broken, as when all of a sudden the music sounds distorted and flat. The "reason" is revealed a moment later: in a record shop (whose shop windows displayed exclusively Beethoven records), we see people listen to recordings played through telephone speakers (as was the practice then). Thus we are to understand that we have been hearing those people's music! The same happens also with the noise track (if more logically): in the *Beethovenhaus,* one hears an irritating ticking noise for some time; again the source is revealed only later when the camera pans to a passing freighter on the Rhine nearby (as in similar cases, one is made aware of the non-existence of unrelated noise without a narrative function in mainstream cinema).

The use of the underscore as some kind of musical interior monologue in voiceover is spectacularly realized in the most famous scene from *Ludwig van,* in which Beethoven examines the music room in the fictional *Beethovenhaus,* designed by Kagel himself after plans by the Czech artist Jiří Kolár (who did not get a visa to participate directly).[27] In the room, all surfaces are plastered over with scores of Beethoven's music, which are heard in real time as the camera slowly passes by, panning and zooming (though the music played does not always conform to the scores displayed on the wall). Since the snippets of music coming into view hardly ever reveal key signatures, tempo markings, or even clefs, the audible result is a curiously defamiliarized version of the original music, although it is always recognizable as Beethovenian. One of the most striking instances is when a mirror comes into view and the resulting music sounds as if it has been turned upside down.

This scene features perhaps the most "musicianly" technique of finding new image-sound relations that Kagel has developed, but it should be seen in the context of his constant quest for such innovations in *Ludwig van* and the earlier films. It is somewhat unfortunate that Kagel turned to fairly straightforward television adaptations of his stage works after *Ludwig van,* even though he took pains to adapt these pieces for the new medium, and continued to use filmic techniques at this disposal in original ways. Nevertheless, none of his later films quite approach the earlier ones in critiquing the nature of acoustic diegesis (whether of music or noise), or exploiting the avant-gardist overcoming of the division between music and noise in making artistic use of the noise track. It is in his earlier films from *Antithese* to *Ludwig van* that Kagel developed challenging vertical montages of image and sound that treat both as independent parameters under "compositional control," this control achieved through the techniques of integral serialism. Adorno never had a chance to see Kagel's later works, but we can surmise that what he valued in *Antithese* was the critical impulse behind the non-hierarchical dialogue between image and sound; in other words, the step from cinematic realism to a genuine aesthetics of multimedia. What would he have made of *Ludwig van*?

Notes

1. Adorno, "Filmtransparente," 358.
2. Adorno and Eisler, *Composing.*
3. Adorno, "Filmtransparente," 357.
4. My approach is diametrically opposed to Hillebrand, *Film als totale Komposition,* in that she focuses on the way preexisting pieces are adapted cinematically, so relegating the films I study to the sidelines. She thus avoids a discussion of precisely those works in which Kagel engages most intimately with the medium and its integral syntax. Her points of comparison are literary adaptations, another genre all too frequently bogged down by its adherence to models outside the actual medium at the expense of filmic techniques properly speaking. Admittedly, my selection is not as hard and fast as it could be, since *Antithese* is also based on an electronic piece and a stage work of the same title (both 1962). However, Kagel has also used another electronic piece, *Transición I* (1958), in the sound track, and the film expands on the earlier versions. Some of the films I have classed as adaptations also considerably enlarge on their respective pieces (for instance, *Match* and *Hallelujah*), but the films I have chosen seem to me to be Kagel's most adventurous from a cinematographic point of view.
5. Klüppelholz, *Kagel: Dialoge, Monologe,* 168ff.
6. Kagel, *Das Burch der Hörspiele,* 316; Reich, "Mauricio Kagel," 4.
7. Attinello, "Kagel, Mauricio."
8. Klüppelholz, *Kagel: Dialoge, Monologe,* 38.
9. Kagel said as much in a recent radio interview with Martin Demmler, broadcast on Sender Freies Berlin (SFB). See also Pauli, *Für wen komponieren sie eigentlich?* 88.
10. Ibid., 89.
11. For the instrumental theater see Kagel, "Über das Instrumentale Theater"; Kagel, "Neuer Raum; " Decroupet and Kovács, "Neue Musik"; Gindt, "Sur les chemins"; Kovács, "Instrumentales Theater"; Roelcke, "Instrumentales Theater"; Sarkisjan, "Instrumentales Theater"; Schnebel, *Mauricio Kagel;* Stoianova, "Multiplicité"; Zarius, "Szenische Komposition"; and Zarius, "Inszenierte Musik." For an account of the traditions of music theater and musical multimedia Kagel builds on, see Kesting, "Musikalisierung des Theaters," and Kesting, "Die Erschöpfung."
12. Quoted in Nicolai, "Türen öffnen."
13. For the distinction between acousmatic and diegetic sound see Chion, *Audio-Vision,* 71ff.
14. Mueller, "Corporealisation."
15. This technique of combining image and sound as well as different sounds in various ways will be described further in my discussion of *Duo* below. Another example, also from *Duo*, shows this effect at its best: at the beginning of the scene one sees treetops and hears

birds chirping (some of which are clearly exotic and cannot be found in Hamburg where the scene is set—another instance of Kagel's subversion of illusion). Then an iron eagle moves into the picture, which soon after turns out to be the top of a ridiculous mock-historical helmet. What is so comical about the scene is that the connection between chirping and the helmet first seems entirely natural, although eagles do not chirp, even if they are not part of an iron helmet. The semantic connection chirping-bird is so strong that for a moment it overrules plausibility.

16. Mueller, "Corporealisation," 36ff.

17. Chion, *Audio-Vision,* 63.

18. Eisenstein, *The Film Sense,* 61.

19. Ibid., 16; emphasis in the original.

20. Ibid., 68.

21. Ibid., 69; emphasis in the original.

22. Ibid., 114–56.

23. Kagel's program note, Donaueschinger Musiktage 1969, quoted in Schnebel, *Mauricio Kagel,* 220ff. The sketch materials for *Ludwig van* contain a similar system (Mauricio Kagel Collection, Paul Sacher Foundation Basle).

24. Some of the titles actually move from left to right, so the words have to be read in reverse order. The explanation for this is that the first shot presents a shop window, and the titles mimic the mirror images of passing cars that can be seen in the background.

25. Schnebel, *Mauricio Kagel,* 111ff.; Klüppelholz, *Kagel: Dialoge, Monologe,* 182.

26. Gorbman, *Unheard Melodies,* 22–23.

27. This can be inferred from letters among the sketch materials kept in the Mauricio Kagel Collection of the Paul Sacher Foundation Basle (Switzerland), which allow detailed insight into the production process of the film.

References

Adorno, Theodor W. "Filmtransparente." In *Ohne Leitbild: Parva Aesthetica, Gesammelte Schriften,* vol. 10/1. 1967. Reprint, Frankfurt: Suhrkamp, 1977, 353–61.

Adorno, Theodor W., and Hanns Eisler. *Composing for the Films.* London: Athlone, 1994.

Attinello, Paul. "Kagel, Mauricio." In *The New Grove Dictionary of Music and Musicians,* 2nd ed., ed. S. Sadie. London: Macmillan, 2001.

Chion, Michel. *Audio-Vision: Sound on Screen,* ed. and trans. C. Gorbman. New York: Columbia University Press, 1994.

Decroupet, Pascal, and Inge Kovács. "Neue Musik—Neue Szene." In *Im Zenit der Moderne: Die Internationalen Ferienkurse für Neue Musik Darmstadt 1946–1966,* ed. G. Borio and H. Danuser, 4 vols. Freiburg im Breisgau: Rombach, 1997, 2:311–32.

Eisenstein, Sergei M. *The Film Sense.* Ed. and trans. J. Leyda. London: Faber and Faber, 1943.

Gindt, Antoine. "Sur les chemins d'Aperghis et de Kagel: Introduction à l'analyse du théâtre musical." *Analyse Musicale* 27 (1992): 60–64.

Gorbman, Claudia. *Unheard Melodies: Narrative Film Music.* London: British Film Institute, 1988.

Hillebrand, Christiane. *Film als totale Komposition: Analyse und Vergleich der Filme Mauricio Kagels.* Frankfurt am Main: Lang, 1994.

Kagel, Mauricio. *Das Burch der Hörspiele.* Ed. Klaus Schöning. Frankfurt am Main: Suhrkamp, 1982.

———. "Neuer Raum—Neue Musik: Gedanken zum Instrumentalen Theater [1966]." In *Im Zenit der Moderne: Die Internationalen Ferienkurse für Neue Musik Darmstadt 1946–1966,* ed. G. Borio and H. Danuser, 4 vols. Freiburg im Breisgau: Rombach, 1997, 3:245–53.

———. "Über das Instrumentale Theater." *Neue Musik: Kunst- und gesellschaftskritische Beiträge* 3 (1961), n.p. (abridged). Reprints: *Nutida Musik* 3 (1960/61), n.p.; *Dansk Musiktid-*

schrift 7 (1962), n.p.; *Hefte des Ulmer Theaters* 7 (1963), n.p.; *Hefte der Kölner Bühnen* 4 (1963/64), n.p.

Kesting, Marianne. "Die Erschöpfung des Kunstwerks: Imaginäre Musik oder musikalisches Theater der Verhinderung." In *Kagel. . . . /1991,* ed. W. Klüppelholz. Cologne: DuMont, 1991, 221–30.

———. "Musikalisierung des Theaters—Theatralisierung der Musik." *Melos* 3 (1969): 101–9.

Klüppelholz, Werner, ed. *Kagel: Dialoge, Monologe.* Cologne: DuMont, 2001.

Kovács, Inge. "Instrumentales Theater." In *Von Kranichstein zur Gegenwart: 50 Jahre Darmstädter Ferienkurse,* ed. R. Stephan et al. Stuttgart: Daco, 1996, 333–39.

Mueller, Adeline. "Corporealisation in Mauricio Kagel's Film *Antithese.*" Master's dissertation, University of Sussex, 2000.

Nicolai, Felicitas. "Türen öffnen für die Fantasie." Interview with Mauricio Kagel. *Musik und Gesellschaft* 12 (1987): 643–45.

Pauli, Hansjörg. *Für wen komponieren sie eigentlich?* Frankfurt am Main: Fischer, 1971.

Reich, Wieland. "Mauricio Kagel." In *Komponisten der Gegenwart,* ed. H.-W. Heister and W.-W. Sparrer. München: text + kritik, 21st delivery, 2001, unpaginated loose leaf compilation.

Roelcke, Eckhard. "Instrumentales Theater: Anmerkungen zu Mauricio Kagels *Match* und *Sur Scène.*" In *Musiktheater im 20. Jahrhundert.* Laaber: Laaber-Verlag, 1988, 215–38.

Sarkisjan, Svetlana. "Instrumentales Theater bei Mauricio Kagel und anderen Komponisten." In *Musikkultur in der Bundesrepublik Deutschland: Symposion Leningrad 1990,* ed. R. Stephan and W. Saderatzkij. Kassel: Bosse, 1994, 381–97.

Schnebel, Dieter. *Mauricio Kagel: Musik—Theater—Film.* Cologne: DuMont, 1970.

Stoianova, Ivanka. "Multiplicité, non-directionalité et jeu dans les pratiques contemporaines du spectacle musico-théâtral (I): Théâtre instrumental et 'impromuz': Mauricio Kagel, *Staatstheater,* Ghédalia Tazartès, *Ghédal et son double.*" *Musique en jeu* 27 (1977): 38–48.

Zarius, Karl-Heinz. "Inszenierte Musik: Systematische Anmerkungen zum Instrumentalen Theater." *Positionen* 14 (1993): 2–6.

———. "Szenische Komposition—komponierte Szene: Kagels neues Musiktheater als Reflexion zwischen den Medien." *Musik und Bildung* 11 (1977): 588–95.

Filmography

(Television stations indicated in parentheses)

TITLE	TELEVISION STATION
Antithese	(NDR, Hamburg, 1965)
Match	(WDR, 1966)
Solo	(NDR, 1967)
Duo	(NDR, 1968)
Hallelujah	(WDR, 1968)
Ludwig van	(WDR, 1969)
Tactil	(WDR, 1971)
Zwei-Mann-Orchester	(SWF, 1973)
Unter Strom	(Radio Svizzera Italiano, 1975)
Kantrimiusik	(SWF, 1976)
Ex-Position	(Radio France, 1978)
Pas de Cinq	(Swiss Television DRS, 1978)
Phonophonie	(Swiss Television DRS, 1979)
Blue's Blue	(Swiss Television DRS, 1981)
Mm 51	(Swiss Television DRS, 1983)
Szenario: Un chien andalou	(Buñuel)(Swiss Television DRS, 1983)
Er: Fernsehspiel über 'Eine Radiophantasie'	(WDR 1984)
Dressur	(Swiss Television DRS, 1985)
Mitternachtsstük	(Swiss Television DRS, 1986/1987)
Repertoire	(ZDF, 1989)
Bestiarium	(WDR, 2000)

THE USSR

SEVEN

Eisenstein's Theory of Film Music Revisited: Silent and Early Sound Antecedents

JULIE HUBBERT

Sergei Eisenstein occupies an enduring position in the history of film theory. In the same way that his films have cast a long shadow, his extensive theoretical writings, especially on the Soviet technique of montage, have commanded a central position in the film theory literature. Eisenstein's discussion of montage technique in sound film, what he called "vertical montage" or "audio-visual montage," has been particularly influential and has inspired both imitation and discussion. Film theorists and historians, from Siegfried Kracauer to Christian Metz to David Bordwell, have scarcely ever failed either to comment on his theories or to absorb them into their own understanding and discussion of film music.

Originally written between 1940 and 1942, the essays "Vertical Montage (Parts One, Two and Three)" were later edited by Eisenstein together with an earlier essay entitled "Montage 1938" to form a complete theoretical text which Eisenstein published in the United States in 1944 under the title *The Film Sense*.[1] While film theorists and historians have made these essays a central part of the theoretical canon, most have also struggled with or ignored altogether those sections of the "vertical montage" theory that deal with music. Eisenstein's discussion of music, especially as it is presented in the second and third sections of *The Film Sense* entitled "Synchronization of the Senses" and "Form and Content: Practice," has produced a wide range of critical responses. Eisenstein enthusiasts, like Kracauer and Raymond Spottiswoode, have simply glossed over the sections in the theory that deal with music, as have detractors, like André Bazin and Metz.[2] Some Soviet film historians and Eisenstein biographers, on the other hand, have made concerted attempts to understand and explain Eisenstein's film music theory. Both Jean Mitry and Vlada Petric, for instance, praise Eisenstein's discussion of music, in particular the way it presupposes a whole and synthetic approach to film, and equality between sound, music, and visuals.[3] Jay Leyda, too, in his critique of vertical montage specifically acknowledges Eisenstein's "organic" approach to film music.[4] Bordwell goes so far as to suggest that discussion of music in the vertical montage theory is the very thing that makes the theory so exceptional: "The concepts of rhythmic and melodic montage enabled [Eisenstein] to launch the most detailed inquiry into sound/image interactions that film theory has yet produced."[5]

From a purely musical perspective, Eisenstein's film music theory has had a far different reception. Hanns Eisler and Theodor Adorno, for instance, disparaged Eisenstein's film music theory as ridiculous and unmusical. His theory, they concluded, relies not just on naive overstatement but on false assumptions. It hinges, they charge, on the "faulty principle of relating picture and music by pseudo-identity or association."[6] For Roy Prendergast, too, Eisenstein's idea of total fusion of film and music is "wholly incorrect," and many of its supporting arguments are "highly questionable," if not altogether "bogus" and "inconsistent."[7] Douglas Gallez also dismisses Eisenstein's conceptualization of music in his theory of vertical montage as "hardly meaningful."[8]

While much of the criticism of Eisenstein's film music theory on both sides is valid, it is limited in the sense that it seeks to explain or place his ideas on music either within the greater discussion of montage technique or within the narrower confines of music proper. Neither side contextualizes Eisenstein's discussion within the more specific history of film music theory. Yet Eisenstein's admittedly difficult, even cryptic, description of music has strong echoes of contemporary film music theory and practice. In both language and content, Eisenstein's theory of music recalls aspects of silent and early sound film music theory, in particular the work of Erik Satie, George Antheil, Kurt London, and Leonid Sabaneev. In the way that Eisenstein focuses on a more abstract and non-narrative role for film music instead of the more conventional approach of illustrating the moods and actions on the screen, his aesthetic is indebted to previous film music theory. In this context, Eisenstein's ideas represent not an eccentric and difficult extreme, but rather the continuation of an alternative, non-illustrative approach to film music.

Eisenstein's Predecessors

During the silent period, film music theory centered to a certain extent on the idea of music as illustration of the images. The goal was to contribute to the "mood" of the picture on the screen through the use of musical stereotypes: the conventions of happy or sad music, for instance, or to realize the sound for specific sonic events pictured on the screen, such as the musical approximation of thunderstorms, trains, animals noises, and so on. Additionally, the practice of assigning themes to identify specific characters, emotions, or events in the film, and repeating those themes in a Wagnerian or leitmotivic fashion to generate thematic coherence, also occupied a significant portion of the early film music discussion.[9]

There was little mention in the playing manuals, however, of a larger purpose for film accompaniment beyond the task of reinforcing the mood, characters, and geographical location of the events visualized on the screen. Even the discussion of tempo seemed inextricably tied to mood.[10] Advice columnist George Beynon, for instance, only briefly considers the impact musical form has on film structure in his film music manual *Musical Presentation of Motion Pictures*. In a brief chapter entitled "Synchrony," he hints at the idea that musical structure—the ends of phrases and forms in particular—can lend a similar sense of cohesion to the visual images on the screen: "Music need not be cut to fit the situation; but, if care be taken in the finishing of phrases, the musical setting becomes cohesive—one complete whole that conveys to the audience that sense of unity so essential to plot portrayal."[11] While Beynon flirts with recognizing a larger, structural function for music, like most of the manuals of the silent period, he is primarily occupied with describing the practical concerns of illustrating the moods and actions of each picture.

Some challenges to this approach did surface, however, especially as filmmakers began to experiment with unconventional visual styles. In the mid-1920s, avant-garde filmmakers—René Clair, Fernand Léger, and Luis Buñuel in particular—began to experiment with a cinematic style that was explicitly non-narrative. Instead of using film to tell a story, they used it to present images that were abstract, surreal, or superimposed, and in a manner that had no logical order or coherence. This new style, captured vividly in films like Buñuel and Dalí's *Un chien andalou* (An Andalusian Dog, 1929) and *L'Âge d'or* (The Golden Age, 1930), abounded in visual non-sequiturs and oblique, disjunct imagery. While offering a sharp departure from narrative conventions, however, these films were meant not to destroy the medium of cinema, but rather to differentiate it further from the other arts. As Clair explained, these experiments represented a desire to develop "a pure language for the cinema," separate from the narrative-based structures film had borrowed from literature and the theater.[12]

Altering the visual language of film, naturally, required a similar adjustment to the musical accompaniment. The idea of "illustrating" a picture that had no visual narrative, much less visual logic, had to be abandoned. Satie's score to *Entr'acte,* Clair's experimental film from 1924, was one of the first attempts to outline an alternative approach to film scoring. Created to play during the intermission between the first and second acts of a ballet called *Relâche* by Jean Borlin, the film, like the ballet, had little in the way of a plot. The scenario, by the Dada poet and painter Francis Picabia, was cryptic and illogical, an inexplicable chain of images and events. One moment the camera pans up a chimney and the exterior of an apartment building, the next the face of a monkey appears. A scene of a ballerina leaping in slow motion in a darkened studio is abruptly juxtaposed with a scene of a pile of matches moving magically about by themselves. Shot selection, too, is elliptical instead of literal. The distorted angles of an exterior of a building, for instance, are superimposed over images of contemporary artists Marcel Duchamp and Man Ray playing chess.[13]

Satie's score for the film was suitably unconventional. With no discrete moods to illustrate or characters to whom to assign a theme, Satie instead accompanied the collage of surreal images with blocks of short repetitive patterns and thematic fragments.[14] The large-scale form of the score was also unconventional, in the sense that there are no transitions between the ostinato groups or patterns. Instead, one pattern or "block" shifts abruptly into the next when the imagery changes on screen.

Satie never discussed his unconventional film score in any formal or theoretical way. When asked about the music for *Entr'acte,* he gave a typically cryptic response: it was meant to be "pornographic, but not enough to make a lobster blush, or even an egg."[15] Satie did make a cue sheet, however, and this condensed sketch or outline suggests the primary function of his musical accompaniment was structural, not illustrative (see Figure 7.1). Satie's concern was to use music to describe not the content, but the length of each individual scene. Each motive is repeated the designated number of times in a section until the visual imagery changes.[16]

While Satie contributed to the practice of avant-garde film scoring, his contemporary, the American George Antheil, contributed to the theory of it. By the early 1920s, Antheil had already scandalized European audiences with his dissonant "mechanical" works, especially the second and third piano sonatas entitled the *Airplane Sonata* (1921) and the *Death of Machines* (1923).[17] His

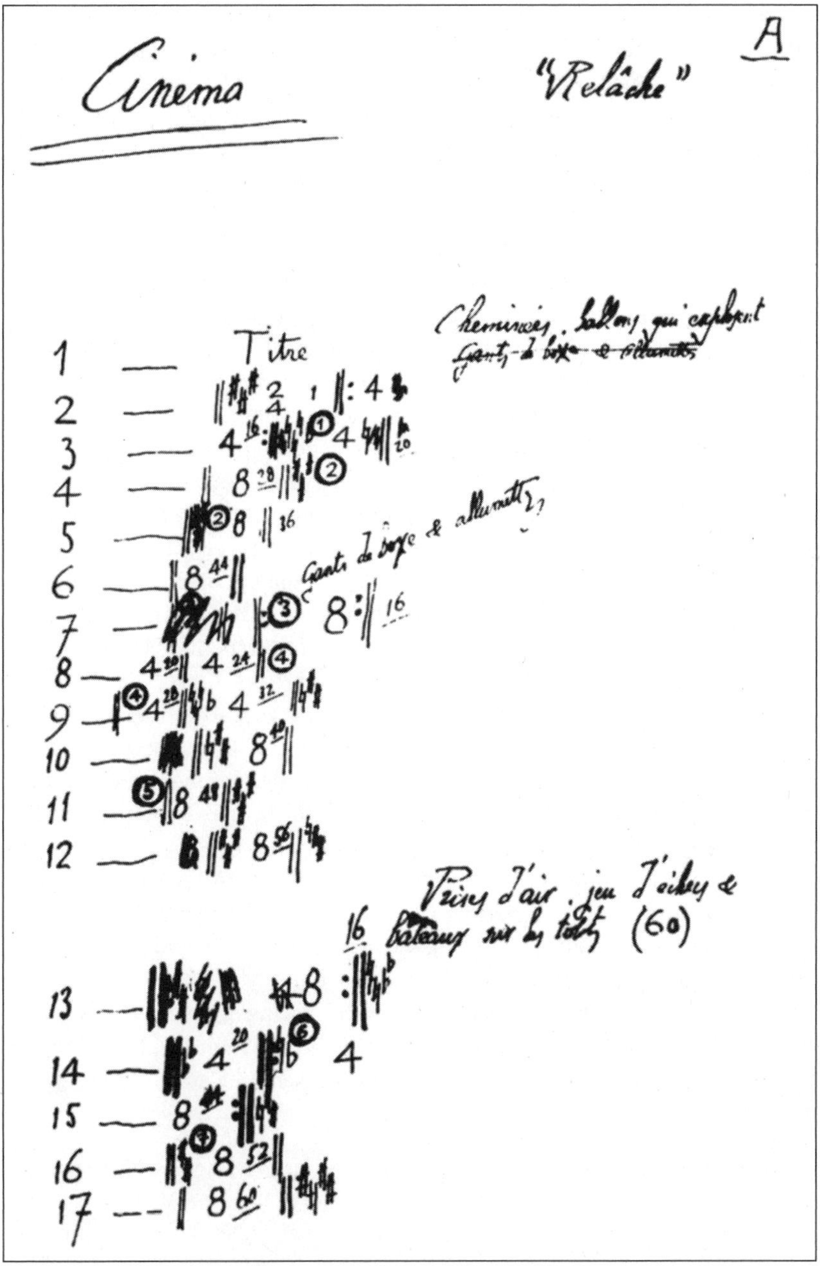

Figure 7.1. Eric Satie's cue-sheet for *Entr'Acte. Reproduced by permission of the Bibliotheque nationale de France.*

Ballet mécanique, begun the next year in 1924, was to have a similar mechanical aesthetic. Its original instrumentation called for three xylophones, electric bells, wood and metal airplane propellers, tamtam, four bass drums, siren, two pianos, and one player piano. It was also originally to have an accompanying film that would match in pictures what Antheil was trying to achieve in sound. As Antheil remembers it, as soon as he began work on the music, he announced that he was seeking a cinematic accompaniment. The painter Fernand Léger responded to the advertisement, and set out with the help of cameraman Dudley Murphy to make a similarly experimental and mechanistic film,[18] suitably composed of "disconnected photos of different pieces of giant machinery photographed in action."[19] Human figures and faces were included, but their actions were intentionally choreographed to mimic machine movements. The image of a girl swinging, for instance, is immediately followed by close-ups of a clock pendulum so that the mechanical movements of the actors are juxtaposed with those of manufactured objects.[20] Although the film was never officially synchronized with the music, there is some evidence to suggest that the original version of *Ballet mécanique* was composed if not as a true film score, then at least with the film in mind. In working with the Pleyel company to construct the player piano rolls for the premiere of the *Ballet mécanique* in 1924, Antheil describes editing the work and removing "many of the repetitions that had been inserted to match with the film."[21]

Antheil's "mechanical" score resembles Satie's surreal accompaniment for *Entr'acte* in a number of ways. Antheil makes use of "block" form or abrupt shifts of different patterns and textures between the sections, and dramatic use of repetition within the sections. In terms of formal structure, Antheil insisted certain parts of *Ballet mécanique* should simply be a single section repeated twenty-five times, or "AAAAAAAAAAAAAAAAAAAAAA."[22] The most striking contrast to Satie's repetitive but tonal style is that most of *Ballet mécanique* is highly dissonant, broadening the sonic palette to include machine and machine-approximated noises.

Antheil defended his unusual compositional techniques by describing them as a manifestation of a larger abstraction he saw in music. Literal repetition, he argued, is what allowed music's most essential element to be experienced: time:

> I did not hesitate, for instance, to repeat one measure one hundred times; I did not hesitate to have absolutely nothing [on my pianola rolls] for sixty-two bars; I did not hesitate to ring a bell against a certain given section of time or indeed to do whatever I pleased to do with this *time canvas* as long as each part of it stood up against the other. My ideas were the most abstract of the abstract.[23]

Antheil's reduction or abstraction of music is simple, but radical. Music, he argues, cannot itself express a specific content or emotion; music is simply a "canvas" for displaying time. Repetition, even of silence, is the compositional element most capable of expressing musical time.

Later, Antheil also ascribed temporal intentions to the work's dissonant tonal language. Music was capable of being reduced or abstracted not only to "time," but also to "sound," or "sound material." While it was this dissonant sound material that, ironically, often prevented listeners and critics from understanding the work, in a letter to the conductor Nicholas Slonimsky, Antheil admitted it too was aimed at making music's temporality audible:

> I personally consider that the *Ballet mécanique* was important in one particular and that is that it was conceived in a new form, that form specifically being the filling out of a certain *time canvas* with *musical abstractions and sound material* composed and contrasted against one another with the thought of *time values* rather than tonal values. Up until the *Ballet mécanique* I think that nobody actually thought of music particularly in the time sense. . . . In order to paint musical pictures one must admit right at the outset that the only canvas of music can be time.[24]

As Antheil sees it, the only way to perceive music's fundamentally temporal aspects is to fill out a composition with "musical abstractions and sound material," or sound effects and mechanical noises.

While on this last point—dissonance instead of common practice tonality—Antheil departs from Satie, their aesthetic is in general similar and similarly unconventional. The avant-garde film score of the 1920s and the music associated with it produced an uniquely abstract understanding of music, one that emphasized music's ability to be purely structural, to express the fundamental elements of length or time alone. It was a small but significant experiment that forced composers especially to think differently about the purpose of music in film. The intentionally disjunct and abstract imagery of the films required composers to find a function beyond the literal and illustrative purposes for which music had conventionally been used. It invited them to think more abstractly about the function of music in film, prompting composers like Satie and Antheil to emphasize the "time values" over "tonal values," rhythm over themes, repetition over melodic leitmotifs.

This conceptual shift toward emphasizing music's temporal qualities over, or in addition to, its emotional qualities, is also reflected in the first serious wave of film music theory that surfaced in the mid-1930s. Kurt London's and Leonid's Sabaneev's book-length studies of film music published in 1935 and 1936, respectively, document the emergence of the new medium of sound film and reflect the adjustments that had to be made to music now that it would be sharing space with dialogue and sound. London's book, *Film Music*, is somewhat anachronistic in that nearly half of it is devoted to the nearly extinct practice of silent film accompaniment. However, his observations of silent film music are significant, especially in the way that they offer clear references to the avant-garde shift toward abstraction. London, a composer and historian who taught classes on silent film music at the Berlin Academy in the 1920s, offers a great deal of practical advice, much like the "playing manuals" of the silent period, but he also observes a broader philosophical assessment of music's function in film. Film music, London asserts, can play an illustrative role, but it has a more fundamental or "rhythmic" role to play in outlining the formal structure of the film:

> The reason which is aesthetically and psychologically most essential to explain the need of music as an accompaniment of the silent film, is without doubt *the rhythm of the film as an art of movement.* We are not accustomed to apprehend movement as an artistic form without accompanying sounds, or at least audible rhythms. Every film that deserves the name must possess its individual rhythm which determines its form. . . . It was the task of musical accompaniment to give it auditory accentuation and profundity. . . . This does not mean only descriptive music . . . but in reality supporting the film in rhythm, in thought, and in structure.[25]

Film, London asserts, is primarily a kinetic art. In a reduction that echoes Antheil's abstraction of music to "time values," London suggests that film music's purpose is fundamentally temporal. Its rhythm and length help delineate the form and structure of the film. If film is the "art of movement," then it is through a similar expression of movement that music supports the film. In other chapters, London acknowledges the emotional value music can add to the moving images through conventional thematic processes and stereotypical styles and tempos. But the prominence that he gives to the structural aspects of film music is striking, resonating with avant-garde artists' earlier efforts to reduce music to the abstractions of time and rhythm.

Like London's text, Leonid Sabaneev's book, *Music for the Films,* contributes significantly to this conceptual shift in film music aesthetics. Because Sabaneev focuses exclusively on sound film, a central issue in his discussion is the division between "photographic" and "non-photographic" filmic planes, or what will soon be more commonly referred to as a distinction between diegetic and non-diegetic space. But his chapter on "The Aesthetics of the Sound Film" is noteworthy for its preoccupation with a more abstract and structural purpose for music. Sabaneev begins with an obligatory mention of music's "emotional" function in film, but he also observes an additional function for music, one that is fundamentally "rhythmic" or temporal.[26] Music can help describe the mood of the images on the screen, he asserts, but it can also help dictate the more abstract aspects of film form and structure:

> Music in the cinema . . . should possess a musical form of its own, in some way subordinated to the rhythm of the screen, but not destroyed by them. Indeed music often dictates its rhythms and tempi to the screen. . . . Music in the cinema cannot sacrifice the principles governing its form; no matter what is happening on the screen, the music must have its melodic structure, its phrases and cadences and it must not be asked to suffer dilution by the rhythms and occurrences of the picture.[27]

As Sabaneev sees it, music can do more than describe film content; it can delineate film structure. Musical form can also be used for the more abstract purpose of dictating the rhythms and tempi of the screen. Where his predecessors expressed this abstraction more generally as one of "time" and "movement," however, Sabaneev gives the correlation between film and music a more precise description and location. In identifying what specific form or structure can create filmic structure, Sabaneev points to melody. For Sabaneev it is the movement of melody or melodic form that can more specifically help articulate the internal shape of a film because the "phrases and cadences" of a melody can reinforce, when coordinated with the length of a specific scene, the rhythm and structure of the film. While Sabaneev's discussion of a non-illustrative function for music is not as exclusive as the avant-garde artists mentioned above, in the sense that structure is just one of several functions music provides a film, it is more substantial than London's, especially in terms of the specific connection it makes between melodic structure and film structure. By tying melodic form to the rhythm or structure of the picture, Sabaneev gives not just music generally, but melody specifically a more abstract and structural role to play in film.

Sabaneev describes a purely structural function for music elsewhere, when describing music's role in the editing process of the film. Whereas with sound the aim in the editing process is to synchronize it with the appropriate actions and objects on the screen, with music the intention is more abstract. It is often used simply to delineate the length of the scene, he asserts. There are "musical backgrounds which have no definite sections [that] require accurate synchronization. As we know, these fragments can be composed before the *montage*; all that is necessary is that their length shall coincide with the length of the scene to which they refer."[28] Especially where little or no dialogue is being articulated, or where no musical performance is being visually represented, music serves to mark time and space. Although Sabaneev goes on to describe a second category of music—diegetic music—that requires the same immediate and localized attention to synchronization that "sound" montage does, this first category—the musical background—is distinct precisely because it is not literal. Because it is not tied to the action on the screen, this non-photographic or background music is particularly capable of being abstract and working simply to articulate film structure. Like London's concept of film music as "movement," Sabaneev similarly locates music's purpose in its "length." If music's content can more conventionally be heard to contribute to the emotional understanding of the images, then its length, its large-scale form and structure, can help articulate the visual form and structure of the film. In fact, it is this large-scale formal aspect of music, this purely temporal aspect, that helps distinguish music from sound. Because music can function independently from the action on the screen, because it can be purely temporal, it can also articulate film structure. In the same way that "melodic form" can structure a film on a localized level, musical "length" can articulate film structure on a larger, more abstract level.

In describing with even greater specificity the role large-scale musical form can play in film accompaniment, Sabaneev's theory is important. His aesthetic of narrative sound film resonates significantly with the ideas and language of his predecessors. By focusing on the concept of musical "length," Sabaneev maintains London's evocative reduction of film music to the "art of movement." In Sabaneev's theory, too, the echo of avant-garde artists and their conceptual shift to a more abstract and temporal conceptualization of music is perceptible. But to the degree that Sabaneev also makes several unique contributions to the discussion of music's function in film, his theory does more than integrate the non-illustrative approach into the discussion of narrative film music. By asserting that not just musical length, but more specifically melodic length—the contour, shape, and phrasing of melody—can also participate in the more abstract and structuring capabilities of music, he gives greater theoretical weight to purely structural function for film music.

Eisenstein

At the outset of his filmmaking career, there was little to suggest that Eisenstein would develop very specific ideas about the musical accompaniment or scores for his films. With his first film, *Stachka* (Strike, 1925), for instance, little is known about the musical accompaniment, nor is there any evidence to suggest that Eisenstein was particularly involved with its construction. At this point in his career, however, Eisenstein was acquainted with the most current and contemporary European filmmaking trends, including the work of the French avant-garde. Biographers place Eisenstein in Paris in 1924, and although he does not seem to have developed a specific relationship with any of the filmmakers mentioned above, he was known to admire their films, Léger's *Ballet mécanique* in particular. In an introductory preface to the film included a short time after its premiere, for instance, Eisenstein's admiration is cited on the title card for the film, where he is quoted as saying that he considered the film "one of the greatest works of the cinema."[29] Although there is no evidence to suggest that Eisenstein equally admired Antheil's *Ballet mécanique,* it seems likely that he was at least aware of it and other avant-garde films such as *Entr'acte.*

Eisenstein's serious interest in film music instead seems to date from *Bronenosets Potyomkin* (Battleship Potemkin, 1925). In post-production work on the film, Eisenstein not only acknowledges the importance of music, but hints at wanting the music for the film to play a non-illustrative or non-narrative role. *Bronenosets Potyomkin* was not particularly well received when it premiered in St. Petersburg, but when the film traveled to Berlin later that year and achieved widespread acclaim, many attributed its success to the exciting original score the German distributor had commissioned from native composer Edmund Meisel. As Meisel remembered it, he composed the score in a miraculous twelve days. Eisenstein arrived on the scene only at the end of the project, just in time to advise Meisel on the music for the last act or reel of the film.[30] Although Eisenstein did not challenge the music Meisel had put to the first four reels, his involvement with the music for the final reel was significant. Where Meisel had given most of the film standard illustrative or "thematic" treatment, Eisenstein insisted that in the final reel, where the ship sails out to meet the Russian fleet, the music should function more abstractly.[31] As Eisenstein remembered it, his instructions to Meisel were brief but passionate:

> It [was] not a matter of editing the film and composing the music in an identical rhythm. Nothing could be more mindless and simplistic. I described to Meisel my requirements for the music as "rhythm, rhythm, rhythm, above all else rhythm"—but by no means in the sense of rhythmic coincidence between sound and picture. What I wanted was that the rhythm of the music should function as a mode of expressivity.[32]

With the repeated emphasis on the element of "rhythm" in particular, Eisenstein strains to find a function for music beyond the conventional boundaries of localized sound effects. Clearly because the imagery at this point in the film focuses on machinery and the mechanized action of a ship at war, Eisenstein is anxious to avoid the clichéd illustrative approach of using music simply to articulate sound effects, such as gunfire or the ship's engines. In wanting rhythm specifically to act not as a sound, but as a "mode of expressivity," Eisenstein hints at a function for music less tied to the discrete images and actions on the screen. Well before vertical montage, Eisenstein was not only thinking about the fundamental relationship between music and film, but suggesting that the relationship could be less literal and more structural.[33]

Although Eisenstein produced one more silent film, *Oktyabr* (October, 1927), for which Meisel also wrote the score, that experience produced no tangible analysis or discussion of music. Aside from a noteworthy passage where Meisel composed a section of music in retrograde to accompany a scene Eisenstein had shot in reverse, Eisenstein was not inspired to comment on the film's music at all.[34] There is also a notable absence of a discussion of music in Eisenstein's earliest sound film aesthetic, in particular the famous "Statement on Sound" from 1928.[35] In the initial transition to sound film, it was not Eisenstein, in fact, but fellow Soviet Vladimir Messman who gave music the most consideration in the emerging theory of sound film.[36] It was not until the essays on "vertical montage" in *The Film Sense* in the early 1940s that Eisenstein returned to the topic of film music. The greatly expanded and substantial nature of his discussion of film music in these works may have resulted from his contact with the composer Prokofiev, with whom Eisenstein worked closely on the score of his first sound film, *Aleksandr Nevskiy* (Alexander Nevsky, 1938). But it may also have resulted from Eisenstein's greater acquaintance with previous film music theory.[37]

In the second section of his "vertical montage" theory in *The Film Sense*, entitled "The Synchronization of the Senses," Eisenstein begins his examination of film music with an abstraction that clearly ties his theory to Sabaneev, London, and the French avant-garde. In the commentary on *Bronenosets Potyomkin*, Eisenstein hinted at giving music a purpose less rigidly or literally tied to film content. Here that wish finds full voice under the familiar umbrella concept of "movement." Music's function, he argues, is dictated by the elements or features it shares in common with moving images:

> Music and visual imagery are actually not commensurable through narrowly "representation" elements. If one speaks of genuine and profound relations and proportions between the music and the picture, it can only be in reference to the relations between the *fundamental movements* of the music and the picture, i.e., compositional and structural elements, since the relations between the "pictures" and the "pictures" produced by the musical images are usually so individual in perception and so lacking in concreteness that they cannot be fitted into any strictly methodological "regulations."[38]

In much the same way that London reduced both film and music to the "art of *movement*," Eisenstein, too, roots film and music in the shared attribute of movement. If film and music can work in concert, it is only because they are both essentially temporal art forms. Eisenstein does more than just reiterate the structural position of the French avant-garde; he gives that position center stage. By questioning whether music can express content as concretely as can a visual picture, Eisenstein not only validates the importance of musical structure, he elevates it. Because music is incapable of representing ideas or images with any sense of concreteness, he argues, structure is the only musical element capable of generating filmic meaning.

Deconstructing the visual aspects of film beyond the abstraction of "movement" is an easy refinement for Eisenstein, because it involves the familiar territory of montage— shot composition, camera angle and perspective, and so on. Reducing musical movement to its component parts, however, presents something of a challenge for Eisenstein. In trying to identify more specifically how "movement" is manifest in music, Eisenstein focuses first on the idea of musical form. Musical movement finds expression in the basic outline or contour of a musical phrase: "We must know how to grasp the movement of a given piece of music, locating its path (its line or form) as our foundation for the plastic composition that is to correspond to the music."[39] Perhaps sensing the terms "line or form" were too general or vague, however, Eisenstein employs more precise and musically literate terms to express the reduction. As his discussion unfolds, Eisenstein also defines musical movement as the "contour" or "outline" of a musical work. A sense of meaning is available in the general coordination of musical contour with the visual movement on the screen:

> We cannot deny the fact that the most *striking* and immediate impression will be gained, of course, from a *congruence of the movement of the music with the move-*

ment of the visual contour—with the graphic composition of the frame; for this contour or this outline, or this line is the most vivid "emphasizer" of the very idea of the movement.[40]

Although he uses different terminology on different occasions to define the concept of musical movement, the focus of each reduction is the same. The contour of music makes vivid or emphasizes the visual and graphic structure of the film.

Much of Eisenstein's discussion of music's structural function centers on describing this generalized correspondence of film and musical "movement." Like Sabaneev, however, Eisenstein, too, strains to find a more localized or concrete expression of this correspondence. Uniquely for Eisenstein, however, the refinement of movement takes place on not just one but four further levels: meter, rhythm, melody, and tone.[41] The most superficial or localized coordination or relationship Eisenstein calls "rhythmic vertical montage." This type of coordination literally pairs musical rhythm and tempo, with the tempo of the action depicted on the screen. Synchronizing music and film in this manner, however, he acknowledges, comes dangerously close to the longstanding illustrative method of silent film accompaniment, the idea of using musical accompaniment to parallel or "mickey-mouse" the moods and actions of the film. This level of correspondence is inferior and represents a "low plane of synchronization"[42] that is tolerable only by circumstance and not design:

> In the rudimentary forms of expression, both elements (the picture and the sound) will be controlled by an identity of rhythm according to the content of the scene. This is the simplest, easiest, and most frequent circumstance of audio-visual montage, consisting of shots cut and edited together to the rhythm of the music on the parallel sound-track. Whether movement exists in these shots is not of serious consequence. If movement in the visual happens to be present, the only demand upon it is that it conform with the rhythm fixed by the parallel [music] track.[43]

As Bordwell has pointed out, in this part of his discussion Eisenstein further reduces rhythm to the component part of "accent," and postulates a characteristically elliptical or contrapuntal juxtaposition of strong musical accents with weak visual gestures, and vice versa.[44] In this coordination of musical rhythm and accent with film structure and gesture, Bordwell finds the influence of Bely and the Russian formalists, who argued for a conceptualization of cinematic montage that paralleled the idea of poetic scansion. While the recognition of this influence is indeed valid, the influence of the early sound film music theorists on this "rhythmic" part of Eisenstein's film music philosophy is equally strong. Both London and Sabaneev also resisted the literal coordination of music tempo with filmic action. For them, it was superficial because it represented a more rudimentary approach connected with the outmoded technique of silent film accompaniment.

The influence of film music theory and Sabaneev in particular is even more pronounced, however, in the mode of coordination Eisenstein calls "melodic vertical montage." In further deconstructing "movement," Eisenstein identifies melody as the musical element most capable of coordinating with film on a more immediate or localized level. It is not just a general musical "line and form," he now argues, but more specifically "melodic line and form" that is most capable of articulating visual structure in a film. Where rhythmic movement represented a lesser order of coordination, for Eisenstein the coordination of melodic form and visual movement represents a higher and more abstract level of synchronization:

> From all the plastic means of expression at our disposal we can surely find those whose movement harmonizes not only with the movement of the rhythmic pattern, but also with the movement of the melodic line. . . . "The higher unity" into which we are capable of organizing the separate tones of the sound-scale may be visualized as a line that unites them through movement. The tonal changes on this line may also be characterized as movement . . . whose characteristics we can perceive as sounds of varying pitch and tone.[45]

While this focus on "melody," or more specifically melodic phrasing and contour (i.e., variations in pitch and tone), is one of the more unusual aspects of Eisenstein's theory, in the sense that it has little or no anticipation in any of Eisenstein's previous theoretical writings, it is not without precedence in the film music literature. Sabaneev before him hinted at just such a coordination of melody and montage. Sabaneev also discussed the structural aspects of melody—phrases and cadences—as the elements best capable of serving the montage, of highlighting the purely structural aspects of film. In the way that Eisenstein similarly reduces melody to its external structure, to its "line and form" and not to a mood, emotion, or character, the influence of Sabaneev's theory of film music seems particularly strong.

Where Sabaneev's, and indeed film music history's, influence becomes weak if not altogether lost in Eisenstein's theory, however, is in the final reduction Eisenstein finds for musical movement, the literal connection he postulates between melodic and visual movement. Although there is no precedence for it in any music theory, film or otherwise, Eisenstein asserts that music notation itself is an expression of musical movement:

> The movement which lies at the base of a work of art is not abstract or isolated from the theme, but is the generalized plastic embodiment of that image through which the theme is expressed. . . . Here we want to emphasize that *pure line,* that is, the specifically "graphic" outline of a composition, is only *one of the many* means of visualizing the character of a movement.[46]

The belief that the structure of melody can be expressed graphically in the physical attributes of music notation, and that additionally this graphic manifestation of music can be perceived aurally as well as visually, is, as many historians have concluded, forced if not altogether far-fetched.[47] Most agree that Eisenstein stretched the abstraction of musical movement beyond its conceptual limitations. To dismiss Eisenstein's music theory because of this over-determination, however, is also, as Bordwell suggests, equally misguided. Bordwell reconciles this awkward moment in vertical montage with a quick tutorial in music perception.[48] Another solution, however, is to contextualize it in the history of film music theory. Eisenstein's attempt to draw a connection between musical notation and musical movement may be overreaching, but it is also an expression, albeit extreme, of the continuing attempt to describe a more general, structural, and non-illustrative function for film music.

Not all of the unprecedented aspects of Eisenstein's theory of film music are missteps. In his analysis of the "Battle of the Ice" sequence from *Aleksandr Nevskiy,* Eisenstein offers a practical application of his theory. In his discussion of Prokofiev's score for this sequence, Eisenstein not surprisingly focuses on melodic structure or contour. He predictably finds correspondence between musical movement (melodic phrases and cadences) and visual montage (change in perspective, camera angle, etc.). Perhaps more surprising is the weight and focus he gives to another familiar element in the search to describe a more abstract and structural function for film music: repetition. Just as visual structure can be articulated by small-scale musical structures such as melodic structure and phrases, he argues, it can also be imposed on a larger scale through the use of repetition:

> One function [of repetition] is to facilitate the creation of an organic whole. Another function of repetition is to serve as a means of developing that mounting intensity. . . . Instead of repeating a single measure of the music *four* times as written in the score, I multiplied this by three, achieving *twelve* exact repeats of the measure. This occurs in the sequence where the peasant militia cuts into the rear of the German wedge.[49]

Whereas earlier in his theory Eisenstein focused on melody or melodic structure as the element of music most capable of generating filmic structure on a localized level, here his concern is broader. Music is capable of creating not just foreground structure, but a larger sense of "organic wholeness," he asserts, through the element of "repetition."

The influence of the French avant-garde seems especially strong here. The emphasis on pure repetition instead of leitmotifs to generate structure instead of narrative meaning recalls Antheil's attempt to use excessive repetition to express music's "time values." The "cue sheet" or analytical sketch Eisenstein made for the "Battle on the Ice" sequence, included as an appendix to the "Form and Content: Practice" chapter, also bears the influence of another predecessor (see Figure 7.2). Just as Satie did in *Entr'acte,* Eisenstein uses music or thematic motifs to mark time, to give structural outline to discreet scenes within the montage. In fact, in its close coordination of melodic phrasing and repetition and visual changes, Eisenstein's cue sheet departs from Satie's only in terms

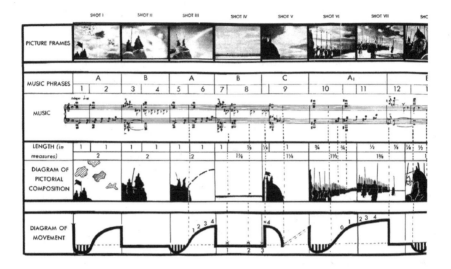

Figure 7.2. Eisenstein's cue-sheet for the "Battle on the Ice." Excerpt from *Film Forum: Essays in Film Theory* by Sergei Eisenstein, English translation by Jay Leyda © *1949 by Harcourt, Inc. and renewed 1977 by Jay Leyda, reprinted by permission of the publisher.*

of detail. It describes the musical and visual movement on a more localized or detailed level, coordinating melodic phrasing not only with scene changes, but also with shifts in camera angles. Conceptually, however, it is remarkably similar in its attempt to describe a purely structural and unemotional function for music.

To reevaluate Eisenstein's aesthetic of film music from the perspective of film music theory challenges both sides of the vertical montage debate. It shows those detractors who view Eisenstein's theory as musically illiterate and overdetermined to have underappreciated the degree to which Eisenstein's arguments reflect a knowledge of silent and sound film music theory. But it also offers a gentle corrective to the contrasting view that Eisenstein's theory offers one of the most complete and important discussions of film music to date. As an overview of the preexisting film music literature reveals, Eisenstein's appreciation of music's function in film was not comprehensive, but was instead more narrowly focused on reaching beyond the conventions of illustrative accompaniment in one particular way. By emptying themes of their emotional content and extra-musical associations, by focusing on the temporal instead of the emotional—contour and shape, movement, length, and repetition—Eisenstein was seeking to describe a more abstract and structural function for music in film. On both a large and small scale, he argued, music can articulate film structure even more than it can express film content. A brief reminder of contemporary

Hollywood theory and practice makes this observation even more emphatic. Placing Eisenstein's vertical montage theory of film music next to Max Steiner's wall-to-wall "theme for every character" model, for instance, does not show Eisenstein to be less musical, as some have suggested.[50] Rather, it shows him to be interested in articulating a more autonomous direction for film music, one that sees music as an integral part of film structure but independent of the characters, moods, and sounds on the screen.

That Eisenstein was guided in this structural approach by the French avant-garde filmmakers and composers who were intentionally looking for an abstract and non-illustrative function for film music, and by those film music theorists who first gave this purpose theoretical consideration, is manifest in both the content and style of Eisenstein's discussion. Certainly by the time of *Bronenosets Potyomkin,* Eisenstein was already beginning to envision a less literal and illustrative purpose for music. The fact that his discussion of music in his mature theory of vertical montage resonates clearly with the language and ideas of Satie, Antheil, London, and Sabaneev is significant. Eisenstein might not have been the first to envision a purely structural function for music in film, but he gave this alternative approach a measure of detail, clarity, and theoretical weight it had never had before. Because he gave prominence to a theory of film music that before him was faint and piecemeal at best, Eisenstein should be recognized as an important voice not just in film theory, but in the history of film music theory as well.

Notes

1. For a discussion of how these essays developed and how they developed out of Eisenstein's earlier essays on montage technique, see Bordwell, *The Cinema of Eisenstein,* 163–198, 291; and Leyda's introduction to Eisenstein, *The Film Sense,* iii–vi. For additional context on these essays, see also Christie and Elliott, *Eisenstein at 90;* Christie and Taylor, *Eisenstein Rediscovered;* Kleberg and Lovgren, *Eisenstein Revisited;* Taylor and Christie, *Inside the Film Factory.*

2. See Spottiswoode, *A Grammar,* 192–93; Kracauer, *Theory of Film,* 133–56; Bazin, *What is Cinema?* 17–40; Metz, *Film Language,* 32–33.

3. Mitry, *Esthétique,* 157; Petric, "Sight and Sound," 27; Gallez, "The Prokofiev-Eisenstein Collaboration," 29–30.

4. Leyda, *Kino,* 350–51.

5. Bordwell, *The Cinema of Eisenstein,* 188.

6. Adorno and Eisler, *Composing for the Films,* 65–68, 152–59.

7. Prendergast, *The Neglected Art,* 223–26.

8. Gallez, "The Prokofiev-Eisenstein Collaboration." Other film music historians have added to Eisenstein's demise not with criticism but with virtual silence; see Marks, *Music,* 12n47; Gorbman, *Unheard Melodies,* 15. Prokofiev's biographers have, understandably, been kinder; see Samuels, *Prokofiev,* 136–37; Nestyev, *Prokofiev;* Egorova, *Soviet Film Music,* 66–68. Leyda also defends Eisenstein's musical literacy, particularly his knowledge of opera (Leyda, *Kino,* 350).

9. See Paulin, "Richard Wagner." Most of the major playing or instruction manuals in the silent period discuss aspects of thematic presentation in film accompaniment. See Bey-

non, *Musical Presentation;* Rapee, *Encyclopedia;* Lang and West, *Musical Accompaniment;* Reisenfeld, "Music."

10. Beynon encourages musicians to organize their repertoire and by extension their accompaniments, first by tempo and second by mood or emotion. The orchestral leader's library, he observes, "should consist of as many pieces of music of varied *tempi* and character as he can possibly procure" (Beynon, *Musical Presentation,* 15). The bulk of Beynon's manual is taken up with giving examples as how to best categorize music according to tempo and mood or emotion.

11. Ibid., 102.

12. Clair, "Pure Cinema," and Clair, "Rhythm."

13. For a good general description of this film and the artistic movement that inspired it, see Shattuck, *The Banquet Years,* 170–74.

14. Two studies have described Satie's score and cue sheet in detail: Gallez, "Satie's *Entr'acte,*" and Marks, *Music,* 167–85.

15. Harding, *Erik Satie,* 229.

16. Marks ultimately characterizes Satie's unusual approach as patchwork or "crazy-quilt" (Marks, *Music,* 172). Contemporary descriptions of the score, however, saw it not only as corrosive but related to the difficult aspects of Stravinsky's work: "Without Strawinsky [*sic*] would Satie have dared to take a melodic and rhythmic group of notes, repeat them without change during a whole scene, and then pass abruptly to another group at the beginning of the next scene?" (Petit, "Music," 34). That Satie was the first to use such an approach also has to be qualified. As Marks notes, some scores that predate Satie's—like Simon's score to *An Arabian Tragedy* (1911)—use a repetitious and rhythmic approach, but not to the extent that Satie does. The *Entr'acte* score is striking, even original, in the way that it exclusively isolated the rhythmic and metrical possibilities of a music accompaniment; see Marks, *Music,* 170, and also Harding, *Erik Satie,* 228.

17. Whitesitt, *The Life and Music,* 8–20.

18. There is also some evidence to suggest that the film *Ballet mécanique* may have existed first and may have prompted Antheil to write his musical score of the same name; see Oja, *Making Music,* 89–90.

19. Whitesitt, *The Life and Music,* 106.

20. Oja, *Making Music,* 89.

21. Whitsett, *The Life and Music,* 107, and Oja, *Making Music,* 85–89. See also Karin Bijsterveld, "A Servile Imitation," 129.

22. Oja, *Making Music,* 87. See also Bijsterveld, "A Servile Imitation," 128–30.

23. Whitesitt, *The Life and Music,* 105–106; and Oja, *Making Music,* 79–84.

24. Whitesitt, *The Life and Music,* 105–106.

25. London, 35–36.

26. Sabaneev, *Music,* 17–18.

27. Ibid., 21.

28. Ibid., 109.

29. Bergan, *Eisenstein,* 172–89.

30. Ibid., 123–24. See also Meisel, "Wie schreibt man Filmmusik?" 57.

31. This is not to suggest that Meisel himself did not contribute to the "rhythmic" sound and approach of the score. In earlier film scores and the incidental music he had written for Piscator's quasi-Marxist theater, Meisel had been the architect and foremost advocate of a particularly modern and noise-filled style of music called "Gerauschmusik." See Sudendorf, "Revolte im Orchestergraben." It was perhaps, however, this more literal use of musicalized noise in both film and theater that Eisenstein was hoping to avoid in the final reel. Indeed, on at least two other occasions, Meisel suggests that in regard to this illustrative approach to film music, he and Eisenstein had diverging opinions. In an essay he wrote for *Pravda,* Meisel describes not only how the Russians (i.e., Eisenstein) were the first to encourage the original score as the only proper counterpart to the great multi-reel epic (i.e., *Potemkin*), but how

the purpose of the original score was to underline the style and "rhythm" of the picture. See "Meisel: An die Prawda," and also Meisel, "Wie schreibt man Filmmusik?" where Meisel later rather uncharacteristically advocates using a Wagnerian approach to film scoring for Fanck's film *Der Heilige Berg* (The Holy Mountain, 1926). In his discussion of Meisel, London, too, singles out the *Bronenosets Potyomkin* score as Meisel's best and most unique, that "his expressionistic style, turning first and foremost on rhythm, was many stages in advance of the films for which he composed" (London, *Film Music*, 93). But London, too, suggests that it is really Eisenstein who should be credited with the unusual aspects of the last reel's score, not Meisel, pointing out that the remainder of Meisel's film scores were hardly of a similar type or quality. Meisel's score for Ruttmann's *Berlin: Die Sinfonie der Großstadt* (Berlin: Symphony of a City, 1927) in particular, London observes, was "energy wasted in useless musical experiments." See London, *Film Music*, 94.

32. Eisenstein, *S. M. Eisenstein*, 236–37.

33. Eisenstein later made this connection overt. After developing the theory of vertical montage, Eisenstein superimposed many of those ideas about music back onto his analysis of his own silent films. In much later discussions of the music for the final reel of *Bronenosets Potyomkin*, for instance, Eisenstein reworks his discussion of "rhythm" to give it a more emphatically structural definition. The purpose of the music in the film was to reinforce the structure and montage of the sequence, he insists, not to illustrate the events in it—the mood of the sailors or the sound of the battleship's engines as it steamed out to meet the Imperial fleet. See Eisenstein, *Film Form*, 177–78.

34. Bergan, *Eisenstein*, 133–34. Eisenstein and Meisel parted company in 1929 after Eisenstein accused Meisel of damaging the reception of the film by projecting it at a speed that, while suiting the music, was much too fast; see Bergan, *Eisenstein* , 166–67.

35. The improper use of sound effects in particular, Eisenstein and Pudovkin warned, could destroy the art of montage, the technique they believed secured film's autonomy from other arts: "Only the *contrapuntal use* of sound vis-à-vis the visual garment of montage will open up new possibilities for the development and perfection of montage. . . . The first experiments in sound must aim at a sharp discord with the visual images" (Taylor and Christie, *Inside the Film Factory*, 234–45).

36. Messman, "Sound Film," 235–36. For Messman, Eisenstein's observation that the new technology would "industrialize" or even destroy the technique of montage was significant. But that sound film also threatened the relationship that film and montage had already established with music was just as important. Music, too, for Messman, needed to be theoretically renegotiated, especially its relationship with the technique of montage. While Messman did not offer any specific suggestions for this, his criticism may have had the unintended consequence of prodding Eisenstein to include music in his evolving theory of sound film.

37. That a full theoretical discussion of music in sound film did not emerge in the immediate wake of *Bronenosets Potyomkin* was partly due to circumstances beyond Eisenstein's control. Stalin and the great Soviet purges between 1929 and 1933 interrupted Eisenstein's work, as did a trip to the United States in the early 1930s. After touring the Hollywood studios, where he considered developing several projects, Eisenstein eventually traveled to Mexico and began working on a new sound film entitled *Que Viva Mexico*. Threatening telegrams from Stalin in 1931, however, recalled him to Moscow, and he was eventually forced to abandon the film. Once back in the Soviet Union, as punishment for his independence and anti-Soviet behavior, Eisenstein was relegated to teaching. A second sound film, *Bezhin lug* (Bezhin Meadow), which Eisenstein had begun shooting in 1935, was banned before it was completed in 1937. See Bordwell, *The Cinema of Eisenstein*, 15–27; and Bergan, *Eisenstein*, 190–217.

38. Eisenstein, *The Film Sense*, 163–64. This particular quotation is also central to Adorno's and Eisler's analysis of Eisenstein's theory. See Adorno and Eisler, *Composing for the Films*, 68.

39. Eisenstein, *The Film Sense*, 168.

40. Ibid., 173.

41. Bordwell, *The Cinema of Eisenstein,* 186–87.

42. Eisenstein, *The Film Sense,* 83.

43. Ibid.

44. Bordwell, *The Cinema of Eisenstein,* 186.

45. Eisenstein, *The Film Sense,* 84.

46. Ibid., 169.

47. Adorno and Eisler, *Composing for the Films,* 152–57; and Prendergast, *Film Music,* 223–26.

48. Bordwell, *The Cinema of Eisenstein,* 188.

49. Eisenstein, *The Film Sense,* 95–96.

50. See Adorno and Eisler, *Composing for the Films,* 155–56. Prendergast also accuses those film theorists who have adopted Eisenstein's approach as having a "superficial knowledge and understanding of music." See Prendergast, *Film Music,* 226. In reality, while Eisenstein may very well have lacked the formal training of a professional composer, his knowledge of the musical literature, especially as it is revealed in *The Film Sense,* was quite sophisticated. See for instance his references to composers from Bach to Gounod, Verdi, and Scriabin in both "Synchronization of Senses" and "Form and Content: Practice," and his discussion of both Wagner's and Scriabin's ideas for a *Gesamtkunstwerk* in *Film Form,* 181–82.

References

Adorno, Theodor, and Hanns Eisler. *Composing for the Films.* London: Athlone Press, 1994.

Antheil, George. *Bad Boy of Music.* New York: Doubleday and Doran, 1945.

Bazin, André. *What Is Cinema?* Vol. 1. Ed. and trans. H. Gray. Berkeley: University of California Press, 1967.

Bergan, Ronald. *Eisenstein: A Life in Conflict.* Overlook Press, 1999.

Beynon, George. *Musical Presentation of Motion Pictures.* New York: G. Schirmer, 1920.

Bijsterveld, Karin. "A Servile Imitation: Disputes About Machines in Music, 1910–1930." In *Music and Technology in the Twentieth Century,* ed. H.-J. Braun. Baltimore: Johns Hopkins University Press, 2002, 121–35.

Bordwell, David. *The Cinema of Eisenstein.* Cambridge, Mass.: Harvard University Press, 1993.

Christie, Ian, and David Elliott, eds. *Eisenstein at 90.* Oxford: Museum of Modern Art, 1988.

Christie, Ian, and Richard Taylor, eds. *Eisenstein Rediscovered.* London: Routledge, 1993.

Clair, René. "Pure Cinema and Commercial Cinema." In *Cinema Yesterday and Today.* New York: Dover, 1972, 99–100.

———. "Rhythm." In *French Film Theory and Criticism, Vol. 1,* ed. Richard Abel. Princeton: Princeton University Press, 1988, 368–70.

Egorova, Tatiana. *Soviet Film Music: An Historical Survey.* Trans. T. Ganf and N. Egunova. Amsterdam: Harwood, 1997.

Eisenstein, Sergei. *Film Form.* New York: Meridian Books, 1947.

———. *The Film Sense.* New York: Meridian Books, 1968.

———. *S. M. Eisenstein: Selected Works. Vol.2, "Towards a Theory of Montage."* Ed. M. Glenny and R. Taylor. London: British Film Institute, 1991.

Gallez, Douglas. "Satie's *Entr'acte:* A Model of Film Music." *Cinema Journal* 16/2 (1976): 36–50.

———. "The Prokofiev-Eisenstein Collaboration: *Nevsky* and *Ivan* Revisted." *Cinema Journal* 17/2 (1978): 13–35.

Gorbman, Claudia. *Unheard Melodies: Narrative Film Music.* Bloomington: Indiana University Press.

Harding, James. *Erik Satie.* New York: Praeger Press, 1975.

Kleberg, Lars, and Haken Lovgren, eds. *Eisenstein Revisited.* Stockholm: Almqvist and Wiksell, 1987.

Kracauer, Siegfried. *Theory of Film.* Princeton: Princeton University Press, 1960.

Lang, Edith, and George West. *Musical Accompaniment of Moving Pictures.* Boston: Boston Music Co., 1920.

Leyda, Jay. *Kino: A History of the Russian and Soviet Film.* Princeton: Princeton University Press, 1973.

London, Kurt. *Film Music.* Trans. E. S. Bensinger. London: Faber and Faber, 1936.

Marks, Martin. *Music and the Silent Film: Contexts and Case Studies, 1894–1924.* New York: Oxford University Press, 1997.

Meisel, Edmund. "Meisel: An die Prawda und alle Kino-Zeitungen Moskaus." *Kinomatograph* 1 (1984): 64–65.

———. "Wie schreibt man Filmmusik?" *Kinomatograph* 1 (Deutschen Filmmuseum Frankfurt, 1984): 57–60. Originally published in *Ufa-Magazine* 14/1 (1927).

Messman, Vladimir. "Sound Film." In *Inside the Film Factory,* ed. R. Taylor and I. Christie. London: Routledge, 1988, 235–36.

Metz, Christian. *Film Language: A Semiotics of the Cinema.* Trans. M. Taylor. New York: Oxford University Press, 1974.

Mitry, Jean. *Esthétique et pyschologie du cinéma,* vol. 2. Paris: Editions universitaire, 1965.

———. *S. M. Eisenstein.* Paris: Éditions universitaires, 1961.

Nestyev, Israel. *Prokofiev.* Trans. F. Jones. Stanford: Stanford University Press, 1960.

Oja, Carol. *Making Music Modern: New York in the 1920s.* New York: Oxford University Press, 2003.

Paulin, Scott. "Richard Wagner and the Fantasy of Cinematic Unity: The Idea of the *Gesamtkunstwerk* in the History and Theory of Film Music." In *Music and Cinema,* ed. J. Buhler, C. Flinn, and D. Neumeyer. Hanover, N.H.: Wesleyan University Press, 2000, 58–84.

Petit, Raymond. "Music for French Films." *Modern Music* 3/2 (1926): 34.

Petric, Vlada. "Sight and Sound: Counterpoint or Entity?" *Filmmaker's Newsletter* 6/7 (1973): 27–31.

Prendergast, Roy. *The Neglected Art of Film Music.* New York: W.W. Norton, 1992.

Rapee, Erno. *Encyclopedia of Music for Pictures.* New York: Belwin, 1925.

Reisenfeld, Hugo. "Music and Motion Pictures," *The Motion Picture in Its Economic and Social Aspects* 128 (November 1926): 58–62.

Sabaneev, Leonid. *Music for the Films,* trans. S. W. Pring. London: Sir Issac Pitman and Songs, 1935.

Samuels, Claude. *Prokofiev.* Trans. M. John. London: Calder and Boyars, 1971.

Shattuck, Roger. *The Banquet Years: The Origins of the Avante Garde in France, 1885–WWI.* New York: Vintage, 1967.

Spottiswoode, Raymond. *A Grammar of the Film: An Analysis of Film Technique.* Berkeley: University of California Press, 1962.

Sudendorf, Werner. "Revolte im Orchestergraben Zur Biographie Edmund Meisels." *Kinomatograph* 1 (Deutschen Filmmuseum Frankfurt, 1984): 7–13.

Taylor, Richard, and Ian Christie, eds. *Inside the Film Factory.* London: Routledge, 1991.

Whitesitt, Linda. *The Life and Music of George Antheil.* Ann Arbor: UMI Research Press, 1983.

Filmography

ALEKSANDR NEVSKIY (**ALEXANDER NEVSKY**)

release:	1 December 1938, USSR
duration:	112 mins
dir:	Sergei M. Eisenstein, Dmitri Vasilyev
prod co:	Mosfilm
actors:	Nikolai Cherkasov (Prince Aleksandr Nevskiy); Nikolai Okhlopkov (Vasili Buslai); Andrei Abrikosov (Gavrilo Oleksich); Dmitri Orlov (Ignat, the master armorer); Vasili Novikov (Pavsha, Governor of Pskov); Nikolai Arsky (Domash Tverdislavich, a Novgorod boyar); Varvara Massalitinova (Buslai's mother); Vera Ivashova (Olga Danilovna, a maid of Novgorod); Aleksandra Danilova (Vasilisa, a maid of Pskov); Vladimir Yershov (Von Balk, Grand Master of the Teutonic Order); Sergei Blinnikov (Tverdilo, the traitor); Ivan Lagutin (Anani, a monk); Lev Fenin (The Archbishop); Naum Rogozhin (The black-cowled Monk)
camera:	Eduard Tisse
music:	Sergei Prokofiev
DVD:	Image Entertainment (21 October 1998), ASIN: 630513104X
	Criterion (24 April 2001); with *Ivan the Terrible*, ASIN: B00004XQN5
CD:	Deutsche Grammophon (23 January 1996), Chicago Symphony Orchestra, ASIN: B000001GQC
	RCA (12 November 1996), St. Petersburg Philharmonic Orchestra, ASIN: B000003G5Y
	RCA (13 July 2004), St. Petersburg Philharmonic Orchestra (original recording remastered), ASIN: B0002DD674

BALLET MÉCANIQUE

release:	24 September 1924
duration:	19 mins
dir:	Fernand Léger
actors:	Kiki of Montparnasse (Alice Prin)
camera:	Man Ray
music:	George Antheil
DVD:	Image Entertainment (18 October 2005); on *Unseen Cinema—Early American Avant Garde Film 1894–1941 (1910)*; ASIN: B000AYEIJA
CD:	Naxos (18 September 2001), ASIN: B00005NCYE

BRONENOSETS POTYOMKIN (**BATTLESHIP POTEMKIN**)

release:	21 December 1925 (Moscow)
duration:	75 mins
dir:	Sergei M. Eisenstein; Grigori Aleksandrov
prod:	Jacob Bliokh
prod co:	Goskino
actors:	Aleksandr Antonov (Grigory Vakulinchuk, Bolshevik sailor); Vladimir Barsky (Commander Golikov); Grigori Aleksandrov (Chief Officer Giliarovsky); Ivan Bobrov (Young sailor); Mikhail Gomorov (Militant Sailor);

Aleksandr Levshin (Petty Officer); N. Poltavseva (Woman with pince-nez); Konstantin Feldman (Student agitator); Prokopenko (Mother carrying wounded boy); A. Glauberman (wounded boy); Beatrice Vitoldi (Woman with baby carriage)

camera:	Vladimir Popov; Eduard Tisse
music:	Edmund Meisel
DVD:	Image Entertainment (7 October 1998), ASIN: 6305090033
	Eureka (17 January 2000), ASIN: B00004SGIS
	Delta (10 March 2004), ASIN: B0001EFTXI
CD:	Sound Track Factory; 19 September 2000; ASIN: B00000811E (with *Der heilige Berg*)

ENTR'ACTE

release:	3 December 1924
duration:	22 mins
dir:	René Clair
prod:	Rolf de Maré
prod co:	Les Ballets Suédois
actors:	Jean Börlin; Inge Frïss; Francis Picabia; Marcel Duchamp; Man Ray; Darius Milhaud
camera:	Jimmy Berliet
music:	Erik Satie
DVD:	Criterion (20 August 2002); with *A nous la liberté*; ASIN: B000067IY4
CD:	Naxos (31 August 1999); Orchestre Symphonique et Lyrique de Nancy; ASIN: B00000JYTF

EIGHT

Aleksandr Nevskiy: Prokofiev's Successful Compromise with Socialist Realism

REBECCA SCHWARTZ-BISHIR

The film *Aleksandr Nevskiy* (Alexander Nevskiy, 1938) is a remarkable achievement for many reasons. It was one of the few films released in the late 1930s Soviet Union that was successful both at home and in the West. It clearly communicated the Communist Party's policy of Socialist Realism. It also brought high praise to its embattled creators. Perhaps most remarkable, however, is that its famous collaborators, the director Sergei Eisenstein and the composer Sergei Prokofiev, managed to assert their artistic independence while working within the confines of the stifling political system.

When Eisenstein was selected to make the film, his career was in need of rehabilitation. His achievements with montage in the 1920s were being rejected as decadent, and his work during the 1930s had been repeatedly stifled by bureaucrats.[1] The approach he took to the film was understandably conservative, but even so it bears his unmistakable style in its editing and timing.

Prokofiev was also under pressure to prove himself both a good Communist and a great Soviet composer during the *Aleksandr Nevskiy* project. His years abroad (1918–36) and close contact with other émigrés, among them Sergei Diaghilev, rendered him suspect. By 1938, his modernist experiments in music, once hailed as progress, were alien to the policy of Socialist Realism. As in Eisenstein's case, *Aleksandr Nevskiy* marked an important point in Prokofiev's career, proving both his loyalty to Communist Party ideals and his talent for working within boundaries. His music fulfilled its basic function of accompanying the picture, but it also enhanced the meaning of the film, making the Socialist Realist message unmistakable. In addition, Prokofiev made his work an outlet for his personal style, and invoked sophisticated musical meanings and methods in the process. Eisenstein's approach to *Aleksandr Nevskiy* and the fact that it resurrected his status as a Soviet filmmaker has received ample consideration over the years. This essay instead considers Prokofiev's compositional choices in light of the political climate.

Socialist Realism

The government policy of Socialist Realism was the standard by which all works were measured in the Soviet Union of the 1930s. The ultimate goal behind Socialist Realist art was to reach the masses with the party doctrine.[2] There were three requirements that all artists' work had to meet. First, the topics of Socialist Realist art had to educate, instill loyalty in, and provide an attractive vision of the future Soviet Union for the citizens of the country. Second, all works had to be easy to comprehend in order for the citizens to understand what to think and feel. Third, Socialist Realist creations were to perpetuate the idea that the party's perspective was the only way to see the world. Any work that suggested otherwise, either in subject matter or presentation, was viewed as a threat.

In the eyes of the party, art was inseparable from politics. Socialist Realism therefore offered artists two choices: conformity or non-conformity. Conforming was expected; not conforming resulted in persecution. The boundaries of Socialist Realism were not as simple as they seem, however, because they were defined by criticism rather than by explicit doctrine. Even those works that appeared to be congruent with Socialist Realist policy were sometimes, for the most insignificant or ridiculous reasons, declared unfit, or labeled subversive. A work was subversive if its creator consciously sought to undermine the party in some way; he or she fooled the party into not noticing that subversion had taken place; and an audience got the messages in the work that the party missed. The charge of subversion was highly flexible and easily applied.

A perfect example is *Derzis' Karluša!* (Karl Brunner, 1936). This film, scripted by Béla Balázs and directed by Aleksej Masljukov, recounts the story of a German boy who is orphaned as a result of his parents' arrest by Nazis for being Communists. A work ideally suited to creating a single, pro-Communist view of the world, the film had to be withdrawn because of a baseless accusation. According to Peter Kenez, "someone maintained that it was based on the true story of the son of Ruth Fischer, a Trotskyist."[3] Leon Trotsky was one the early architects of the USSR and a rival of Stalin. Although Trotsky was politically impotent by the time of *Derzis' Karluša!,* the mere suggestion that someone in the audience would make the connection between the film, Fischer, and Trotsky twisted the film's meaning into a threat to Stalin's authority. In spite of Balázs's protests that he was unaware that Fischer had a son, he could not save the work.

Another label used to censor works was "formalism." "Formalism" began as a movement in literary criticism that surfaced before and occurred after the 1917 Revolution. It was based on the idea that literature is autonomous and each work is self-contained. As the party leadership became more conservative and paranoid after the end of the NEP (New Economic Policy) in 1928, the term was used to brand works that were foreign, modern, and/or decadent. Where cinema was concerned, "formalism" was used to point out "any concern with the specifically aesthetic aspect of film-making, any deviation from a simple narrative line, and artistic innovation."[4] Musicologist Glenn Watkins clarifies "modernism" and "formalism" as the terms were applied to music by the Soviet censors. He writes that "'formalist perversions' . . . meant a separation of form from content, which in practice meant 'modernism' of any sort."[5] The term "modernism" we will take to refer to musical techniques that were associated with composers from Western Europe and the United States and that were forbidden in 1930s USSR. Among these techniques are "particularly angular, unsingable melodies, primitivist rhythms, Futurist noises, and especially dodecaphony."[6] Rather than empower artists with the freedom to select subject and method, the Socialist Realist policy put creative interpretation into the hands of the censors. For Soviet artists, the great challenge of the 1930s and 1940s was to make a work one's own while still following a set of restrictive and unclear "rules" imposed *after* one's work was finished.

An emblematic case is Dmitri Shostakovich's opera *Lady Macbeth of the Mtsensk District,* which premiered in 1934. This work recounts the miserable life of Katerina Izmailova, her sexual experiences, and the murder she commits. Portraying her as a victim of circumstance, much of the music graphically represents what is taking place on stage: in the most sensational scene, intercourse with her seducer Sergei is evoked by trombone slides. Over the course of the next two years, the work was performed numerous times in the Soviet Union as well as abroad, mostly to critical acclaim. The reception of the opera as the great achievement of Soviet music, however, was reversed after Stalin attended a performance on 26 January 1936. An anonymous review two days later in *Pravda* denounced the work as "Chaos Instead of Music" and labeled the work "formalist."[7] The opera that had been regarded as evidence of the success of party policy and the rejection of Western methods and society was now judged a "bourgeois" work.[8] The fallout from this response jeopardized Shostakovich's life, all but paralyzed the music community, and traumatized Soviet artists in general.

Socialist Realism and artistic censorship were just part of Stalin's totalitarian control of the entire population. During 1938, when *Aleksandr Nevskiy* was completed, the Great Purge taking place terrorized everyone in the Soviet Union, from party officials to intellectuals to peasants. Show trials weeded out the leaders of "fascist conspiracies," some of whom were military and cultural heroes. Among the well-known people singled out were General Mikhail Tukhachevsky, a leader in the Red Army and a patron of Shostakovich, who was executed in 1937; and Vsevolod Meyerhold, the renowned theater director, who was arrested in 1939 and tortured before his death in prison. In this political context, individuality was both threatened and regarded as a threat; appearing non-conformist in any way was virtually signing one's own death warrant.

Prokofiev and *Nevskiy*

Did Prokofiev break the "rules" of Socialist Realism in *Aleksandr Nevskiy*? If Prokofiev did indeed break these "rules," were his choices subversive? What, if any, compromise did he achieve between his artistic style and Socialist Realism? Both the *Aleksandr Nevskiy Cantata Op. 78* and the film music with its visual counterpart are considered in this investigation. The film reveals how music and image work together to teach the Socialist Realist message of the story. The *Cantata* score allows a close analysis of Prokofiev's counterpoint, harmony, tonalities, phrasing, and other musical elements.[9]

The film *Aleksandr Nevskiy* is based on the thirteenth-century historical figure of the same name. In 1242, the Russians are under attack from the Teutonic Knights as well as the Mongols, and ask Prince Alexander to help them defend the town of Novgorod. Nevskiy, who led his countrymen in a defeat of the Swedes in 1240, agrees to lead the merchants and peasants, but announces there will be no defense. Instead, they will attack the Teutons. The film chronicles the Russians' preparations for battle, the Teutons' assault on the people, and Nevskiy's military victory in the battle fought on the ice at Lake Chudskoe. The victory and the ensuing celebration reveal the thinly veiled moral of the story: Russians owe their loyalty to their homeland, which is in danger, and must sacrifice everything in order to save it. The scenario was well suited to Socialist Realist policy: it taught a positive history that was an analogy to the present; it instilled loyalty; and it implied an idealized vision of the future (in this case the defeat of modern-day Germans) as foreshadowed in the past.

Collaboration on the image-sound relationship made the film highly effective. When Prokofiev began work on the film music, he considered incorporating medieval Catholic chants and Russian folk tunes. He soon concluded, however, that authentic thirteenth-century chants and folk music would be too "remote and emotionally alien"[10] for the Soviet audience of the 1930s, and with Eisenstein decided that he should modernize the musical past in order to encourage the audience's imagination. This would work better: the more the audience was able to relate to the topic at hand, the more readily it would accept its lessons.

Eisenstein believed that music was essential to the communication of the drama in this film, and was willing to alter scenes to fit the music.[11] His willingness to collaborate likewise pleased Prokofiev, and is one of the reasons the composer accepted criticism from the director that made his music more effective.[12] Another reason is that Prokofiev had great respect for Eisenstein's musicianship.[13] Eisenstein's estimation of the audio-visual relationship was so great that he searched for a direct correlation between the temporal progression of sound and film, which he named his theory of "vertical montage."[14]

Prokofiev's working methods helped his music coordinate with the action onscreen, augmenting the message of individual sections. He composed music for finished scenes by tapping his fingers in order to measure the progression of musical time to the time in a scene.[15] In a letter to Jay Leyda after the film was finished, Eisenstein wrote: "I think there could be said more about the visual and sound unity and composition: in some of the sequences we've reached with Prokofiev the results I was dreaming about pretty long ago."[16]

Prokofiev explored the available sound technology in order to match audio and visual messages. In some cases, he used modernist, "formalist" techniques as a means to his end. For example, he used distortion, caused by loud sounds played directly into the microphone, in conjunction with the Teutonic buglers. Prokofiev believed this manipulation was an imaginative approach to the modern representation of sounds that "must have been unpleasant to the Russian ear [of the thirteenth century]."[17] For the Soviet audience, this sound would have been unfamiliar and unmusical. Another recording method, which he referred to as "inverted" orchestration, called for the simultaneous juxtaposition of loud instruments (e.g., trombone) played far away from the microphone, and soft instruments (e.g., bassoon) played in proximity to it.[18] Although Prokofiev does not identify where inverted orchestration was used, the most likely place is during the Teutons' attack on Pskov, when the Germans march through and destroy the town. In this case, the bassoon's sound is much louder than that of the trombone, which is not normally the case, and the result is the creation of a strange new timbre. This trick dashes conventional expectations and takes the predictability out of orchestration.

The composer also experimented with mixing techniques. One technique he used was the separation of sound choirs (e.g., brass in one studio, vocal choir in another) in order to control the balance. Another mixing technique involved the use of three microphones to record a performance whose streams of sound were tempered and combined in the final cut. In all these cases, sounds were manipulated in order to intensify the aesthetic effect and were a departure from the written score. Prokofiev and the sound engineer Boris Volsky's experiments were stepping beyond the boundaries of permitted practice by treating his score as a flexible music-play akin to a screenplay. Given that film directors of the day were not allowed to deviate from their screenplays, the experiments with musical sound were risky.

Sound technologies in the USSR developed later than and largely independent of those in the West; thus Prokofiev's experiments appear both positive, highlighting the progressiveness of the Soviet cinema, and rather innocent, reflecting his inquisitive nature. A more subversive reading of Prokofiev's choices, however, is that he was attempting to duplicate "decadent" methods he had learned about in February and March of 1938 while visiting several motion picture studios in California. According to Russell Merritt, Prokofiev was especially impressed by Walt Disney's accomplishments in sound and picture synchronization. Merritt suggests that experiments made by *Fantasia* conductor Leopold Stokowski—among them "sound mixing, microphone placement, [the use of] sound filters, variable acoustics, and even electronic instruments" in the recording of *The Sorcerer's Apprentice*—affected Prokofiev's work on *Aleksandr Nevskiy*.[19] Dukas's music had been recorded just before Prokofiev arrived, so he would not have witnessed the experiments taking place with that portion of the film, but it is likely that he discussed the methods with his friend Stokowski. Incorporating the West's artistic innovations into the sound track was going against the doctrine.

Furthermore, it was in Prokofiev's nature to challenge musical authorities and their stodginess and assert his individuality. During his years at the St. Petersburg Conservatory, Prokofiev resisted Nikolai Rimsky-Korsakov and Anatol Liadov's teaching methods, as well as his piano teacher Anna Yesipova's choice of music and playing technique, as boring and unsuited to his style.[20] Prokofiev composed and played in a way his professors found passable, while he continued to develop his compositional voice and pianistic technique outside of his classes. In 1914, he performed his own First Piano Concerto in the conservatory's Rubenstein competition, rather than one by Mozart or Beethoven as per tradition. After heated debate, the judges declared Prokofiev the winner and awarded him the coveted prize, a grand piano. Prokofiev was prepared for the Socialist Realist challenges during his work on *Aleksandr Nevskiy* by his conservatory experiences, which taught him how to compromise while operating within a conservative system, and ultimately succeed.

Prokofiev's recording experiments changed *how* sounds were made in the USSR: mixing and distortion were a direct and intrusive manipulation of the recording method, revealing an emphasis on aesthetics. In addition, his deliberate manipulation of the sounds themselves changed *what* his audience heard. The typical Socialist Realist musical work was boring and "deliberately cultivated" to be tedious.[21] In contrast, Prokofiev's music for *Aleksandr Nevskiy* was exciting and alive with fresh sounds. Prokofiev, therefore, did break the basic "rules" of Socialist Realism by using "formalist/modernist" techniques in the sound track. Ironically, by embracing modernism—and thus subverting one major tenet of Socialist Realism—Prokofiev furthered the primary goal of reaching the masses and giving them the Socialist Realist point of view.

Prokofiev also broke the doctrine's "rules" with his compositional choices. At the heart of *Aleksandr Nevskiy*'s message is the distinction of cultures through stereotype. Compositional techniques, founded in the Socialist Realist distinction between Russian (classical, folk) and Western European (modernist) music of the day, explicitly set the Russian protagonists apart from the Teuton antagonists. The importance of recognizable musical stereotypes is that they were another way of teaching the audience the difference between good and bad, which reinforced the Russian and Teuton images on the screen. The distinction of cultural stereotypes, however, gave Prokofiev creative freedom.

The music characterizing the Russian defenders is conservative in that it is based on musical conventions like tonal harmony and conjunct lyrical melodies. The chorus and its text, which celebrates Nevskiy's earlier victory over the Swedes, tell us of the battle-readiness of the Russians. These characteristics suggest familiarity and imply heroism. In order to portray the Teuton invaders as foreign and evil, Prokofiev composed music that was based on contemporary practices, utilizing "modern" techniques like polytonality, montage-like structures, and melodies that move in disjunct motion.[22] The exception in the Teutons' music is the Latin chant: it is singable, but percussive and monotonous, not lyrical, and links by its nature to religion. These musical characteristics are used to suggest alien qualities and to imply brutality. Two movements from the *Cantata,* "Song about Alexander Nevskiy" and "The Battle on the Ice," demonstrate these musical stereotypes.

"Song about Alexander Nevskiy" is distinguished by its conservative musical traits. It is tonal (in B-flat major) and diatonic, free of what some might consider confusing chromatic notes. As a result, its sound is predominantly consonant (harmonically stable). Its melody is conjunct, simple, and tuneful. Altos and tenors sing in melodic and rhythmic unison in the first and last sections of the *Cantata,* and there is no vocal polyphony. Call and response gives the text and the antecedent-consequent phrase structure a rhetorical quality. It is orchestrated for strings, woodwinds, and mixed choir. It suggests a Russian characterization that is united (the hymn-like rhythmic and melodic unison, the call and response rhetoric of the chorus), heroic (the use of a major key and diatonic scale, and the predominance of men's voices), and at peace (its consonant harmony, which moves in largely predictable progressions).[23] Nothing here is complex or subversive, but manifests the Soviet ideal: beautiful music that can move the masses.

In contrast, "The Battle on the Ice" would fit a Socialist Realist definition of "progressive." Most of the music is dissonant, and it changes keys so often that rarely does the listener get a definite sense of a tonal center. In this piece, key area plays an important part in the meaning behind the music. The presence of polytonality (simultaneous melodies written in two or more different keys) adds to the instability and fills the score with tension. The Teutons' battle herald is written in C-sharp minor every time it appears, perhaps to symbolize their machine-like single-mindedness. In contrast, the Russians' music changes keys regularly, arguably as a symbol invoking their flexible military strategy, which in the end is what helps them outsmart the enemy. As the opposing forces clash, so do the keys.

In "The Battle on the Ice" movement, polytonality represents a state of tonal anarchy (a fight over which key is in control, if any, until the battle is won). This anarchy not only complicates the sound of the piece, but also bears a textural similarity to cinematic montage, for which its pioneer, Eisenstein, had been denounced as "formalist" in 1935. Because of this kinship, Prokofiev was taking a chance. Furthermore, the juxtaposition of multiple key areas was a gamble because Prokofiev used a "decadent" technique, polytonality, which complicated the music. From this perspective, his music seems subversive.

In fact, the meaning of tonalities in "The Battle on the Ice" movement has two implications, one highlighting the difference of the Russians and Teutons, the other revealing their likeness. "The Battle on the Ice" movement begins in C-sharp minor, the key of the Teutonic Knights. When the Russians' music enters it begins in B-flat, a full step and a half lower than the Teutons' C-sharp minor, but ends the movement in D-flat major, a key name above the Teutons' C-sharp. This is likely to be a deliberate prediction of the "underdog" Russians' future victory over the static Teutons, rather than mere coincidence or a mistake on the part of the composer. Here Prokofiev's music would seem to fulfill its Socialist Realist mandate: he predicts a victorious future for the Russians through their music. The emergence of the major tonality assures the listener that the Russians have won in the music as well as on screen.

A more subversive implication of the tonalities is the enharmonic relationship of the keys, C-sharp major and D-flat minor. Although each pitch is of a different name and its respective tonality is distinguished by the ordering of the major and minor scales, the pitches do share the same location on the keyboard, a black key. Prokofiev seems to compare the Russian and Teutonic fighters by associating each faction with the same pitch, thus highlighting their similarity.

If intended, this was a significant risk, because the essence of the suggestion is that the "evil" Teutons and the "good" Russians have something in common. Using a musical paradox, he could both adhere to Socialist Realism and expose it for its contradictions. It is a compromise with Socialist Realism that at the same time compromises the doctrine.

The movement's texture also evokes aspects of "formalism." "The Battle on the Ice" sounds complex in part because of the polyphonic texture. There is nothing modern about polyphony, but for Prokofiev, just as it had for Church officials nearly four hundred years earlier during the Catholic Counter-Reformation, polyphony had the potential to create consternation amongst the censors. Polyphony bears a kinship to montage because it combines one distinct musical line with another. The significance of polyphony is that it is more difficult to follow for the average listener than homophonic or hymn-like texture, and hence is a source of possible aesthetic distraction.

Prokofiev's setting of the Teutons' chant is percussive and heavy, and in contrast to the lyrical nature of "Song about Alexander Nevskiy." The fact that it is in Latin also distances it from the Russians' "Song." It alludes to the strangeness of the Teutons: "Peregrinus expectavi/Pedes meos in cymbalis."[24] Perhaps this text was an effort to further the depiction of the Teutonic Knights as inhuman instruments of destruction, and advance the distinction between the Russians and the invaders. There is a strong connection between the Teutons' metallic sounds and images, such as their metal helmets and percussion instruments, throughout the film. Perhaps the text is a subtle pun based on the origins of the Russian word for Germans, "nemets," which meant "foreign" but also "mute." The link between the Teuton chant and this Russian term may have been yet another reinforcement of a long-held, indigenous belief about Germans: to the Soviet audience, the nonsensical nature of the chant text might have mimicked the incomprehensible sounds of a non-Russian speaker. Perhaps, as Morag Kerr proposes, the text was a private joke directed at Igor Stravinsky's Symphony of Psalms. Kerr suggests that Prokofiev might have composed his Teutonic chant by taking a word or two from each movement of Stravinsky's Latin texts and stringing them together.[25] Maybe Prokofiev, in his tongue-in-cheek way, was reinforcing the party's position that a composer who abandons Russia for the West becomes incomprehensible to those at home.

Unlike the "Song about Alexander Nevskiy," "The Battle on the Ice" is orchestrated for extensive percussion and "shrill" brass that augments the dissonant sound of the music and evokes the sense of battle.[26] Its traits allude to a Teutonic stereotype that is repulsive (the lack of lyricism in the melodies), inhuman (the use of percussion; shrill brass; technologically manipulated sounds; and a foreign, incomprehensible language), and barbaric (significant dissonance and lack of strong key center).[27] Much in the music associated with the Teutons is sophisticated and subversive: this music does not attempt to meet the requirements of Socialist Realist art. Instead, it flaunts musical modernism and "formalism" in the face of the censor and the viewer.

What can we conclude about the relationship of Socialist Realism and creativity in the music of *Aleksandr Nevskiy*? Much of the music looks and acts like Socialist Realism, but in several instances it is not. The *Cantata* score and the film music reveal that Prokofiev broke the "rules" of Socialist Realism in his portrayal of the Teuton stereotype. He manipulated the sound track and embraced modernist techniques of composition. He separated the message's form from its Socialist Realist content with his aesthetic choices. He called forth the complex composition and multiple interpretations of montage with his tonal choices and polyphonic texture. This was a gamble during the time of the Great Purges.

Were Prokofiev's choices subversive? It depends on one's perspective. From the party's point of view, where music and politics were one and the same, Prokofiev's modernist choices look like an effort to get around the "rules" of Socialist Realism. His musical "formalism" could easily have been twisted to mean political subversion. From Prokofiev's perspective, however, music and politics were distinct, and one suspects that his subversion of musical restrictions had nothing to do with politics. Instead, he was following his instincts, creating the best music he could while meeting the requirements of the assignment, just as he had done at the conservatory. Prokofiev had not had much praise since returning to the Soviet Union in 1936, and he needed musical success as much for his safety in Soviet society as he did for his own ego. He found a loophole in the Socialist Realist message of the film—to portray the bad guys with the worst sounds he could in order to reinforce the images' message. He subverted musical restrictions, not party politics.

Did the audience comprehend Prokofiev's modernist choices? No evidence has been uncovered that suggests it did. But the potential for understanding was there amongst the musical elite. The USSR of the 1920s had been a hot-bed of musical modernism that included experiments like the Termenvox, the first electronic instrument, built in 1920 by the Soviet acoustics engineer Leon Theremin; constructivist pieces like Alexander Mossolov's *The Iron Foundry* (1928), which evoked the sounds and the mechanical drive of modern factories; and new works from Western Europe such as Alban Berg's opera *Wozzek* and Stravinsky's burlesque *Le Renard,* both of which premiered on the Maryinsky stage in 1927. Surely some of the musicians in the audience must have realized how different and formalistic many of Prokofiev's choices were. Just as the potential association with Trotsky had been enough to end work on Balazs's *Bezhin lug,* the mere possibility that Prokofiev's music might reach the musically educated with a deeper message was enough to render it suspect, if not subversive.

Why, then, was Prokofiev not admonished for his choices? The political ends justified the musical means. One may assume that distinction of stereotypes was of primary importance to the censors, just as it was to Eisenstein and Prokofiev. It appears that *how* Prokofiev represented the differences between the two foes was less important than achieving the goal of differentiation itself. Also, Socialist Realism allowed the censors to be subjective. It is possible that if the censors recognized the "modern" traits in the music they ignored them because the sound of it clarified the difference between Russian and Western music, and the nature of the contrasting societies, so well. In addition, Eisenstein's plot is a combination of historical contradictions and narrative "compression and ellips[es],"[28] and Prokofiev took advantage of the opportunity to match these contradictions with his music. Ironically, this increased the effectiveness of the Socialist Realist message. Last, at this time it was especially important to have works that could be acknowledged as evidence of the success of the Socialist Realist policy. The film and its music send a clear message about the Soviet people and their future.

Richard Taruskin points out that "what a piece of music says is not always, or only, what its composer meant to say."[29] I argue that *Aleksandr Nevskiy* makes its party line very clear, but that is not the only message in Prokofiev's work. The music in this film is evidence of Prokofiev's (at that time) still independent voice. It is undoubtedly in his style, and exhibits the elements that he himself identified as his "basic lines," those of classicism, modernism, lyricism, a toccata-like drive, and a mocking quality.[30] Although it seems contrary, Prokofiev was both conservative—a classicist who respected and relied on conventions of the past—and progressive—an explorer of modernist trends who incorporated them in his music when they suited him. These two traits served him especially well in the case of *Aleksandr Nevskiy,* because he accomplished the unlikely feat of using modernism to conservative ends. The music for this film is a successful compromise with Socialist Realism because it is as much about Prokofiev's style and talent as it is about the cinematic message.

Notes

1. An excellent example is the film *Bezhin lug* (Bezhin Meadow, 1937), which was denounced as a failure by the head of the Soviet film industry, Boris Shumyatsky. During the making of this film, which was never finished, Eisenstein suffered production delays as well as health problems.

2. Both "policy" and "doctrine" henceforth refer to Socialist Realism.

3. Kenez, *Cinema and Soviet Society*, 130.

4. Ibid., 93.

5. Watkins, *Soundings*, 414.

6. Ibid. In 1948 Prokofiev was charged with writing music marked with "formalist distortions." See Slonimsky, *Music since 1900*, 1364; for Prokofiev's letter of apology, see 1373–74.

7. Translated by Slonimsky, *Music since 1900*, 619. The authorship of this article remains uncertain.

8. Schwarz, *Music and Musical Life*, 141.

9. The two versions of the *Aleksandr Nevskiy* music are henceforth referred to as the *Cantata* and the *Film music.*

10. Blok, *Sergei Prokofiev,* 34.

11. Nestyev, *Prokofiev.*

12. Barna, *Eisenstein,* 215–17.

13. Blok, *Sergei Prokofiev,* 34.

14. Eisenstein's theory, known as "vertical montage," may be found in chapter 4, "Form and Content: Practice," of his first book, *The Film Sense.* For analysis of the concept, see Aumont, *Montage Eisenstein;* Prendergast, *Film Music;* Bordwell, *The Cinema of Eisenstein;* Brown, *Overtones and Undertones;* and Eagle, "Visual Patterning."

15. Prendergast, *Film Music,* 50.

16. Leyda, *Kino,* 350.

17. Blok, *Sergei Prokofiev,* 35.

18. Ibid.

19. Merritt, "Recharging *Alexander Nevsky,*" 42.

20. Shlifstein, *Sergei Prokofiev,* 24–25, 27–28, 36.

21. Frolova-Walker, "Stalin," 103.

22. Conjunct, meaning stepwise, versus disjunct, made up of leaps, affects the ease with which a melodic line may be sung. Melodies in conjunct motion, such as the tune "Brother John," are consistently easier to sing than melodies in disjunct motion, such as "The Star Spangled Banner." The significance lies in the fact that the Russians' tunes could probably be sung by the average audience member.

23. James Goodwin also takes this view of the musical characterization of the Russian stereotype (Goodwin, *Eisenstein,* 173). See also Egorova, *Soviet Film Music,* 63.

24. "A foreigner, I expected/My feet to be shod with cymbals" (Goodwin, *Eisenstein,* 172).

25. Kerr, "Prokofiev," 609.

26. Goodwin, *Eisenstein,* 173. Brass and percussion instruments have a long and prevalent association with military music and marches.

27. Ibid.; Egorova, *Soviet Film Music,* 62.

28. Merritt, "Recharging *Alexander Nevsky,*" 36.

29. Taruskin, "Art and Politics," 61.

30. Shlifstein, *Sergei Prokofiev,* 36–37.

References

Aumont, Jacques. *Montage Eisenstein.* Trans. L. Hildreth, C. Penley, and A. Ross. Bloomington: Indiana University Press, 1987.

Barna, Yon. *Eisenstein.* Bloomington: Indiana University Press, 1973.

Blok, Vladimir. *Sergei Prokofiev: Materials Articles Interviews.* Moscow: Progress, 1978.

Bordwell, David. *The Cinema of Eisenstein.* Cambridge, Mass.: Harvard University Press, 1993.

Brown, Royal S. *Overtones and Undertones: Reading Film Music.* Berkeley: University of California Press, 1994.

Eagle, Herbert. "Visual Patterning, Vertical Montage, and Ideological Protest: Eisenstein's Stylistic Legacy to East European Filmmakers." In *Eisenstein at 100: A Reconsideration,* ed. A. LaValley and B. P. Scherr. New Brunswick, N.J.: Rutgers University Press, 2001, 169–190.

Egorova, Tatiana. *Soviet Film Music: An Historical Survey.* Amsterdam: Harwood, 1997.

Eisenstein, Sergei. *The Film Sense.* New York: Harcourt, Brace and World, 1947.

Frolova-Walker, Marina. "Stalin and the Art of Boredom." *Twentieth-Century Music* 1/1 (2004): 101–24.

Goodwin, James. *Eisenstein, Cinema, and History.* Urbana: University of Illinois Press, 1993.

Kenez, Peter. *Cinema and Soviet Society: From the Revolution to the Death of Stalin.* New York: I. B. Tauris, 2001.

Kerr, Morag G. "Prokofiev and his Cymbals." *The Musical Times* 135/1820 (1994): 608–9.

Leyda, Jay. *Kino: A History of the Russian and Soviet Film.* Princeton: Princeton University Press, 1983.

Merritt, Russell. "Recharging *Alexander Nevsky:* Tracking the Eisenstein-Prokofiev War Horse." *Film Quarterly* 48/2 (1994–95): 34–47.

Nestyev, Israel V. *Prokofiev.* Stanford: Stanford University Press, 1960.

Prendergast, Roy. *Film Music: A Neglected Art.* New York: W. W. Norton, 1992.

Schwarz, Boris. *Music and Musical Life in Soviet Russia 1917–1970.* New York: W. W. Norton, 1972.

Shlifstein, S., ed. *Sergei Prokofiev: Autobiography Articles Reminiscences.* Trans. R. Prokofieva. Honolulu: University Press of the Pacific, 2000.

Slonimsky, Nicolas. *Music since 1900.* New York: Charles Scribner's Sons, 1971.

Taruskin, Richard. "Art and Politics in Prokofiev." *Society* 29/1 (1991): 60–63.

Watkins, Glenn. *Soundings: Music in the Twentieth Century.* New York: Schirmer Books, 1995.

Filmography

ALEKSANDR NEVSKIY (ALEXANDER NEVSKY)

release:	1 December 1938, USSR
duration:	112 mins
dir:	Sergei M. Eisenstein, Dmitri Vasilyev
prod co:	Mosfilm
actors:	Nikolai Cherkasov (Prince Aleksandr Nevskiy); Nikolai Okhlopkov (Vasili Buslai); Andrei Abrikosov (Gavrilo Oleksich); Dmitri Orlov (Ignat, the master armorer); Vasili Novikov (Pavsha, Governor of Pskov); Nikolai Arsky (Domash Tverdislavich, a Novgorod boyar); Varvara Massalitinova (Buslai's mother); Vera Ivashova (Olga Danilovna, a maid of Novgorod); Aleksandra Danilova (Vasilisa, a maid of Pskov); Vladimir Yershov (Von Balk, Grand Master of the Teutonic Order); Sergei Blinnikov (Tverdilo, the traitor); Ivan Lagutin (Anani, a monk); Lev Fenin (The Archbishop); Naum Rogozhin (The black-cowled Monk)
camera:	Eduard Tisse
music:	Sergei Prokofiev
DVD:	Image Entertainment (21 October 1998), ASIN: 630513104X
	Criterion (24 April 2001); with *Ivan the Terrible,* ASIN: B00004XQN5
CD:	Deutsche Grammophon (23 January 1996), Chicago Symphony Orchestra, ASIN: B000001GQC
	RCA (12 November 1996), St. Petersburg Philharmonic Orchestra, ASIN: B000003G5Y
	RCA (13 July 2004), St. Petersburg Philharmonic Orchestra (original recording remastered), ASIN: B0002DD674

....

In Marginal Fashion: Sex, Drugs, Russian Modernism, and New Wave Music in *Liquid Sky*

MITCHELL MORRIS

In the beginning, there was the bewildering plot. An extraterrestrial being that resembles an eyeball/embryonic egg in fluorescent aspic visits New York in a ship the size of a Frisbee, and settles on the roof of a penthouse apartment in SoHo inhabited by an androgynous New Wave fashion model named Margaret (Anne Carlisle) and her psychotic, drug-dealing performance artist girlfriend, Adrian. Soon after the diminutive saucer arrives, a German scientist named Johann Hoffman disembarks from a plane at JFK in pursuit. As Hoffman will explain in the film, the extraterrestrial lives off opiates; it has settled above Margaret's flat because of Adrian's heroin supply. Very quickly, it discovers an even better food source: the endorphins released in the human brain at the moment of orgasm. The creature is in luck; Margaret is the indifferent-to-sullen object of constant sexual advances, many of them violent. And she is having a very bad week.

About twenty minutes into the film's cross-cut narrative, Margaret is beaten and raped by a club tourist from whom she has been trying to get cocaine. Her morning after is dominated by insults and intrusive treatment both by Adrian and a junkie client named Paul. But later on that same day, after Margaret has agreed to allow her old college acting teacher, Owen, to have sex with her, something extraordinary happens: Owen dies upon orgasm, pierced through the brain by a large glassy splinter. Later that afternoon, Paul returns to the apartment with rape on his mind. He dies as well. Margaret, who is never close to orgasm during sex, lives on, fantasizing that she is being avenged by "an Indian" (he shoots arrows, after all) in the form of the Empire State Building. Her new abilities by proxy are fraught with vengeful promise.

Margaret's lethal self-assertion begins during a fashion shoot in her apartment even later that same evening when, irritated past all bearing, she seduces a narcissistic, hostile junkie model named Jimmy (also played by Anne Carlisle) so that he will come to death. General dismay and puzzlement ensue. Adrian, not one to forgo a deadly risk, forces Margaret to have sex with her, and meets a predictable fate. At this point, Margaret snaps, and leaves her apartment in search of the man who raped her the night before. When she finds him, she brings him home to kill him too. Until this point, the kinky homicides have been missed by Hoffman; although he has found an apartment from which he can spy on the alien, it is occupied by a TV producer named Sylvia, whose hilarious attempts at seduction prevent him from working. (In another of the film's magnificent implausibilities, Sylvia is the mother of the obnoxious model Jimmy.) When Hoffman finally witnesses the extraterrestrial's predation, he rushes to the apartment to warn Margaret of danger; her response is to stab him, change into a wedding dress, and inject herself with a massive overdose of heroin to seduce the creature herself. Sylvia sees the scientist's murder through his telescope and rushes over in alarm. Arriving at Margaret's building, Sylvia runs into a complete stranger (Paul's wife, Katherine, in search of her errant mate), also heading for the penthouse. As the two watch in astonishment, the saucer emits a beam that appears to absorb Margaret entirely, and flies into the night sky.

What are we to make of such a weird plot, told with the cheesiest of special effects, ham-fisted editing, wooden acting, stilted and implausible dialogue, and a score whose materials often consist of sound effects and peculiar fragmentary musical bits taken from Carl Orff, Marin Marais, and the nineteenth-century German American composer Anthony Philip Heinrich? Upon its release in 1982, *Liquid Sky* was greeted with both acclaim and passionate loathing, and it rapidly became a cult film. Those things that sent it to the margins of audience in the first place guaranteed, of course, that it would continue to flourish there, accruing praise and vilification, as any Google search will reveal. But the difficult features of the film are not the result of technical incompetence; instead, they arise out of the fertile interactions of two belated aesthetic worlds: the Soviet Union in the Brezhnev years, the "era of stagnation"; and America in its post-Watergate/Vietnam War hangover. I first delineate the complex sensibility that seems to underwrite *Liquid Sky,* and then turn to a brief consideration of music as it contributes to the intricate modernist structure of the film while also addressing some important cultural moments in early-1980s America.

Ostranenie

Liquid Sky was directed and partly written by a Soviet emigré, Slava Tsukerman, in collaboration with no fewer than ten other Soviet emigré artists,[1] and many details of the film's shot structure, editing, and mise-en-scène reflect his time spent at the most important Soviet film school, VGIK (the All-Union State Institute of Cinema).[2] This was a lofty cinematic lineage. Admission to VGIK during the late Soviet era was almost exclusively restricted either to members of the *intelligentsia* (the traditional "idea" class of Russia/the USSR), who could acquire intensive experience of film technique and repertory, or members of the *nomenklatura*/bureaucratic class, who could gain admission on the strength of their political connections.[3] Tsukerman, an *intelligent,* had been making home films since his teens.[4]

The Soviet background matters to our understanding of the film because *Liquid Sky* relies heavily on characteristically Russian aesthetic choices and narrative strategies. At the time of production, Tsukerman had been in the United States for only three years, and the film views the rarefied subcultures of downtown New York in the late seventies/early eighties as a reformulating of High Modernist concerns about life and/as art. Tsukerman has noted that "the thing is that I am fond of the Russian avant-garde art of the twenties and Brecht's epic theater. Surely, American pop art and New Wave continue this trend."[5] Specifically, Tsukerman has related the central action of the plot, Margaret's campaign of vengeance, to the song "Pirate Jenny" from the Brecht/Weill *Threepenny Opera.*[6] And although it is true that the film's costumes, make-up, and scenic designs are recognizably New Wave, they also display strong affinities to the design principles that undergirded the work of Russian Constructivist artists and their associates: Malevich, Tatlin, Popova, Rodchenko, Lissitsky, to name just a few.[7] Like many other Russian emigrés confronted with the bizarreries of downtown New York, Tsukerman and his compatriots found that the best lens through which to view their new world was one that, though it departed from the (conceptually) familiar, still placed greatest value on the charm of strangeness.

Brecht called it *Verfremdung:* when the protocols of a genre are violated and we are suddenly forced to *look,* not only at the mundane assumptions that had governed our perceptions until the deliberate interruptions of art turned into rough trade, but also at how, when the object of our gaze is jarred loose from its comfortable habits, it once more becomes an extraordinary thing. The term came to Brecht from the Russian Formalist school of literary critics and cultural theorists, who located the effects of estrangement (*ostranenie*) at the center of their notion of art. Viktor Shklovsky, the most exuberant of the Formalists, coined a set of terms to identify specific manifestations of *ostranenie:* "hampered form" (*zatrudnyonnaya forma*), in which artistic conventions were deliberately made cramped and awkward to block automatic reading and false senses of clarity; "deceleration" (*zamedlenie*), in which ostentatious adherence to formal details would take precedence over communicative function; or "laying bare the device" (*obrazhenie priyoma*), using a convention as a self-evident artifice.[8] These characteristic preoccupations are connected with the Formalists' intense involvement in the avant-garde of their day (the 1910s and 1920s), both within Russia/the USSR and Central Europe as well. (The development of montage in the early Soviet cinema, to name only one instance, shows a strong resonance with the tastes of cultural critics such as Shklovsky in its embodiment of *ostranenie.*) This rich tradition of thought and practice about narrative representation inflects the production of *Liquid Sky.*

For instance, the lengthy sequence which recounts the fashion shoot in Margaret's apartment is articulated by a pair of scenes, each composed of photo sets. The first of these follows Adrian's sly come-on to a bitchy reporter, offering to tell the story of Margaret's childhood with a series of snapshots in a scrapbook. These pictures show Margaret before her punk androgynification: as a fresh-faced teen; her hair is long, an undyed brown, emblematic of her conventional upbringing in the midst of suburban comforts. Adrian has viciously derided Margaret earlier in the film as "an uptight WASP cunt from Connecticut," and Margaret's own recollections of childhood have had a distinctly prelapsarian quality (apple pies, not to be eaten until they had cooled!), but the photos Adrian shows the reporter are the audience's first visual connection to the negotiations of Margaret's nostalgia.[9]

The music that accompanies these girlhood photos is Heinrich's "Laurel Waltz" from 1840, a piece of parlor music used for its simple, sentimental style. The A section of the tune, the only part played, observes strict quadratic phrasing of 4x(2+2) bars, and uses simple diatonic harmony with a tame diminished seventh chord appliquéd on; melodically and formally, it adds a set of naive chromatic decorations to dot the melody—in an A/A'/A"/B phrase structure—with wan prettiness. The deployment of the Heinrich is a strong defamiliarizing gesture, inasmuch as the grounding of any *ostranenie* is always a type of incongruity; based on the character of Margaret presented up to this point in the film, there is no way for the audience to take the photos as instantiations of pastness without plunging into deep ironies. The estrangement is intensified dramatically, however, by the music's clangorous timbre (realized on a New York City public-access synthesizer). The brilliant metallic sound envelopes of the arrangement allow the audience to project the image of some giant damaged music box, a sounding icon of Margaret's mind and body. The next appearance of "The Laurel Waltz" is appropriately enough an accompaniment to the series of photographs of Margaret on her roof for the magazine spread, in lurid New Wave fashions. It is worth emphasizing how the complex manipulations of focus and exposure in these photos are managed so as to resonate with the color and design of costumes and makeup, as well as the awkward positions and angles of Margaret's body within many of the separate frames.[10] And the music contributes its share of *ostranenie* again, chiefly through its re-orchestration.

Gesamtkunstwerk

Tsukerman and his group made *Liquid Sky* on the astonishing budget of only $550,000, in significant part because their taste for *ostranenie* allowed them to make an aesthetic virtue of "unrealistic" effects. The conjunction of Soviet homemade sensibilities with American punk's "Do It Yourself" attitude was another fortuitous coincidence. The major expense of the production was not materials or salaries, but the time spent to manage the relationships between script, mise-en-scène, and sound track to create the abstract thematic unity of the film. I have already mentioned the interrelationships in the photography shots that appear in the fashion sequence shoot; this dense patterning is characteristic of the entire film. Linda Trefz has asserted:

> The intent was to bring every possible aspect of the medium into play—both by blatant visual "overkill," and with subtler mood effects—to represent realities of that world [the punk scene of late-seventies SoHo] as well as to convey the sensibilities of an alien perspective which they, as émigrés, could furnish firsthand.[11]

By Tsukerman's recollection, he had met actress Anne Carlisle on a previous film project, and when he showed her his initial script treatment for *Liquid Sky,* she commented that it reminded her of the punk scene. Since Tsukerman had already visited CBGB's in the company of Vitaly Komar (of the émigré art duo Komar and Melamid), he decided to locate his science fiction story in that milieu.[12] He and his central team spent hours in downtown locales such as the legendary Mudd Club doing research. They did not aim at illusions of verisimilitude, but rather stylized recreations of what the Russian émigrés perceived as the "effect" of punk with respect to visual style, musical taste, and linguistic and gestural decorum.[13]

The original music composed for the scenes in the club, for instance, is not punk or New Wave as it actually appeared in downtown New York during the late seventies. That music—the Ramones, Blondie, Patti Smith, Richard Hell and the Voidoids, Television, the Talking Heads—though it incorporated jagged melodic dissonances and sought to fold in substantial amounts of noise to its pitched sounds, nevertheless depended more often than not on complex second-order relations to older rock styles and genres. New Wave in this context was usually meta-music. But the Russians could not be expected to know this; instead, they seem to have heard it as continuous with the experimental traditions of early "classical" modernism. The dance music in *Liquid Sky*'s club is sonically a few steps closer to the written-tradition avant-garde to give it qualities of increased depersonalization as well as more generic neutrality.[14]

Along with attention to *ostranenie* went centralized artistic control: Tsukerman's credits encompass the roles of director and producer, plus partial responsibilities for the screenwriting and music. Moreover, close associates such as his wife, Nina Kerova, who had partial credit for the screenplay and appears onscreen as well, and Neyman and Levikova, who managed the cinematography and design, can arguably be combined with Tsukerman to make a kind of collective auteur. (Anne Carlisle was the only major American collaborator; in addition to her starring role, she was given co-credit on the screenplay.) The intensive planning of detail carries over into the acting as well: although the performances often appear haphazard, stiff, and under-prepared, Tsukerman has insisted, "There was no improvisation at all. Each word was a thousand times thought over and rehearsed."[15]

Such despotic control over every aspect of the film suggests it be understood as an attempt at a *Gesamtkunstwerk,* and Tsukerman has readily agreed to this description.[16] The obvious reference is Wagner's theory of the utopian "total art-work" that would stem from his own music dramas. By coining the technical term Wagner wished to characterize and predict an *Aufhebung* of ancient Greek tragedy in which all aspects of a work would be unified into one sublime dramatic whole, creating transcendental effects in its audiences. It is worth remembering that Wagner shied away from claiming that his own works were actually such monuments. They were forerunners of the works-to-be. In fact, the real home of aspiring *Gesamtkunstwerke* tended to be fin-de-siècle Russia. The most ambitious instance of this is Skryabin's projected *Mysterium,* but many of the famous productions of Sergei Diaghilev's *Ballets russes,* perhaps most notably *The Rite of Spring,* operated along similar principles. Interest in "total artworks" continued into the Revolution, when cyclopean projects were constantly imagined and occasionally attempted.

The fact that Tsukerman presents *Liquid Sky* as a *Gesamtkunstwerk* is significant because it encourages a paranoid style of reading the film. That is, we are incited to "over"-interpret, because the implicit claim of the film's underlying aesthetic is that nothing that we experience is fortuitous. This taste for saturated intentionality is perhaps an especially Soviet inflection of the Wagnerian concept, because the history of censorship and the arts from the tsarist regime through all of the Soviet era had led to the development of endlessly subtle systems of double-coding. "Aesopean language," as it was called, depended on *sub rosa* rules of allegorical substitution as well as elaborate connotational shadings of linguistic/visual/gestural/musical style in order to make political reflection available to common reflection. From such specific uses, the mode of representation can quickly pick up substantial philosophical (moral, epistemological, ontological, metaphysical) weight. This is especially apt for science fiction from a late Soviet point of view: one thinks not only of Tarkovsky's films *Solyaris* (Solaris, 1972) and *Stalker* (1979), but also of the Dantean/gnostic fantastications that filled the wildly popular Soviet SF novels of Arkady and Boris Strugatsky.[17]

A closer look at the opening sequence of the film shows how this hyper-synthetic mindset plays out in the film's total texture. After the title pops onto the black screen, accompanied by the sound effect that will mark most instances of sudden (de-)materialization in the film, another cut brings the camera into a tight close-up on the stylized mask (abstract, but hinting at both *commedia dell'arte* and *kabuki*) of Margaret's face—the mask that hides Adrian's heroin stash—hanging above the bed in the apartment. From this point, the camera slowly dollies back through the apartment to a stridently orchestrated dissonant march. Although the music here is original (credited to Brenda I. Hutchinson and Tsukerman), it has strong affinities with the borrowed music that will soon appear to accompany the extraterrestrial's arrival and initial surveillance. This later music, a chant-like passage from a work by Carl Orff, is, like so much of his music, overwhelmingly influenced by Stravinsky in both ritualistic style and tonal language.[18] The original music of the first, brilliantly dissonant march is designed around some of the same textural and tonal relationships, so that both pieces of music taken together help constitute one of the major sonic spaces of the film.

Returning to the series of shots: the camera backs away from the mask until it reaches a medium shot, then suddenly bumps out to medium long in a cut signaled in the sound track by a sound effect that thuds contradictorily against the metrical and periodic structure of the ongoing march. The next shot, which moves from the outside of the apartment to an extreme distance from the building, finishes the film's initial subsequence. Extended dollying back is an important gesture in the film, and the three combined shots feel quite long thanks to the contrast between the graduation of the camera's movement as set against the rapid tempo of the music. It is at this point that the film will begin to cross-cut between the apartment/city and the downtown club. Music is keyed to each location, diegetic in the club and non-diegetic for the apartment/city.

The return to the apartment after the first insertion of a shot from the club tracks the same motion from Margaret's mask out of the apartment, only this time from looking outward, eventually arriving at a shot of the Empire State Building partially cloaked in mist. After another shot of the club, and rapid shots of mask and apartment (again marked by sound effects), the camera turns to the skyline for the extraterrestrial's arrival. The ship brings in new music, the Carl Orff passage mentioned above, from *Il Trionfo di Aphrodite*.[19] After a series of brief shots in which the ship settles down on the roof, the important business of ending the sequence takes place. A long tracking shot establishes sight lines between the ship and Margaret's mask through a mirror image, and the camera turns to the film's version of "alienvision," a computer-adjusted filtering process that gives the film the look of heat-sensitive photography, albeit with altered color values.[20] Once the alienvision is established, the film tracks slowly back into the apartment to a close-up of Margaret's mask (the time roughly matches the time of the initial move away from the mask), followed by the film's abstract representation of the extraterrestrial's visual "feeding."

A Wilderness of Mirrors

At stake in the opening sequence of *Liquid Sky* are a number of questions about perception, reality, and aggression. The totalizing aspects of the film are so prominent and structurally apparent that our experience tends toward the synaesthetic; sight and sound, in particular, are related in innumerable ways, small and large. As I have mentioned, this is a characteristic of most film, but in *Liquid Sky* the stagy attention to detail pushes us to foreground the mixed-modal qualities of our perceptions. Borrowing from the old distinctions of Charles Peirce, we could classify some of these interrelationships as indexical signs, in the film's source music most obviously, but also in a sense during the moments that arise from the conjunction of sonic and visual special effects; as iconic signs, again in the conjunction of sonic and visual special effects, but even in such details as the way the metallic timbres of much of the sound track find resonance in the garish neons and mirrory glintings of Margaret's apartment; and as symbols, seen especially in the historical resonances of the previously composed music.

These confusions of senses confuse the sense. We are forced to question ourselves on more abstract levels about our perceptions. How do we apportion our cognitive and affective experiences of the moments in the film among the various domains of the film as a whole? What distinctions may be made between kinds of synaesthesia, and is it possible to establish levels of intensity within these kinds? Although sight and hearing are in an important sense "passive," to what degree may they be thought of as active as well? That is, what is the effect of perception on reality? Such questions probably arise inevitably in any film with a significant degree of self-reflexivity, as well as—as theorists of the gaze have repeatedly demonstrated—in many films that avoid such artifice by attempting to naturalize their own representational apparatus. Nevertheless,

Liquid Sky's passion for *ostranenie*—its ostentatiously alien gaze—places extra weight on our ability to recognize and interrogate the structure of intersensory modalities, as well as their trajectories of signification.

Sight is the most rapacious sense in *Liquid Sky*. Repeatedly, Margaret's personal difficulties arise from being looked at, because in the film's world, looking always leads to her spoliation—not exclusively rape, but other physical and verbal violences as well. And yet she is a model; her occupation is precisely to be looked at. The extraterrestrial's ocular anthropophagy is only a literalization of the rule that underlies all the interactions between Margaret and everyone else. Moreover, the despotism of the glance is not confined to matters of sexual and gustatory desire. The extraterrestrial's characteristic visual feeding pattern is a circle that expands, transforms in color, and diminishes to nothing. In a lovely parallel, its shape is echoed in the concentric red circles that define the lens of Hoffman's telescope. As a scientist, he appears to be driven by such an intense epistemophilia that he does not even notice Sylvia's deranged horniness; but the voyeuristic/cannibalistic overtones of the telescope are inescapable, and place his thirst for knowledge within the same continuum.

The ambivalent gaze, however old a trope, is nowhere more central to *Liquid Sky* than in the characteristic scenes that present Margaret as a self-object, in front of her mirror. The first of these is the opening shot in the sequence that begins the morning after Margaret has been raped. For the first and only time in the film, we see her without makeup and dressed hair. This is her plain face, marked only by the affects worn in the musculature, registering the damage within. What is she doing here, if not looking to see what remains of her self? If in Lacan's terms the mirror image is a captivating fiction, here in *Liquid Sky* its most "realistic" accents are those of melancholy, the looking glass as a broken promise. The humanizing simplicity of Margaret's plain face is all the more moving because the film has already shown, and will repeatedly show, that it is no match for the delirium of art, perhaps because it is so vulnerable to the charge that the plain face is simply an especially subtle instance of the art to which it seems to be set in opposition. One deep calls to another in the "natural order" in *Liquid Sky*. As Georges Bataille would say, "Coitus is the parody of crime."[21]

Constructing Melancholies

In an interesting reading of gender roles in *Liquid Sky*, Janet Bergstrom has stressed the abstraction and artifice of the denizens of the downtown club as a externalization of their rejection or bereavement of "everyday" human life, such that in our eyes as well as the extraterrestrial's eye, the members of the punk scene are the "real aliens."[22] This is true, but Bergstrom's points could be pushed further by asking: What is it about the "everyday" that inspires such hatred among the characters of the film? Although a deep reading of the film would turn to the failures of nurturance in both the Soviet and American states that became so glaring during the sixties and seventies, the most immediate source of loathing of the everyday arises from a pervasive distrust of details in the dominant fiction of postwar America: the mythology of the bourgeois suburban nuclear family, and especially the gender politics that underwrote it. Once again, this is a place where late Soviet and American post-countercultural sensibilities find powerful points of resonance.

Russian émigrés to the United States, as well as many gay and lesbian activists in the former Soviet Union, tend to understand gender and sexuality in strongly anti-essentialist terms. To a great extent this is a contradictory legacy of Leninist-Marxism. On the one hand, the intense utopianism and idolatry of humanity in Soviet ideology demanded a hyper-pure form of constructionism. Lysenko's updated Larmarckism had such a disastrous effect on Soviet biological research during Stalin's reign, precisely because its theoretical assumption of genetic "progress" was so ideologically compatible with the current theory of the state.[23] (A glance at classic Soviet films will show instances of this constructionist mindset with respect to gender.)[24] The Soviet belief in the infinite malleability of human nature can seem an irrevocable concomitant to any notions of optimism even in post-Soviet Russia. On the other hand, Soviet administrative tastes for fixing individual identities with respect to categories (class, "official nationality") quite naturally led to a resistance to categorization. From either side of the (post-)Soviet point of view, American notions of naturalized, fixed gender identities and sexual orientations seem false and constricting, and American attempts to build social groups and quasi-ethnic identifications out of such individualized impulses seem to be folly.[25] By contrast to the American populist model, the manifestations of erotic desire in *Liquid Sky* are always fractured, incoherent, situational, aleatory, understood as different shadings within a continuum. The film asserts that differences in gender identity and in sexual orientation exist—and should exist—along a blurry continuum.

Take the moment of dialogue early in the film when the junkie, Paul, has come to the apartment looking for a fix. He talks to Margaret while Adrian retrieves the heroin, and begins to query her sexual identity as part of a creepy come-on:

> PAUL: Do you like girls better than boys?
> MARGARET: I'm always curious about people who have to make those kind of sexual definitions.
> PAUL: What do you mean?
> MARGARET: Homosexual, heterosexual, bisexual. Whether I like someone doesn't depend on what kind of genitals they have. As long as I find them attractive, don't you think?

Today, after the rise of queer theory, with its obsessive sloganeering on behalf of constructionism and "the performative," Margaret's attitudes hardly seem unusual. But in America of the early eighties they were expressed against a mainstreaming gay rights politics that, in modeling itself on the civil rights movement, was heavily committed to a "10 percent born-gay" point of view, as well as against the intense essentialism of much Lesbian Cultural Feminism during the seventies. The nineties' popular T-shirt slogan "I fuck with categories" fits the ethos of *Liquid Sky* perfectly.

Understanding the film as resolutely opposed to gender-separatist and minoritizing attitudes also entails our awareness of the film's distaste for the sixties' American social activism out of which the seventies' gay and lesbian movement grew. Indeed, Margaret makes this clear in her flirtatious but serious argument with Owen. Here is some dialogue from its central passage:

> OWEN: All your costumes. They're just participation in some kind of phony theater. I'm only telling you this for your own good. It's a freak show.
> MARGARET: Are you trying to say that your blue jeans weren't theater?
> Owen: It's not the same thing.
> Margaret: So your professor wore a three-piece suit and blamed you for your jeans. For him your jeans were too much. And he didn't understand that his suit was also a costume. You thought your jeans stood for love, freedom, and sexual equality. We at least know we're in costume.

Binary oppositions—gay/straight, man/woman, sixties/seventies, politics/theater, street clothes/costume—are set up, only to fail almost immediately. Note the appearance of bisexual in Margaret's list. Or note the occurrence of the three-piece suit in the battle between jeans and New Wave extravagance. These terms are not introduced simply to break the binary into a ternary; they are meant to undo the possibility of stable and meaningful contrasts altogether. Margaret's experience has seemed to indicate that such paranoid/schizoid logic always signals a ploy by someone to get her into bed, and her indifference to "yes" versus "no" questions is an attempt at mustering resistance. Margaret hates binaries. Oppositions that entail visual representation are especially vulnerable to suspicion in *Liquid Sky*. Sound, by contrast, often appears outside of the film's oppositional patterns, as something which more often than not tends toward some kind of truth. The film suggests that there is more truth in sound than in sight, because it does not construct sound within polarizing distinctions.

Adrian's performance piece, for instance, a song entitled "Me and My Rhythm Box," is spoken over an extended synthesized groove that we are to understand as located in the drum machine strapped to her hip. The accompaniment in fact emanates both from the drum machine and from noumenal space outside the film's diegesis; the film does not make this heterogeneity an occasion for *ostranenie* because other matters take precedence here. First and foremost is the complex representation of what we might call an aspiration for posthuman embodiment.[26] The lyrics of the song flatly praise the drum machine as an object of desire in the gnostic terms that will reappear as cyberpunk's hostility toward "meat" in the nineties: the rhythm box "never eats / it never shits . . . it's a tool / it doesn't drool . . . It. It is. Preprogrammed. So what?" For the expression of such a body-hating rant, we might expect a "mechanical" sounding voice from which most overt markers of affect have been removed; but instead, Adrian's speech carries an intense burden of grief and rage. Her speech melody frames the mechanophilia of her lyrics, so that we understand the love of her rhythm box as a reaction formation (i.e., an irony) against the messy disappointments of biology.[27] If we understand the operations of denotation and connotation in speech as analogous to the functions of sight and sound in the film, once again we are in a position where the denotative functions are always to be read as secondary to the connotative functions. In a maneuver of Aesopean filmic language, sound must be privileged over sight, all the more so because of its noumenal superiority.

Liquid Sky's intense dislike of stable categories is embodied in its favorite ways of relating sound and vision. For significant stretches of the film, the narrative is broken up by fairly rapid cross-cutting, only occasionally parallel. In the opening section following the titles, for instance, we move back and forth between the club, Margaret's apartment and its furnishings, and the skyline of New York. The music initially corresponds strictly to these changes in the mise-en-scène. After the sub-sequence of the extraterrestrial's arrival and first fix, the film moves to an extended set of cross-cuts between Adrian's performance at the club and a fight between Margaret and Jimmy at the apartment. As "Rhythm Box" begins, its ominous force breaks up the pattern of musical and visual correspondence established in the opening sequence. The rage and despair carried in Adrian's music begins to leak into Margaret's apartment, even while Margaret and Jimmy realize they must return to the club to make up for a fashion show.

In thinking through this sequence in *Liquid Sky,* we might want to consider the question of cyborg identities; we might puzzle over the casting of Anne Carlisle as both Margaret and Jimmy, and the peculiar ways it pulls at our normativizing understandings of identity in the narrative; and so on. But most simply we might observe that the overriding strength of "Rhythm Box" as a song effectively disrupts our expectations that the film's separate spatial/social worlds will continue to be marked by sound as well as image. Music and sound effects act as primary conduits between ontological locations; characters and visual qualities follow what we will already have heard. Perhaps more important, the sound track's gradual smearing over the film's visual cuts adumbrates interpretive issues addressed in three central moments that occur during the film's *peripateia,* the fashion shoot.

First there is the disorienting sub-sequence where, deranged by the consumption of many varied drugs, Margaret is seated to allow the stylists to work on her hair and make-up. At this point she is approached by the columnist from *Midnight* magazine, who makes catty remarks about Margaret's status as a model. As the columnist utters damning words—"tacky," "strange," "clothes"—the sound track of the film moves vertiginously in a *trompe l'oreille* effect between objective auditory space and Margaret's drug-laden auditory subjectivity. The drugginess is presented by electronic manipulations of the columnist's words, to the point that they begin to resemble the rest of the synthesized score. Are these words on the way to music? What, in the end, and in this world, is the real difference between music and words? As this and so many other moments attest, *Liquid Sky* is in love with instability.

But this instability brings no joy. Violence and gratuitous cruelty are everywhere in Margaret's world. She is raped twice (arguably thrice), forcibly "seduced" twice, slapped, threatened with a knife, and verbally abused over and over again by nearly everyone who interacts with her. Maybe it's just a really bad week; or maybe her life is like that all the time. The great problem with her hyper-constructionist politics is that at the same time that she can preserve an illusion of autonomy and strength, she has no genuine refuge from the brutality that these politics seem to underwrite within the film. It's as if the grim capitalist selfishness of Ayn Rand (another Russian émigré, after all) suddenly appeared dressed up with full makeup, accompanied by a synthesizer. The viciousness of Margaret's everyday world explains why the extraterrestrial appears to Margaret in such a beneficent light; from her point of view "the Indian" is the only entity who has seemed to do something purely for her sake. We assume this is a savage irony, although Margaret's absorption into the spaceship at the film's close might leave us wondering.

More disturbingly, perhaps, the banal evils visited on Margaret by her surroundings seem to be a crucial part of her internal world as well. The next key moment in the fashion shoot sequence brings back "Rhythm Box" as part of the non-diegetic sound track. The self-loathing so strongly implied in the original performance lends an additionally unsettling quality to the antagonism between Margaret and Jimmy during this, their final encounter. The participants in the fashion shoot, drugged and bored, have provoked Jimmy by challenging his narcissism; he responds by taunting Margaret and stomping on her foot. This sets the occasion for Margaret's seduction/murder act of revenge. But remember that Anne Carlisle is playing both characters, so that with the brief assistance of a body double, she fellates "her"-self to death in a gesture that seems to embody the film's questions about mirroring, gender, and internalization in the most dizzying of ways.

The last of these key sequences seems to suggest an answer to the dilemmas posed in the earlier spectacles of cruelty greeted first passively, then by vengeful response. After Adrian's death, Margaret turns off the neon lights that fill her apartment and tips over a tree made of broken mirrors, leaving only a black light to illuminate Margaret's face as she applies makeup. She chooses fluorescent creams, making her face resemble the mask of her face as seen in the opening shot. It is this face, as it acquires its new and living mask, with overtones of Picasso's *Demoiselles d'Avignon,* that recounts Margaret's savage parody of a *Bildungsroman.* The music during this section, from the toppling of the mirror tree onward, is "The Laurel Waltz," reorchestrated in an increasingly grand style. The narrative that it frames is crucially concerned with Margaret's history of subjection to girlhood: her story is structured by the phrase "and I was taught that." By the end of her narrative, she exclaims that all her teachers are dead, and savagely challenges the befuddled onlookers from the photo shoot: "Come on, teach me!" The sweetness of the music comments ironically on Margaret's description of the way she has been "girled."[28] It is at this moment that the delirious ambiguities the film has seemed to admire suddenly disappear, making way for what Margaret has come to understand as a counter-pedagogy of terrifying power. Think of the end of Sylvia Plath's "Lady Lazarus": "Out of the ashes I rise with my red hair / And I eat men like air."[29]

What are solutions to Margaret's problem, then, to the inadequacy of the scenes of instruction she sought throughout her life, and by which she has so decisively been betrayed? The film has no clear answers here; indeed it cannot. In the late Soviet contexts that decisively shaped *Liquid Sky,* irony was often not particularly funny, at least not in the ways that Americans might expect.[30] And such a complex mode of representation, aimed so confusingly in all directions at once, was arguably ideal for that cultural moment in 1982 America. It is becoming increasingly clear that the United States was beginning to mourn the irrevocable collapse of its postwar dominant fiction (though sadly, the process of mourning seems to have turned into a spiteful melancholia). One sign of this collapse came from increasing dissatisfaction with that dominant fiction's picture of gender and sexuality; but there was not a great deal to be offered in its stead, even in the rarefied circles of the downtown New Wave scene depicted in *Liquid Sky.* To its credit, the film refuses to offer a comfortable solution, but instead continues to count the costs of holding so austerely to the illusions of individual autonomy.

Notes

1. Batchan, "The 'Alienation' of Slava Tsukerman," 16.

2. Trefz, "Photographing *Liquid Sky,*" 63. Cinematographer Yuri Neyman was, like Tsukerman, an honors graduate of VGIK; his wife, Marina Levikova, who created the sets and costumes, was a graduate of the Moscow Textile Institute who had also worked for Mosfilm, the largest and most prestigious of the Soviet film studios.

3. Faraday, *Revolt of the Filmmakers,* 45. For more details on the late Soviet film industry, see Golovskoy, *Behind the Soviet Screen.* For the transition into the era of *glasnost',* see Lawton, *Kinoglasnost.*

4. Batchan, "The 'Alienation' of Slava Tsukerman," 18.

5. Tsukerman quoted in Batchan, "The 'Alienation' of Slava Tsukerman," 26–27. In a perfect instance of talking at cultural cross-purposes, the very features of the film that Tsukerman means to be taken as updated 1920s modernism appear to film critic Vivian Sobchak as

textbook postmodernism: the "clutter" and "pastiche" of the film's "dispersed and decentered mise-en-scène," as well as the organization of the narrative in terms of spatial values; see Sobchack, *Screening Space*, 245, 269–70. Both director and critic are entirely correct in their analyses, of course.

6. Batchan, "The 'Alienation' of Slava Tsukerman," 27.

7. The characteristic color schemes offer the domain of greatest divergence between Levikova's New Wave and Russian art of the 1920s.

8. Shklovsky's literary work appears in Russian in *Sobranie Sochinenii*; his writing on film may be found in the collection *Za sorok let': stati'i o kino'* (Forty Years: Articles on Film). Some film articles are translated into German in *Der Sowjetische Film*. Overviews and histories of Russian Formalism are not especially common in English; the standard account is still Erlich, *Russian Formalism*; see also Bann and Bowlt, *Russian Formalism*.

9. Although the question of Margaret's abject whiteness is important to the film, it is beyond the scope of this paper. In a more specifically Russian vein, let me point out that one of Adrian's structural roles in the film is to put into perspective Margaret's statements about her own past. The purest example of this is her hilarious/appalling riposte to Margaret's "apple pie" story: Adrian recalls a time when her schizophrenic mother, suddenly believing herself to be Jesus, "baptized" an entire restaurant by urinating on the diners from a balcony. This sour parody of *Heilsgeschichte* is not meant to negate Margaret's tale altogether, however, but to "carnivalize" it in an appropriately Bakhtinian manner.

10. It is unlikely that Nijinsky's legendary choreography for the original production of *The Rite of Spring* is part of the film's repertory of references, but any glance at stills of that production or modern recreations offers an excellent parallel to this passage in *Liquid Sky*; although it is worth mentioning that Millicent Hodson's recreation of *The Rite of Spring* stems from 1960s fashion shoots.

11. Trefz, "Photographing *Liquid Sky*," 62–63.

12. Batchan, "The 'Alienation' of Slava Tsukerman," 26.

13. Trefz, "Photographing *Liquid Sky*," 65.

14. This neutrality tends to be lost on contemporary audiences for the film because of the increased cross-fertilization between the old avant-garde and punk traditions during the eighties and nineties.

15. Batchan, "The 'Alienation' of Slava Tsukerman," 32.

16. Ibid., 28.

17. The majority of these novels date from the sixties and seventies. See Howell, *Apocalyptic Realism*.

18. The most important piece for understanding Orff's essentially derivative style is Stravinsky's *Svadebka* (*Les Noces*, or *The Wedding*) from 1923. Although I do not discuss the formal details of the music in much detail here, these two marches depend upon octatonic tonal formations, themselves developed extensively in nineteenth- and twentieth-century Russian compositional practice.

19. This work is a theater piece for soloists and chorus based on the poetry of Sappho and Catullus. Although space does not permit a full discussion, the ironic contrasts between Orff's vision of ritual marriage, where a premodern community celebrates sexual intercourse in terms of the sacred union or *hieros gamos* that brings fertility and blessing to everyone, and the frantic, fragmented, and dissociated sexual relationships in the film, filled with hostility and despair, are quite rich.

20. Trefz, "Photographing *Liquid Sky*," 69.

21. Bataille, "The Solar Anus," 5.

22. Bergstrom, "Androids," 44–49.

23. See Soyfer, *Lysenko and the Tragedy of Soviet Science*.

24. Shapinskaya, "Social Construction of Gender Roles," 150–55.

25. Pointed comments to this effect are offered anecdotally in Tuller, *Cracks in the Iron Closet*.

26. An attempt to situate this film in terms of posthuman identities and popular culture at this time would necessarily take up an enormous number of examples. For my purposes, let me just list three: David Bowie's career during most of the 1970s; SF-inspired New Wave albums such as Devo's *Q: Are We Not Men? A: We Are Devo!* (1978) and Gary Numan's *Replicas* (1979); and Laurie Anderson's technological musings in *United States Parts I-IV*, which premiered at the Brooklyn Academy of Music in 1983 after extended development in performances of the late seventies and early eighties.

27. The overtones of nurturance and maternity are also obvious, here and at many other points in the film. We might wonder how far these resonances ("Mother Russia"? "Mom and Apple Pie"?) inflect other aspects of the film.

28. For more on this point, see Bergstrom, "Androids," 48–49.

29. Plath, *Collected Poems*, 244.

30. See Vishevsky, *Soviet Literary Culture*.

References

Bann, Stephen, and John E. Bowlt, eds. *Russian Formalism: A Collection of Articles and Texts in Translation.* New York: Barnes & Noble, 1973.

Bataille, Georges. "The Solar Anus." In *Visions of Excess: Selected Writings 1927–1939*, ed. and with an introduction by A. Stoekl, trans. A. Stoekl, with C. R. Lovitts and D. M. Leslie Jr. Minneapolis: University of Minnesota Press, 1985, 5–9.

Batchan, Alexander. "The 'Alienation' of Slava Tsukerman." In *Before the Wall Came Down: Soviet and East European Filmmakers Working in the West,* ed. G. Petrie and R. Dwyer. Lanham, Md.: University Press of America, 1990, 15–34.

Bergstrom, Janet. "Androids and Androgyny." In *Close Encounters: Film, Feminism, and Science Fiction,* ed. C. Penley, E. Lyon, L. Spiegel, and J. Bergstrom. Minneapolis: University of Minnesota Press, 1991, 32–61.

Erlich, Victor. *Russian Formalism: History, Doctrine.* New Haven, Conn.: Yale University Press, 1981.

Faraday, George. *Revolt of the Filmmakers: The Struggle for Artistic Autonomy and the Fall of the Soviet Film Industry.* University Park: Pennsylvania State University Press, 2000.

Golovskoy, Val S., with John Rimberg. *Behind the Soviet Screen: The Motion Picture Industry in the USSR 1972–1982.* Trans. S. Hill. Ann Arbor, Mich.: Ardis, 1986.

Gregor, Ulrich, and Friedrich Hitzer, eds. *Der Sowjetische Film 1930 bis 1939, v.1: Eine Dokumentation.* Frankfort am Main: Verband der deutschen Filmclubs, 1966.

Howell, Yvonne. *Apocalyptic Realism: The Science Fiction of Arkady and Boris Strugatsky.* New York: Peter Lang, 1994.

Lawton, Anna. *Kinoglasnost: Soviet Cinema in Our Time.* Cambridge: Cambridge University Press, 1992.

Plath, Sylvia. *Collected Poems.* New York: Harper & Row, 1981.

Shapinskaya, Ekaterina N. "Social Construction of Gender Roles in Soviet Film." In *Gender in Film and the Media: East-West Dialogues,* ed. E. H. Oleksy, E. Ostrowska, and M. Stevenson. Frankfurt am Main: Peter Lang, 2000, 150–55.

Shklovsky, Viktor. *Sobranie Sochinenii* [Collected Works]. 3 vols. Moscow: "Khudozhestvennaia literatura," 1974.

———. *Za sorok let': stati'i o kino'* [Forty Years: Articles on Film]. Moscow: Isskustvo, 1965.

Sobchack, Vivian. *Screening Space: The American Science Fiction Film.* 2nd ed. New York: Unger, 1993.

Soyfer, Valery N. *Lysenko and the Tragedy of Soviet Science.* Trans. L. and R. Gruliow. New Brunswick, N.J.: Rutgers University Press, 1994.

Trefz, Linda. "Photographing *Liquid Sky:* Parasitic Extraterrestrials Make the Manhattan Punk Scene/Photography for *Liquid Sky.*" *American Cinematographer* 65/2 (1984): 62–72.

Tuller, David. *Cracks in the Iron Closet: Travels in Lesbian and Gay Russia.* Chicago: University of Chicago Press, 1996.

Vishevsky, Anatoly. *Soviet Literary Culture in the 1970s: The Politics of Irony.* Trans. M. Biggins and A. Vishevsky. Gainesville: University Press of Florida, 1993.

Filmography

LIQUID SKY

release:	August 1982 (premiere at Montreal World Film Festival); 15 April 1983, USA
duration:	112 mins
dir:	Slava Tsukerman
prod:	Slava Tsukerman
prod co:	Z Films Inc.
actors:	Anne Carlisle (Margaret/Jimmy); Paula E. Sheppard (Adrian); Susan Doukas (Sylvia, Jimmy's Mother); Otto von Wernherr (Johann Hoffman the Scientist); Bob Brady (Owen); Elaine C. Grove (Katherine); Stanley Knapp (Paul); Jack Adalist (Vincent); Lloyd Ziff (Lester)
camera:	Yuri Neyman
music:	Brenda I. Hutchinson; Slava Tsukerman
	Carl Orff, *Il Trionfo di Aphrodite*
	Anthony Philip Heinrich, "The Laurel Waltz"
DVD:	Mti Home Video (15 February 2000), ASIN: 6305660328
CD:	Home Entertainment (10 September 1996), ASIN: B000005B6F

Contributors

BJÖRN HEILE is a lecturer in music and head of department at the University of Sussex. He has published extensively on new music, as well as The Music of Mauricio Kagel.

JULIE HUBBERT is an associate professor of music history at the University of South Carolina. Her articles on film and music have appeared in *American Music*, *The Musical Quarterly*, and several edited collections. Her book of source readings, *Celluloid Symphonies: Texts and Contexts in Film Music History*, is forthcoming.

ED HUGHES is a composer and lecturer in music at the University of Sussex. He has worked on several scores for contemporary filmmakers and visual artists including Lizzie Thynne (*Playing a Part: The Story of Claude Cahun*) and Sophy Rickett (for a film commissioned by Glyndebourne Opera/Photoworks). He has recently completed a three-year project to score Eisenstein's *Battleship Potemkin* and *Strike* for live ensemble and electronics. These scores were released as sound tracks on DVD in surround (5.1, DTS) by Tartan Video in 2007.

CHRISTOPHER MORRIS is a lecturer in music at University College Cork. He is author of *Reading Opera Between the Lines*, a critical exploration of the role of orchestral interludes in late-nineteenth- and early-twentieth-century opera. His articles on the operas of Wagner, Richard Strauss, and Berg have appeared in *The Journal of Musicological Research*, *The Musical Quarterly*, and *The Journal of the Royal Musical Association*.

MITCHELL MORRIS teaches in the Department of Musicology at UCLA, and works on American, German, and Russian music of the early 1900s, Rock and Soul, and questions of musical subjectivity with special attention to gender and sexual identity. His book *The Persistence of Sentiment: Essays on Display and Feeling* is forthcoming.

ROBERT E. PECK is a research supervisor in the School of Media, Arts, and Design at the University of Westminster. He specializes in German film history and has published in *Media History, The Historical Journal of Film, Radio and Television, Filmblatt,* and *Media, Culture and Society.* He has also contributed to the anthology *Titanic, Memory and Myth,* edited by Tim Bergfelder and Sarah Street.

PHIL POWRIE is Professor of French Cultural Studies at the University of Newcastle upon Tyne. He has published widely in French cinema studies, including *French Cinema in the 1980s: Nostalgia and the Crisis of Masculinity* (1997); *Contemporary French Cinema: Continuity and Difference* (1999); *Jean-Jacques Beineix* (2001); *French Cinema: An Introduction* (co-authored with Keith Reader, 2002); and *French Cinema* (2006). He is co-editor with Robynn Stilwell of *Changing Tunes: The Use of Pre-existing Music in Film* (2006) and with Susan Hayward of *The Films of Luc Besson: Master of Spectacle* (2006). He is the general co-editor of the journal Studies in French Cinema, and is currently co-authoring a monograph on film adaptations of the Carmen story (2007).

REBECCA SCHWARTZ-BISHIR is a Ph.D. candidate in historical musicology at the University of Michigan. Her dissertation is on *musique dansante* and the art of ballet. She also works as the editorial assistant at MUSA (Music of the United States of America), which publishes a series of scholarly editions of American music.

ROBYNN J. STILWELL is Associate Professor of Music in the Department of Art, Music, and Theatre at Georgetown University. Her publications include *Musicals: Hollywood and Beyond* (co-edited with Bill Marshall), and articles in *Beethoven Forum, Music & Letters, Acta Musicologica, Popular Music & Society,* and *Screen,* as well as chapters in several books about popular music, film, and French culture. She is co-editor with Phil Powrie of *Changing Tunes: The Use of Pre-existing Music in Film.*

REIMAR VOLKER works for the Goethe-Institute. His thesis, awarded in 2001, was published as *Von oben sehr erwünscht: Die Filmmusik Herbert Windts im NS-Propagandafilm.*

MARC A. WEINER is Professor of Germanic Studies and Adjunct Professor of Comparative Literature, Communication and Culture, and Cultural Studies at Indiana University. He is the author of *Arthur Schnitzler and the Crisis of Musical Culture; Undertones of Insurrection: Music, Politics, and the Social Sphere in the Modern German Narrative;* and *Richard Wagner and the Anti-Semitic Imagination,* which won the Eugene M. Kayden National University Press Book Award for best book

Index

Page numbers in italics refer to illustrations.